D0872362

Amos Tutuola Revisited

Twayne's World Authors Series

African Literature

Bernth Lindfors, Editor
University of Texas at Austin

TWAS 880

AMOS TUTUOLA.
ADEFUNPE OJEYEMI.
Photograph provided by Bernth Lindfors.

Amos Tutuola Revisited

Oyekan Owomoyela

University of Nebraska, Lincoln

Twayne Publishers
New York

Twayne's World Authors Series No. 880

Amos Tutuola Revisited
Oyekan Owomoyela

Copyright © 1999 by Twayne Publishers

Twayne Publishers
1633 Broadway
New York, NY 10019

Library of Congress Cataloging-in-Publication Data

Owomoyela, Oyekan.
    Amos Tutuola revisited / Oyekan Owomoyela.
        p.   cm. — (Twayne's world authors series ; no. 880. African
    literature)
    Includes bibliographical references and index.
    ISBN 0-8057-4610-2 (alk. paper)
    1. Tutuola, Amos—Criticism and interpretation.   2. Nigeria—In
    literature.   I. Title.   II. Series: Twayne's world authors series ;
    TWAS 880.   III. Series: Twayne's world authors series. African
    literature.
    PR9387.9.T8Z83   1999   1999
    823—dc21   99-14327
                                                        CIP

This paper meets the requirements of ANSI/NISO Z3948-1992 (Permanence of Paper).

10 9 8 7 6 5 4 3 2 1

Printed in the United States of America

For Joan, companion, partner, friend; with love.

Contents

Preface

Amos Tutuola was born in 1920, when colonialism in Nigeria (as in the rest of British West Africa) was at its most confident. The years between the two great wars gave the colonizers little cause to doubt that their hold on their empire would last a thousand years or even more. Their confidence had its impact on a considerable number of their colonized wards, who, for a variety of reasons, were oblivious of, or unimpressed by, the nascent anticolonial movement in their territories. For such people, the colonialists were persuasive in their prescription for the good, meaningful life: rejection of traditional (African) ways and embrace of the "modern" European culture. The new schools (missionary for the most part) started their students on the path to Europeanization, with a promise that those of them fortunate enough to complete the course would emerge "white," with all the privileges whiteness entailed.

Tutuola was not one of the fortunate few, for familial circumstances curtailed his schooling; the stories he would tell throughout his life about those early years convey his lament at his misfortune. His educational handicap notwithstanding, Tutuola embarked (by chance, to be sure) on a literary career that history must judge at least remarkable. Although historians of African literature customarily name his compatriot Chinua Achebe as the father of modern African writing, it is in fact Tutuola who pioneered the field, and from whose whetting of the European literary appetite about "emergent" Africa Achebe and later African writers would benefit.

Evidence of Tutuola's educational and literary handicaps always abounded in his writing, but an indulgent reading public, European in the first instance but later African also, excused or sublimated his stylistic idiosyncrasies, praising them as ingenious, unconventional, and forceful freshness. Harold Collins's earlier volume on Tutuola in the Twayne series is exemplary in this regard. The worldwide adulation he enjoyed sustained him through nine novels and two collections of short stories, but his writing life was never without its disillusionments. Tutuola never achieved recognition at home commensurate with his regard abroad, a point he lamented close to his death. He died in 1997 in destitution and neglect.

The controversy that swirled around him in his lifetime left little room for sober analyses of his life and work: what they say about desire and choice under colonialism, and the convenient fictions that rationalized the accommodations that the colonized found expedient. To the extent that the constraints that existed under colonialism have survived the official end of the regime, Tutuola's life and career will continue to deserve our attention for the insight they can offer into the African condition in our time.

Chronology

1920   Amos Tutuola born in Abeokuta, Nigeria. His father, Charles Tutuola Odegbami, is a cocoa farmer.[1]

1932   Enters Salvation Army School in Abeokuta.

1934   Moves to Lagos, attends Lagos High School.[2]

1936   Returns to Abeokuta and attends Salvation Army School.

1939   Father dies. Amos withdraws from school.

1940   Goes to Lagos to live with brother and begins to learn blacksmithing.

1942   Joins RAF as blacksmith.

1945   Discharged from RAF as grade two blacksmith. Fails in attempt to establish blacksmith shop.

1946   Finds employment as messenger in Department of Labour, Lagos. Writes *The Palm-Wine Drinkard*.

1947   Marries Victoria Alake.

1952   *The Palm-Wine Drinkard* published by Faber and Faber.

1954   *My Life in the Bush of Ghosts* published by Faber and Faber.

1955   *Simbi and the Satyr of the Dark Jungle* published by Faber and Faber.

1957   Transferred to Nigerian Broadcasting Corporation, Ibadan. Employed as storekeeper.

1958   Works with Professor Collis of the University of Ibadan, who is writing a play version of *The Palm-Wine Drinkard*. *The Brave African Huntress* published by Faber and Faber.

1962   Publication of Gerald Moore's *Seven African Writers*, which contains the first readily accessible criticism of Tutuola's work. Publication of *Feather Woman of the Jungle*. Staging of the Yoruba version of Tutuola's *The Palm-Wine Drinkard* in the Arts Theatre, University of

Ibadan; in other places in Nigeria; and at the University of Ghana.

1967   *Ajaiyi and His Inherited Poverty* published by Faber and Faber.

1969   Harold R. Collins's *Amos Tutuola* published by Twayne.

1975   Bernth Lindfors's *Critical Perspectives on Amos Tutuola* published by Three Continents Press.

1979   Writer in residence, University of Ife.

1981   *The Witch-Herbalist of the Remote Town* published by Faber and Faber.

1982   *The Wild Hunter in the Bush of Ghosts* published by Three Continents Press.

1983   USIA International Visitor Program.

1983   Fellow of the Iowa Writing Workshop.

1983   Honorary Citizenship, New Orleans.

1984   Grimzane and Cavour Prize (Italy).

1986   *Yoruba Folktales* published by Ibadan University Press.

1987   *Pauper, Brawler, and Slanderer* published by Faber and Faber.

1988   "Work and Play in Tutuola's *The Palm-Wine Drinkard*" published in *Hopes and Impediments: Selected Essays, 1965–1987,* by Chinua Achebe.

1989   Honorary Fellow of the Modern Language Association (United States).

1990   *The Village Witch-Doctor and Other Stories* published by Faber and Faber.

1992   Pan-African Writers Association Diploma of Noble Patrons (Ghana).

1995   Meridian Award (Odu Themes Meridian).

1996   Special Fellowship Award. National League of Veteran Journalists, Oyo State Chapter.

1997   Dies at home in Odo-Ona (June 7).

Chapter One
The Tutuola Phenomenon

Amos Tutuola is undoubtedly one of the most controversial of African writers; indeed, many would assert that he is indisputably, and by far, the most controversial. In the assessment of a writer and his art, or in the exploration of literature, controversy could lead to unusual and profound insights that in the end deepen understanding and broaden perspectives, but in the case of Tutuola and his writing, controversy has tended to cloud judgment and obscure fruitful discussion. The reason is that circumstances at the time of his emergence imposed an unfortunate and sometimes acrimonious imperative for a certain degree of subterfuge and defensiveness on those who engaged in the debate on his genius. Harold Collins's otherwise most useful monograph on Tutuola bears ample testimony to that fact.[1] A revisit with the author almost a half century into his remarkable career, and almost 30 years after Collins's book, offers an opportunity for a more dispassionate contemplation of the man, his achievements, the reception they have enjoyed, and the historical significance of it all.

Paradoxes

On the appearance of Tutuola's second published book, *My Life in the Bush of Ghosts,*[2] Eric Robinson compared it to the earlier *The Palm-Wine Drinkard and His Dead Palm-Wine Tapster in the Deads' Town*[3] and expressed his misgivings about the author's future. Despite the "pungency" of Tutuola's English (which Robinson nevertheless found to be an unreliable instrument), he remarked on the repetitiousness of the author's comparisons, phrases, and even images, not only within the later work but also from the earlier to the later. Robinson agreed with W. S. Pritchett's description of *Drinkard* as "a freak," saying that the freak had now been repeated. With some dismay, Robinson continued:

> We are told that still other manuscripts exist, presumably of a similar kind. Is there sufficient strength in Mr. Tutuola's work to justify publication of further works; do they point the way for a true Nigerian literature

1

in English? There must be grave doubts whether there is a strong possibility of development in or from the two books.[4]

In spite of such doubts, Tutuola's productivity has been durable, spanning almost the entire second half of the twentieth century. He has produced nine novels and two collections of short stories, and many of these have been well enough received to be translated into several European languages.

But these accomplishments notwithstanding, only a few critics would consider naming him among the more important figures in African literature. Writers whose careers have been considerably shorter, whose output has been more meager, and who have not enjoyed as wide a reading as Tutuola have had a far easier time making that list than he. More serious critics would place Gabriel Okara, for instance, with his one novel, *The Voice* (1964), ahead of Tutuola in significance, although both authors share the distinction of writing in unconventional or nonstandard English. Furthermore, although *Drinkard* was published in 1952, six years before the publication of his compatriot Chinua Achebe's *Things Fall Apart*, students of African literature are more likely to name Achebe, rather than Tutuola, as the pioneering figure in modern Nigerian (or African) literature; indeed, Simon Gikandi's introduction to the 1996 revised edition of *Things Fall Apart* credits Achebe with inventing African literature.[5]

What I propose to argue, however, is that in some important regards, Tutuola is far more significant than even the most celebrated African writers, Achebe and the Nobel laureate Wole Soyinka among them. That seems a daring assertion, but it is easily demonstrated and maintained. No matter how critics and posterity might judge his literary merit, Tutuola—more than such accomplished literary luminaries as mentioned—symbolizes the African condition and its persistence from the colonial to the postcolonial (or, as some would prefer, neocolonial) period. The turbulence that his debut with *Drinkard* generated, I suggest, is itself best understood in that light.

Tutuola and the African Condition

Modern African historians agree that when, after World War II, the colonizers recognized the inevitability of terminating brute colonialism—colonialism, that is, in its naked, conventional guise—they adopted the strategy of cultivating a complaisant elite *(interlocuteurs valables)* among the colonized, to whom the colonizers could grant a formal transfer of power, a semblance of independence, but on whom they could neverthe-less rely to cede effective control of the nominally independent states to the supposedly departed colonizers. The creation of colonial universities in the waning days of colonization (where none had been deemed neces-sary before) answered the need to create this cadre of surrogates, from among whom the literary elite has as a rule emerged. For the colonized person, the conditions for achieving elite status within this scheme cen-tered on his or her assimilation as far as possible (and permissible) into the culture of the colonizer. The determination of the specifics of qualifi-cation, and the extent to which an aspirant to assimilation had met them, were naturally reserved for authoritative figures in the colonial metropoles.

Language

One of the features of elite preparation was a deliberate process of enforced adherence (in schools especially) to the languages of the colo-nizers, which rendered those who went through it more or less incompe-tent users of their native languages. The process was reinforced by Euro-centric indoctrination that induced in participants the regard of their native cultures as pathologies and, inevitably, a resultant desire to dis-tance themselves from traditional allegiances and their markers. Accord-ingly, the truly assimilated colonized person, the exemplary elite, was not only clad in three-piece woolen suits even in the heat of the tropics, and a staunch adherent of one or the other of the Christian denomina-tions, but also a proud and often exhibitionistic client of the appropriate European language. Fluency in the colonial tongue was arguably the most persuasive means of demonstrating one's qualification for elite status in the colonial scheme. It also was an emblem that announced one's insider status with regard to the culture of the masters. V. Y. Mudimbe has testified that in colonial Zaire, French was "the 'property' of the elite, and knowledge of it was meted out with great cautiousness. The colonized peoples desirous of its social status came to view French as the means to social promotion and prestige."[6]

Writing on the discussion during the colonial period of the desirabil-ity of encouraging the adoption of Yoruba for school instruction, and eventually for general use in the Yoruba area of Nigeria, Agboola Olo-gunde cited as one of the hurdles to such a development "the pride of certain parents in seeing their children speak only English in their homes."[7] In *Aké: The Years of Childhood,* Wole Soyinka indicates his greater competence in English than in Yoruba when he was a youngster. He insisted in a conversation with his friend Osiki that the *egúngún* must be able to speak English, for only so would he be able to converse with them in his desired reincarnation as one of them.[8] The pursuit of Anglophonism usually went far beyond mere comprehension and ordinary facility. In the Yoruba world, those acknowledged as possessing the deepest mastery of the language, the elders and *babaláwo,* for example, have at their disposal arcane words and phrases that (although part of the language) are intelligible only to others like themselves—accessible, that is, to those privy to *awo* (mysteries) but closed to the *ògbèrì* (noninitiates). The colonized elite wished for a command of English comparable to the Yoruba initiates' command of Yoruba, in other words, command of a brand of English that would be virtually incomprehensible to many who believe that they understand the language.

It was not a trait exclusive to the Yoruba. At the time of Tutuola's emergence as a literary figure, one of the country's most popular politicians was Dr. Nnamdi Azikiwe, nicknamed "Akwukwo" in his native Igbo language ("Books" in English). His popularity rested to a considerable degree on the public perception of him as the most learned person in the country, a perception he assiduously promoted. Wherever his name was listed (as contemporary almanacs will attest), it was followed by a string of his academic degrees, earned and honorary, among the latter being the doctorate that legitimized the title that was always attached to his name. The story was told of the manner in which a worshipful follower once introduced him to an admiring crowd. Said he of Azikiwe, "Eh-mu A, he get am; Elli-elli.D, he chop am; Pee Ayeshee.D, he knack am; them degree wey he no get, them dash am!"[9] One of the means Azikiwe adopted to reinforce the public perception of his erudition, and therefore election, was his customary resort to bombastic English terminology and phraseology. Students at University College, Ibadan (now the University of Ibadan), in the 1960s regaled themselves with accounts of a famous Azikiwe campaign rally opener: "I will not begin my speech today with any concobility."[10]

Soyinka offers an exposé of this desire for opacity in *Ibadan: The Penkelemes Years,* in which his recollection of his life as a student at Government College Ibadan includes accounts of several run-ins with the senior boy Ezeoba. The latter responds to new boy Maren's (Soyinka's) assertion that he is not from a village with:

Then that wooden receptacle for what I presume must be your private paraphernalia strikes my judgement as incompatible with your protestations, which I am inclined to accept, since your phonetical articulation of the English language is passable, intelligible, and you may not require remedial coaching to save the House public embarrassment.[11]

He notes that the senior boy was disappointed when Maren, by asking if Ezeoba's opening reference was to his box, indicated that he understood what he was talking about. Of course, some critics contend that Soyinka's own career has been built on a demonstration of his breathtaking mastery of obscure English.

The perceived necessity on the part of African writers (Anglophone ones at least) to thus flaunt their virtuosity in English has provoked the ire of critics such as Chinweizu and his colleagues against Soyinka and other impenetrable poets (such as Chris Okigbo), whom the critics characterize as afflicted with Hopkins's disease, and whose style they dismiss as "wrapped up in obscurantist turgidities . . . [and] elaborate mountains of pompous chaff."[12]

The will to assimilate expressed itself in other ways than language— for example, identity. Long after they had replaced Tutuola as the focus of European literary attention, new African writers were objecting to being described as "African" writers, or "African" dramatists, or "African" poets. They objected to the "African" because to them the descriptor (or qualifier) somehow took the luster from "writers," "dramatists," and "poets." In "Africa and Her Writers," Achebe referred, with apparent disapproval, to reports that the Ghanaian writer Ayi Kwei Armah asserted that he was not an African writer but just a writer.[13] Achebe also quoted his fellow Igbo writer Christopher Okigbo as declaring, "There is no African literature. There is good writing and bad writing— that is all" (Achebe 1976, 37).

Precocious Curiosity

When Eric Larrabee interviewed Tutuola in Lagos after the publication of *Drinkard,* he said of the book, "The grammar is not correct at all. I made many mistakes."[14] On the face of it, Tutuola had poor grammar on his mind, but Larrabee astutely read the statement as indicative of Tutuola's sense "of his own naivete, of being treated as a curiosity" or as "a freak." Larrabee was correct, and Tutuola was not alone in suspecting that Europeans regarded Africans and African writers as curiosities.

Africans reading contemporary European reviews of Tutuola's early
books felt that there were reasons to suspect a subtext in the opinions
the reviewers voiced. To those Africans, the indulgent European readers
and critics, having concluded that the African brain was comparatively
undeveloped, had decided on rather lax standards by which to measure
African writing. Their suspicion was of course in line with the belief
entertained in some scholarly circles that Africans and African cultures
were living mosaics, artifacts in which earlier stages of European mental
and cultural development were vivified. Dylan Thomas's description of
Tutuola's usage as "young English written by a West African" certainly
betrayed that subtext, as did V. S. Pritchett's priceless description of
Tutuola's voice as "like the beginning of man on earth, man emerging,
wounded and growing."[15]

Consequently, as the debate raged on whether Tutuola's novels pre-
saged a new departure for African creativity, whether his reliance on
folktales and already familiar materials was defensible, and whether his
version of English was art or drivel, a Yoruba student at Durham (who,
significantly, had not read the books that prompted the debate) offered
his views on Tutuola's disservice to people like him. Startled by what he
considered the suspiciously speedy translation of *My Life* into French, I.
Adeagbo Akinjogbin attributed European interest in Tutuola's writing
to its pandering to Europeans' quest for the exotic by purveying "some
of the unbelievable things in our folklores."[16] Akinjogbin lived in
Britain, we must remember, at a time when anecdotes were rife among
African dwellers and travelers in Europe about requests from Europeans
that they confirm, by stripping, the rumor that Africans had tails—at a
time, that is, when certain Europeans still believed Africa to be the land
of the Niam-Niams.

Yet, curiosity or not, Tutuola has proved precocious in a sense, as well
as exemplifying the African condition: he opted for English *before* the
emergence of later writers whose particular situations—the linguistic
consequences of the manner of elite formation—would lend the most
powerful and the most credible support to the argument that the African
writer's preference for a European language was and is inevitable. But
instead of an admission of the truth that colonial refashioning rendered
the embrace of African languages impractical, the preferred supportive
contention one hears is that no available African alternative is viable
because of the multiplicity of African languages (and its implications for
audience size). According to Charles Larson, one of the earliest propo-
nents of this thesis,

the African writer who writes in a European language has chosen to do so out of expediency rather than from any real desire to communicate in a non-African tongue. Because Africa is a continent with so many different ethnic groups, with somewhere around a thousand different languages and dialects, the African writer has had little option in choosing the language for his writing. If he should choose to write in his native tongue . . . he seriously limits the size of his reading audience. For better or for worse, because of the colonial era, English and French seem fated to be the two major languages of communication on the African continent.[17]

Let us quickly and summarily dispose of Larson's suggestion that the writers had no "real desire" to communicate in European languages, as it contradicts what one knows about the psychology of colonialism, which most certainly inculcated in the exemplary colonized mentality a desire to emulate the colonizer in all important regards, including, as we have seen, language.

When he concedes volition to the writers in this matter, Larson contrives nevertheless to severely undercut it: they have chosen, but with "little option in choosing." Abiola Irele's reading of the situation recalls Larson's but differs in a significant respect. African writers, according to Irele, express themselves "in a language that they have not deliberately chosen."[18] He explained the lack of choice, though, in terms of another mark of the African condition—the mandatory extraversion of African artistic expression. "Modern African literature," he argued, "necessarily had to be directed at a foreign audience to start with, firstly because of the language factor and secondly because the habit of reading was, and is, still new in these parts" (Irele 1971, 11). The newness of the reading habit, we are to understand, translates to a limited audience for the writer.

My use of "audience" instead of "market" is deliberate. One would normally assume that the concern with audience size was ultimately an economic consideration, for the number of books a writer sold would determine his or her monetary return, and therefore whether the writer's chosen vocation (or avocation) would support the style of living to which he or she hoped to become accustomed. But although the economic argument would have some merit today, it did not, and could not, when Tutuola began his career, or when the two scholars offered their observations. In 1952 Africans simply did not perceive writing as a lucrative profession. In Nigeria the aspiration of most upwardly mobile people was to become doctors, engineers, senior civil servants, perhaps lawyers, and thence politicians, but *hardly ever* writers.

One can safely contend that Tutuola was most probably unconcerned about what the implication of the language in which he chose to write would be for the size of his royalties. He simply had no model of any person making a living, let alone a good living, out of writing. Indeed, the model he had—his benefactor in more ways than one—was D. O. Fagunwa; and Fagunwa was an education officer, the position from which his prestige and living derived, *and he wrote in Yoruba*. Larson made his observation in 1972, 20 years after the publication of Tutuola's first book and well after Achebe and Soyinka had become world famous. Significantly, Larson also wrote, "there is still no African writer who lives solely on the income he derives from his work" (Larson 1972, 277). Tutuola began writing, to reiterate, *before* the emergence of writers such as Achebe and Soyinka, whose careers would *eventually* demonstrate the lucrative potential of the foreign market. Besides, Tutuola's champions and critics agree that he was far too unsophisticated to have based his language choice on material calculations.

The suggestion that European languages were *imposed* on the subject people is itself unsupportable. The argument could conceivably be defended with regard to the translocated African populations of the New World, but the African in Africa was only *induced* to adopt a European language; for all the inducement, though, he or she made a deliberate choice. Moreover, the application of the argument to Tutuola, even after the foregoing amendment, would be problematic, because those inducements (to become Europhone, or, properly, more so) came into play only at some point *after* the subject person had become effectively insinuated into the Europhone orbit and had lost the better part of his or her native-language competence. Such a person would have advanced far enough in the Europhone direction that going back into Afrophonism would have become more difficult than advancing further in the direction he or she was already headed. Tutuola had not reached the point of no return; he had received only enough education to qualify for menial employment in the colonial structure, such as the position of messenger he held at the time he embarked on his literary career; he did not belong among those select subjects on whom the colonizers had lavished their attention, and whom they had assiduously cultivated to assume postcolonial leadership. His choice nevertheless to self-insinuate into the predicament (if such it was) was thus that much more deliberate, and remarkable.

Validating the Colonizing Project

If, as Larson indicates, African writers did not opt for European languages and extraversion in response to a utilitarian or subsistence imperative, according to which doing so would assure them of a meal ticket, their outward directedness, their preference to address themselves to *European* audiences, must be otherwise explained. The explanation, as I hope the discussion so far has shown, is that the choice was an evidence of their desire to win approbation from those who conferred elite status on their worthy subjects. It was, moreover, a matter of prestige, a cause for pride for having proved oneself an exemplary product of the refashioning, the so-called "civilizing," process.

The record admittedly shows that in the colonial metropoles, attitudes toward the aspirations of the colonized subjects to become true copies of the colonizers were not uniform. For example, whereas the French wished to convert their colonial subjects to black French men and women and accordingly applauded those of their subjects who achieved the near crossover, the British were put off by the spectacle of black English men and women. English fictional representations of Africans aping Europeans were in the nature of circus freaks, and early photographs of visiting Africans to Britain (cross)dressed in tuxedos and top hats seemed intended to provoke reactions reminiscent of the sentiments a contemporary Yoruba satirical song expressed: *"Mo rêèmò lÉréko ajá wèwù ó róso"* [I saw an abominable sight at Eréko market: dogs wore shirts and wrappers]. Even today, black citizens of Britain, such as Paul Gilroy, author of *The Black Atlantic*,[19] complain that they are still excluded from Englishness. But, for all that, one can aver that the Europeanized African elite, on the whole, served the colonial agenda by endorsing the colonial thesis that Europeanness was preferable to Africanness, thus relieving the colonizers of any guilt complexes that might have arisen from having to confront and acknowledge the truth of their destructive assaults on other cultures and civilizations.

Ungrammatical and unsophisticated Tutuola is thus something of an exception that proves a rule, the rule of success through a necessary mastery of the master's language and manners. His success proved a counterrule—that the colonized person who somehow validates and valorizes the colonizing project may thrive by the grace of the colonizer, *in spite of deficiencies in those qualities normally considered requisite for doing so.*

If Tutuola sensed that he was something of a curiosity, he was not entirely wrong, as the tenor of the critical writing about his first books indicates. The pattern of the critical reception of the work might have bemused contemporary observers, but hindsight shows that it could hardly have been different. *Drinkard* and the "young English" of its author bewitched Dylan Thomas, who was also affected by the fantastically antipodean nature of the many features and creatures that populate it—its "spirit-bristling bush," the Faithful-Mother's "technicolour night-club" tree house, and the Drinkard's destination, Deads' Town. The enthusiasm with which Thomas and other European readers embraced the new work's departure from the run-of-the-mill characters and settings of the realistic novel was essentially of the same order as the fascination that nonrealistic figurative African art held for European artists (such as Pablo Picasso). In describing the work, Thomas said that it was "nearly always terse and direct, strong, wry, flat and savoury," and that "nothing is too prodigious or too trivial to put down in this tall, devilish story."[20] That description contains a truth that has endured: applause for Tutuola's later work has always been predicated on an indulgent, willing suspension of the usual standards for evaluating literature, a suspension Kingsley Amis, for one, confessed he could not manage.[21]

Language and the Surveillance Imperative

The suppression of the colonized person's native tongue in favor of the colonial language was an integral component of the strategy for dominating and controlling the colonized subjects. In this regard, all colonizing cultures were at one. They contrived to linguistically assimilate those of their subjects who would affect the course of affairs for very much the same reasons that the slave owners in the New World forced their slaves to express themselves in the master's language. The objective was to facilitate surveillance over the subjects and minimize the possibility of insurrection by them. Mudimbe thus reports the Belgian colonial authorities' thinking with regard to their inaugurating the Francophone journal *La Voix du Congolais* as an organ in which the Congolese *évolués* could express themselves on their grievances against the colonizers, and indeed on any matter: "They can write to their heart's content; their texts—generally dealing with apparently inoffensive matters such as traditional life and customs, the politics of assimilation, or fiction—are, indeed, when accepted, carefully checked and edited by an editorial board, and then published" (Mudimbe 1994, 123).

Robert Plant Armstrong was certainly not functioning as an agent of empire (at least not deliberately) when he praised Tutuola for his choice of language, but Armstrong's reasoning was in concert with this surveillance imperative. He applauded Tutuola in part because in rendering Yoruba materials in English, and in a manner that (in Armstrong's view) preserved their traditional tenor, "he has doubly blessed the serious student who does not command enough of Yoruba to understand the traditional texts as they are traditionally communicated by writing in English."[22] His "serious student," one must assume, is not African. In this view, then, what Tutuola has done is consistent with the role reserved to the African writer in the colonial economy—to make the ways and thoughts of his or her people available to "the [European] serious student," who is, however, not serious enough to take make the effort to learn the language of the subject. O. R. Dathorne, in agreeing with Armstrong in this regard, rejected the notion that Tutuola might write even in "raw" pidgin English, for, according to Dathorne, pidgin would be "unintelligible to European readers."[23]

Subterfuge and Its Consequences

The strange turns that the discussion of Tutuola and his career has taken (turns that will be apparent in the pages that follow) have resulted because it has often tended to skirt fundamental considerations, such as the ones I have laid out in the foregoing pages. Tutuola's example of rejecting his native Yoruba, the language in which he was most fluent, in favor of the alien English, his control of which was most precarious, is quite obviously an example of a Kafkaesque opting for the status of courier (or slave) over the available alternative of kingship. The main difference is that in this case, the desire is to *emulate* the colonial master. Tutuola's is only an extreme version of the same syndrome that afflicts the colonized African elite, and that they remain intent on cultivating and preserving. The necessity to sublimate that syndrome explains the various versions of the contention that mastery of language is irrelevant to literary art, or indeed that linguistic incompetence is a literary asset. It also explains, I suggest, the eagerness of some accomplished African Anglophone writers (for example, Chinua Achebe, Taban Lo Liyong, and also Wole Soyinka) to embrace Tutuola as a literary genius, for thus they demonstrate their freedom from any ivory-tower, proprietary-protective impulses toward the English language, and also toward mastery of the *received* art of fiction.

The ensuing exploration of Tutuola's work and the Tutuola phenomenon is intended not only to offer a deeper understanding of the man and his work but also to shed more light on the African condition during this momentous twentieth century.

Chapter Two
Tutuola and the Civilizing Project

In many regards, Tutuola is a triumph of the European missionizing and civilizing enterprise in Africa—that is, of the impulses directly responsible for the present African condition. His opting to write in English despite his better facility with Yoruba is a measure of his captivation by European or Western values and habits. The makeup of the (other) worlds in which his heroes and heroines live their fictional lives, and the otherworldy experiences they have therein, also demonstrate and respond to that captivation, inasmuch as they are intended to appeal to the taste indicated in Dylan Thomas's testimonial to *The Palm-Wine Drinkard*. Other instances abound in Tutuola's works.

Besides the rum with which European slavers reportedly stupefied the African chiefs they dealt with, and the guns with which they incited Africans to war against one another, the scintillating, colorful, but virtually valueless trinkets the Europeans proffered also proved most fatally attractive to their African dupes. Well into the period of colonialism, the elite types proudly proclaimed their election with displays of their acquisitions of such emblems. The family photograph almost invariably included pictures of the patriarch, clad in a suit and appropriately trussed with a necktie, perhaps also sporting a pith helmet and nonprescription eye glasses. Around him would be his dependents, also well turned out in Western attire, and his status symbols. These might include a His Master's Voice gramophone atop a cabinet (covered, of course, with an antimacassar), a bicycle, and the like. The attraction of European baubles and gadgets has survived the ending of the slave trade and colonization and manifests itself in myriad guises wherever one cares to look on the continent. The items offered for display would be different today, of course, upgraded to reflect advances in technology, affluence, and sophistication, but the culture is the same.

Material Indices of Mental Colonization

The allure of Westernisms manifests itself in a variety of guises in Tutuola's work. In general, though, it amounts to his association of

Westernesque, Europeanesque, or modern material paraphernalia and institutions with the good life. In other words, the more different the item or locale is from the typically Yoruba or African, and the closer it is to the European or Western, the greater its value and appeal. The Faithful-Mother's white tree house establishment in *Drinkard* provides a good illustration. Its first feature to capture the Drinkard's fancy is the great dancing hall in the center of the tree, large enough to accommodate 300 dancers. We can assume that the dancing is very different from traditional Yoruba dancing, which is typically done outdoors, anyway, not in dance halls. It is ballroom dancing, with music supplied by "uncountable orchestras [and] musicians." The ever-present "dancers and tappers" who "were always dancing and tapping" (68) on the more than 20 stages in the hall keep the orchestras always busy. Because dancing is virtually incessant (as is drinking), the Drinkard and his wife become good dancers within one month.

The walls of the glittering dance hall are decorated at the cost of "one million pounds £ " and bear "images" (photographs), among which the Drinkard and his wife find theirs: "But our own images that we saw there resembled us too much and were also white in color." The lights "were in technicolours and they were changing colours at five minutes intervals" (69). Three hundred and forty cooks work in the kitchen, and "all the rooms in this house were in a row," in contrast to the traditional Yoruba arrangement whereby all rooms face a central courtyard. There is also a hospital where the "patentees" (who treat the patients) attend to the wounds the traveling couple have suffered at the hands of the people of the "Unreturnable-Heaven's Town" (69). Finally, a special room to "play gamble" is available to the inhabitants of the tree house.

Recognizable in these details are the features characteristic of the new towns in the Yoruba world as laid out by the Europeans. Also recognizable are the favorite haunts of the affluent, urbanized, and westernized inhabitants of Nigeria's cities of the 1950s—gaily lit dance halls and nightclubs where they could dance to brass bands and consume European "hot" drinks.

In his books, Tutuola consistently portrays the inhabitants of cities as better and wiser, or more "civilized," than the dwellers of the bushes and jungles, as he does, for example, in *The Witch-Herbalist of the Remote Town*.[1] The valorization of urbanism and its attributes recurs quite frequently in Tutuola's writings, as, for example, in the description of Heaven, the last stop of the hero of *The Wild Hunter in the Bush of Ghosts* before returning to the world of the humans: "In every part of the

Heaven no place where music was not: the Orchestras of the Heaven were uncountable and every one of them were Angels."[2] The place brooks no darkness, and "as a matter of fact, all the lights in heaven were in Glorious Technicolours." The "Wraith Island" (of *Drinkard*), which the Drinkard and his wife had visited before their arrival at the Faithful-Mother's tree house, also features stage plays (*Drinkard*, 47). Among the Western urban features of *My Life* are the assize court of which the hero's cousin is the judge, and the medical services establishment of which the cousin's wife is the director. The parting gifts the Faithful-Mother gives to the Drinkard and his wife on their departure, besides a plentiful supply of roasted meats and drinks, a cutlass, a gun, ammunition, and cigarettes, also include the "many costly clothes etc." she gives to the wife (*Drinkard*, 71).

In *My Life*, Tutuola further itemizes his wish list for the good life. He does so, for example, in the account of the hero and his wife crossing the bridge over the Loss or Gain Valley. Being rather poor, the ghosts in those parts have devised a means of stripping better-off travelers of their attire in exchange for the ghosts' pitiful clothing. The only means of crossing the valley being a rickety, narrow bridge not strong enough to support the weight of people wearing any clothing, travelers must strip and cross naked to the other side, hoping there to find clothes discarded by people who had crossed earlier from that side. The ghost-bush wanderer and his wife cast off their expensive clothing, which cost as much as £100, and make the crossing, but they find no clothes waiting for them on the other side. When eventually "a couplet ghosts, wife and husband" come by, they are clad only in animal skins. These they strip off before crossing the bridge:

> Having reached [the other side] they did not waste time, but the husband wore my costly clothes as trousers, shirt, tie, socks, shoes, hat, golden ring with my costly wrist-watch. After this his wife wore my wife's clothes as—underwear, gown, golden beads, rings, hat, shoes, wrist-watch, after that she handled her (my wife's) lofty hand-bag. (*My Life*, 132)

The list of items is similar to the one that defines the affluence of the wealthy wild people of the jungle on the way to the remote town of the Witch-Herbalist in the novel named for her: "Every one of them wore very costly garments, etc. . . . . And also every one of them put on neck, wrists, ankles, etc. the most costly gold, corals, diamonds, silver, etc.

and the kind of cap on each head was just like a crown of a king" (*Herbalist,* 45).

The Ethics of Loot

The underlying motivation for the European adventure in Africa (as in other colonized lands), whose consequences continue to ramify in African lives, is the appropriation of the resources of the continent for the benefit of Europe. Tutuola demonstrates his internalization of Western values in the manner in which he rationalizes some of his adventures, and the actions of some of his heroes and heroines, which recall the ethics manifest in European adventures among non-Europeans in the non-European world. Just as early European travelers in Africa assumed the right to indenture any African they encountered into involuntary labor, so the hero of *Wild Hunter* says matter-of-factly, "when I was going about . . . I saw a young Ghost under a banana-tree, then I went to him, and captured him as a slave, then I gave him my both gun and my hunting-bag to carry, and I put him at my front and walked closely, so that he might not run away with my gun and bag" (*Wild Hunter,* 37). The ghost escapes while his captor is asleep. Although he had left his gun lying carelessly about, the ghost, more "humane" than his captor, does not harm the now vulnerable abuser; he is interested only in his freedom.

Also in accord with European colonial practices is the assumption that the despoiler's rights embrace not only the targeted victim's person (his or her freedom and labors) but also his or her possessions, including land and all its resources. The assumption is manifest, for example, in *Feather Woman of the Jungle.* The entertainment of the fourth night includes the account of the narrator's capture, after he has fallen from his hiding spot in a tree and landed on top of a spirit-king. Held captive in a cave, the narrator sees "many pots of corals, raw gold and silver, money, expensive beads, etc.," and he begins to hyperventilate. "I thought of two things," he says, "how to save my life from him [his captor] and how to take some of that treasures away."[3] The narrator's trusty dogs (who can hear his summons from great distances) come to his rescue, and once free he engages in some armed robbery: "I took my gun and hunting-bag and after that I went back to him. I was threatening him with my gun to give me some of his treasures. When he agreed to do so, I dragged him to his room and he allowed me to take some of each" (*Feather Woman,* 65).

The narrator-hero later offers the unlikely and unconvincing disclaimer that "if he had not agreed to give me some of his property, I would not attempt to take them for I did not like to be an extortioner." The pretense to moral scruples is exploded by the evidence of the entertainment of the 10th night, which continues the elaboration of the hero's ethics of loot. In the town of wealth, he and his companion Ajasa ask to lodge with the chief, who asks them if they want a job. They tell him quite directly that they are not after jobs but have come to take some of the wealth back to their own town. "He was greatly shocked to hear like that from us," the narrator says, and no wonder (*Feather Woman,* 127). They seize their opportunity and attempt to sneak off with stolen gold bricks one night when the household is asleep, but they are caught and severely beaten for their pains.

The episodes set on the Diamond Mountain are also informed by the same ethics of loot. While the hero is the guest of the Goddess of Diamonds, he spends all his time plotting how to steal her diamonds. After he has taken Sela as his wife, he sneaks off with her (because the Goddess will not grant Sela permission to leave the mountain), carrying stolen diamonds, some acquired through the iconoclastic breaking off of the heads of diamond statues (*Feather Woman,* 93). In a later episode, returning to the mountain to retrieve Sela (who has been abducted and returned there by agents of the Goddess), he escapes with her—but also steals enough diamonds to set them up handsomely for life (131).

In fairness, it is possible to argue that the roguish tendencies of the hero of *Feather Woman* are simply other expressions of Tutuola's penchant to shock his readers with outrageously grotesque and contrary characters. The caveat is necessary, given the care the hero takes to inform his listeners that he tried to caution the people who joined him on his sixth journey against expectations of easy riches. The wealth with which he returned on his previous journeys, he told them, "had not been stolen nor had I been monopolized people of their properties, but I had done a lot of dangerous and risky works for them before they had given them to me as rewards" (*Feather Woman,* 105). That is not entirely true, of course.

Otherization

Tutuola's characteristic practice when setting up his adventures is to invest his heroes, heroines, and their world with the attributes of normality, and then to imagine the grossest possible departures from those attributes for the challenges with which the hero or heroine must contend. Brawler, one of the three principal characters of *Pauper, Brawler, and Slanderer,*[4] is a noteworthy exception to the characteristic normality of the hero/heroine in that she is afflicted with the curse of involuntary and incessant "brawling." She is an exception, though, only if one takes her to be one part of a trio of principal characters. As an alternative, she can be seen as just another challenge—the same as Slanderer—for Pauper, the real hero, and thus as an example of Tutuola's tendency (quite in keeping with European practice) to pathologize difference. The common assumption has always been that the world of Tutuola's books, because his education is so limited, is fundamentally informed by Yoruba values and ethos. The discussion thus far has touched on some manifestations, to the contrary, of his admiration of the colonizers' stock in trade. In examining his work, one finds that the complex of attributes he associates with normality (or with utopia) includes, in addition to those already mentioned, Christianity and Western education.

The grotesqueness of the contrary spirits and monsters—such as the Long-Breasted Mother of the Mountain, the Abnormal Squatting Man of the Jungle, and the Crazy Removable-Headed Wild Man, all of *Witch-Herbalist*—who make life difficult for his heroes and exciting for his readers serves a vital purpose, for without it Tutuola would be deprived of his means of creating a worthwhile sense of conflict or any excitement. In several instances, though, he invites criticism because his valuation grid reflects his hostility to difference; and since his norm is Western and European, the result is that when one looks carefully at his work, one finds a pronounced anti-African strain.

Quite naturally, his anthropocentric inclinations dispose him to position humans at the top of his great chain of being, and to judge other creatures by human standards. The "most beautiful creatures in the world of the curious creatures" of the "wraith-island" in *Drinkard* are most beautiful simply or mainly because "whenever these island creatures dress, you would be thinking they were human-beings" (47). When he provides more specific descriptive details of the beings who occupy the apex of the great chain, one discovers that their features are decidedly European. The nymph queen of the water people in *Feather Woman* is representative: "Her nose was quite pointed like that of an image" (*Feather Woman*, 74), a comparison in keeping with the Yoruba practice of setting up carved images *(ère)* as the ultimate standard of beauty. The monstrous Giant and Giantess are by contrast markedly different: "Their nose were very big and the nostrils were full of hair" (116).

Because Christianity is legitimately associable with Aryanness, the Drinkard's description of the woman who would eventually become his wife as "very beautiful as an angel" (*Drinkard,* 18) is consistent with this valuation scheme. Also consistent with the thinking that produces such a comparison is the description of certain creatures the wild hunter and company encounter on their way to heaven. These creatures live atop a mountain and "resembled goats, but only their bodies were resembled that of HUMAN-BODIES but their heads were resembled that of SHE-GOATS" (*Wild Hunter,* 141). The travelers later discover that "they were among the traitors who betrayed Jesus Christ when He was in the earth."

Tutuola reinforces the Eurocentric tenor of his value system by adopting Negrophobic color symbology that is derivative of colonialist prejudices, and that betrays his innocence of its anti-African nuances. The blissful and life-affirming locations in his works are usually characterized by light and whiteness, as is the Faithful-Mother's white tree house in *Drinkard,* and the Witch-Herbalist's assembly hall. The ghosts in Victoria Juliana's town are all in "white dressings" (*Wild Hunter,* 77); but the gatekeeper of the fifth town (which is ruled by King "Devil") "was very black like charcoal," and when the hero and his companions enter the town, they see "two soldiers" who "resembeled human-beings, but they were not, and these soldiers were as black as black paint" (111). Furthermore, the inhabitants of the town are evil natured, "and the whole of them were very black as coals, their heads were entirely covered with hair and it was very hard to see their eyes or faces, and there we saw a child of one day who was as black as coaltar" (115).

In *Ajaiyi and His Inherited Poverty,*[5] the Devil is also clothed in blackness: he appears in "black garments, black slippers, black cap, black bracelets on both wrists and ankles, all of him was as black as black paint. His disciples were about fifty all were in black dresses" (*Ajaiyi,* 184–85). He also rides a black horse. And in *Herbalist,* the Crazy Removable-Headed Wild Man is "so black that it darkened that spot on which he was turning around" (73).

The same mentality that informs the color symbology in question here is evident in Tutuola's reference to "the primitive customs of Laketu town" and of the Town of Women in *Pauper* (3, 121), and the description of the people of the Rocky Town, the home of the hero of *Witch-Herbalist,* as "pagans" (11); it is also manifest in his frequent use of such terms as "witch-doctor," "witch-herbalist," "jungle," "heathen," and the like.

Education

In Tsitsi Dangarembga's *Nervous Conditions* (1988), the pull of Western education becomes a sufficient incitement for Tambudzai, a young Shona woman, to will the death of the person she sees as the main obstacle to her acquiring it, even though the person is her brother by the same mother. Dangarembga wrote her novel about Tambu's impulsion toward Western education in 1988; almost 40 years earlier, Tutuola was already composing devotionals and testimonials to this particular bequest of the colonizing and civilizing project. The best examples come from the Bush-of-Ghosts novels. In life, the wife of the hero's cousin in the 10th town of ghosts in *My Life* was a native of "a town in Zulu country" and had achieved the ultimate, what in colonial times was described as capturing the golden fleece—she had gone "abroad" to the land of the whites and had acquired the highest possible education. Her father had sent her to "a part of England as a doctor student," but on returning home after qualifying as a doctor, she had died in an accident (*My Life,* 149). Her story is repeated in some important regards by that of Victoria Juliana of the fourth town of ghosts in *Wild Hunter.* She, too, was born in South Africa, her parents having migrated (presumably from England) there in 1800. She had died at the age of 12 after a fall down the stairs in her father's home. Because her death was premature, she was prevented from entering heaven, a fortunate development for the ghosts of those parts, for she devoted her time to establishing a Salvation Army church, just as her father had done in South Africa, and building schools. Her schools, incidentally, are an ideological apparatus of British imperialism, for she has her ghost-pupils celebrating Empire Day (*Wild Hunter,* 83). Thanks to her, the hero captures his own golden fleece: she educates him, makes him the headmaster of her schools, and leaves him in charge when she is finally translated to heaven to the accompaniment of beautiful music and a symphony of colors.

Christianity

Michael Adas has pointed out in *Machines as the Measure of Man* (1989) that the Europeans who first encountered Chinese civilization, unable to claim the superiority of their own on the basis of technological advance, substituted their possession of Christianity as the proof that their culture was superior. Tutuola reflects the durable service that religious persua-

sion had done for the westerners in their construction and pathologiza-
tion of otherness. Because Christian missions were the primary agents
who introduced Western education into Africa, it is not surprising that
Christian prejudices would be closely associated with its acquisition.
Given the importance of names and naming in the Yoruba world, it is of
interest that when the Wild Hunter tells Victoria Juliana that his name
is Joseph Adday, she is happy, because it is a name that "pertained to
God" (*Wild Hunter,* 79). As James Coleman has noted, the abandonment
of African names was one of the conditions European missionaries (and
their African helpers) forced on the Africans who fell under their sway,[6]
on the conviction, obviously, that African names did not "pertain to
God." This is only one of the instances of the intrusion of unexamined
and uncritical Christian biases into Tutuola's work.

In *Simbi and the Satyr of the Dark Jungle,* Dogo's town is "Sinners'
town," because of the inhabitants' devotion to gods other than the
Christian one. Worshipers of "gods" (as distinct from the Christian
"God") and adherents of traditional, non-Christian religions are consistently demonized and contrasted to Christians, who are good. Dogo is
"an expert kidnapper of children and he was a native of a town called
'Sinners' town,' the town in which only sinners and worshippers of gods
were living."[7] Each of the traits that cluster to define evil in this regard
implies the others. The detail that all the inhabitants of his town worship "gods" thus removes any doubt about their perdition.

The surrogate missionizing purpose (coupled with its customary educational adjunct) also informs the Bush-of-Ghosts novels, as it does
Ajaiyi. In *My Life* the hero's cousin has earned himself the respect and
admiration of the inhabitants of the 10th town of ghosts because he has
established Christianity there and gone to great lengths to convert them
to the religion. A "staunch member of the Methodist church" before he
died, he had resolved to "carry on the services until the last day, which is
the 'judgement-day' " (146). He has accordingly built more than a
thousand churches, schools, and hospitals, and he serves as bishop
(ordained by God himself), maintaining his headquarters in the 10th
town, where he presides over the annual synod.

In *Ajaiyi,* when the defrauded hero finally recovers his stolen wealth
from the witch doctor, instead of spending the money on himself, he
decides to build churches with it. He builds one in each town where he
had received some favor in his days of suffering. "Then," he reports,
"with a few people I started to worship the God Almighty in them every
Sunday. I was then teaching the people the little I learned about God

from the town of the Creator" (234). Many more worshipers come when news spreads that the prayers in his churches cure sicknesses:

> All the evil worshippers, idol worshippers, etc. threw all their idols, etc. away and they joined us. Later on, this Witch Doctor too threw away all his gods and he joined us and it was not so long when he became one of the leaders. After some months, all the members of the churches, having understood that the God Almighty was the only to be worshipped and having seen that their prayers were heard by God, without asking them to help me with money. (*Ajaiyi*, 234)

It is in *Herbalist*, though, that Tutuola offers his most extensive elaboration of the evil represented by worship of any other than the Christian god. Based on a Yoruba trickster tale in which Àjàpá's enslavement to his gullet brings him to grief, the story (rather similar in this regard to that of Antere) is about a devoted husband's mission to a distant land to procure the medicine that will cure his wife's barrenness. The tone that pervades the entire narration is set in the opening paragraph:

> In the Rocky Town, the inhabitants worshipped only the god of iron, god of thunder, god of oracle, and god and goddess of the rivers. All kinds of images and idols and the "god of the state" which belonged to the government of the Rocky Town, were also worshipped. The inhabitants lived among the wild animals such as tigers, lions, wolves, leopards, etc. This was so because jungles, forests, etc. were more than the inhabitants of the town. (*Herbalist*, 11)

The proximity of wild animals and the abundance of "jungles, forests, etc." already mark the habitation as repulsive. To those familiar with the Yoruba world, of course, the Rocky Town recalls the author's ancestral Abeokuta, and the various gods and goddesses mentioned are recognizable as Ogun, Sango, Orunmila, Olokun, and Oya.

The hero's father, being the most intelligent person in the town, occupies the office of "the chief priest of oracle and the chief of pagans." The town allows no freedom of worship, for "if any of the inhabitants had no god, idol, or image, which he or she worshipped, both children and grown-ups of the town would not like him or her as an unbeliever, and the rest of the people would not even go near him or her at all" (*Herbalist*, 12). The compulsion of religious conformity is the more onerous because of the diabolic nature of the objects of worship, exemplified by the "god of the state," so designated because it is the most powerful and the most terrible of the gods, save for the god of thunder (Sango). Its objective representation is a fearful colossal image dressed in Rocky Town–style garments made of assorted animal skins. It is "too terrible and fearful for the eyes of human beings to see, because it held above its head a very long and big spear by the right hand in such a fearful way as if it was preparing to stab to death without any hesitation one who might go near it or stand a short distance before it" (12). Tutuola devotes a page and a half to impressing on his reader the grotesqueness and fearsomeness of this representative god, which is also "the imitation of the god or spirit of the river" (14). This god or spirit is both kind and cruel, able to open the wombs of barren women so that they can become mothers, but it is also given to destroying lives by drowning its victims. Moreover, part of the annual worship of the god or spirit is the sacrifice of a young man and a young woman.

The god or spirit will not aid the hero's "barren" wife, though (as the "deathless" paramount chiefs of the remote town will later tauntingly remind him), for her condition in fact resulted from his inadequacy as a "BORN AND DIE baby," an *àbíkú,* who is reaping the rewards of the grief he has caused many mothers in his earlier incarnations. His desperation in the absence of help from the god necessitates the pilgrimage to the remote town. The author alternatively refers to the benevolent matriarch of the town as Witch-Herbalist, Omniscient Mother, Omnipotent Mother, and Witch-Mother, because she is "omniscient and she had a very powerful omnipotence" (*Herbalist,* 141); her people and her grandchildren call her "the Omnipotent, Omnipresent and Omniscient Mother" (143). These are clearly attributes of the Christian deity. Further, the assembly hall where she holds her audiences, attended by "almost deathless" paramount chiefs, features an altar, an organ, and a resident organist. The worship in it is announced by a bell "like that of a church" (150), and the singing is accompanied by an organ. The Christian tenor of the worship is otherwise explicitly stressed:

> Then she announced loudly again that we should kneel down and close our eyes. When we did so, she praised the God Almighty for about twenty twinklings. Then she told us to sit back on our seats. But I wondered greatly that all of the songs which we sang were from the Gospel Hymn Book. Although the people called her Witch-Mother, she did not pray to the witches but to Almighty God. It was not idols, gods, images or witches that they worshipped in the Hall of Assembly. (*Herbalist,* 151)

Always, the Mother's prayers are addressed to God Almighty (*Herbalist*, 152). Moreover, when the "burdensome" people whom she has healed rejoice and praise her, she admonishes them "not to praise her but God Almighty" (157). The spectacle is reminiscent of the biblical account of Jesus healing the multitude: "Now when the sun was setting, all they that had any sick with divers diseases brought them unto him; and he laid his hands on them, and he healed them. And the devils also came out of many, crying out, Thou art Christ the Son of God. And he rebuking them suffered them not to speak: for they knew that he was Christ" (Luke 4:40–41).

When it is the hero's turn to present his burden to the Mother, "her deathless paramount chiefs, noble men and women mocked funnily at my father and the gods, idols, etc. of my town. They said with laughter: 'But your burden which has cost you many years of journey to this town, is quite simple enough for your father, the chief priest and pagan and all the gods, idols, spirits, etc. of your town to make your wife pregnant' " (*Herbalist,* 168). Traditional gods are in effect as ineffectual as Baal, a point the compassionate Mother stresses even as she kindly shields the supplicant from further embarrassment: "There is no need to mock his father and gods, idols, spirits, etc. of his town who had failed to make his wife pregnant," she cautions, "because, without the approval of God Almighty, people will fail in all attempts" (169).

Not surprisingly, the saga ends not with the hero and his wife achieving their desire to become parents but (if we discountenance, as we should, the adventitious trial of the hero's First and Second "Minds") with the termination of their town's evil practice of human sacrifice. They themselves become victims of the practice, owing to the husband's pregnancy, a consequence of his eating some of the medicine intended for his wife. The town regards them as an abomination and sacrifices them to the god of the river, who eventually releases them, together with all earlier human sacrificial victims, in exchange for the two severed heads that are the hero's ever-present prop. The god (and his goddess wife) charge them to deliver the message to Rocky Town people to end their practice of sacrificing human beings. "They said that they do not eat human beings," the hero reports (*Herbalist,* 197).

For some of his readers, Tutuola's aversion to traditional African religions is a trait deserving of admiration and praise. In defending him against charges that he garbles and otherwise misrepresents traditional Yoruba texts, Harold Collins argued that Tutuola's myth "is distinctly

denatured; it is anything but pure Yoruba polytheism and animism."
This is as one should expect, Collins suggested, because "Tutuola is a
Christian and not a nominal Christian either." Collins also endorsed Ulli
Beier's observation that "it is Tutuola's *uninformed Christian horror of the
old gods* that makes his monsters so conspicuous and so frightful" (Collins
1969, 88; italics mine). Yoruba (and Nigerian) critics of Beier's career in
the country have faulted him for several reasons, but disrespect or disregard for traditional beliefs and institutions is not one of them. His
description of the horror of the old gods as uninformed was deliberate
and signals his judgment on Tutuola's unexamined internalization of
Christian prejudices. This fact was apparently lost on Collins.

Collins's seemingly unconditional admiration of Tutuola enabled him
to excuse "the superficial paganism of Tutuola's romances" by citing the
"clear reflections of his Christian beliefs and his personal gentleness,"
and also "the great humanity of his gentle Christian soul, unembar-
rassed by the African past" (Collins 1969, 128). An example of what
such tolerance of intolerance can engender is Tutuola's treatment of
"pigmies" in *The Brave African Huntress*.[8]

Killing the Pigmies

Tutuola follows the familiar colonialist practice of demonizing candidates for exploitation or decimation as a prelude to and excuse for the
onslaught. Because the huntress's people consider the pigmies and the
animals in the Jungle of the Pigmies evil and dangerous, "they made a
meeting to kill all the wild animals, etc., and all the pigmies" (*Huntress*,
12). The description of the first pigmy she encounters is typical:

> This huge pigmy was the "obstacle" of this jungle because he was too
> cruel and fearful. He was so huge and short that if he stood at a distance
> you could not believe that he was a living creature but the stump of a
> tree. Each of his fingers was as big as a big plantain and it was perma-
> nently slightly curved. His arms were very long and thick. He had a big
> half fall goitre on his neck and he had a very big belly which, whenever
> he was going or running along, would be shaking here and there and
> sounding heavily. (*Huntress*, 61)

Tutuola further *blackens* the pigmies by having them sacrifice "a large
number" of their captives annually to their king's god (*Huntress*, 89),
and beat to death those whose work is not to the "pesters' " satisfaction

(90). Having thus prepared the reader's mind, Tutuola indulges in a homicidal orgy, dispatching multitudes of pigmies by blowing them up, incinerating them, crushing them under falling rocks, and shooting them (97–99). When the huntress returns home, she is met with a celebration worthy of a heroine, for the news has preceded her that she has accomplished the task of killing off all the pigmies.

The claim that Tutuola's work reflects the Yoruba world would seem to be sustainable on the basis of his incorporation of several Yoruba folktales in his fiction, of such episodes as the prenatal scene in Heaven where the soon-to-be-born choose their destinies (*Wild Hunter*, 147–49), or the employment of the *àbíkú* phenomenon (as in *Herbalist*). But the hostile attitude toward Nature (wild animals, jungles, forests, etc.), toward things visibly nonwhite and non-European, toward non-Christian "gods" and worship, toward names that do not "pertain to God," and such like, and the willingness to contemplate and even applaud the wanton elimination of those who are different from one, in this instance the pigmies, bespeak a spirit quite unlike that of the Yoruba.

Precontact or Postcontact

The foregoing discussion has highlighted the impact of colonialist and Christian indoctrination on Tutuola. My intention has been to show that the impact is in fact considerable and determinate, as is evident in the Europhilic and Westernesque features of his works. It is therefore necessary to acknowledge and consider, however briefly, Collins's speculation on the historical contexts of Tutuola's writings. Collins asserted that "one of the most conspicuous qualities of Tutuola's ghost novels is the pristine, pre-contact, old African atmosphere of them" (Collins 1969, 69), because none features a white character "or explicitly mentions a white person." But the actual or direct involvement of a white character is not the only manner in which white presence can express itself. A white sensibility may be pervasive even though a white figure is nowhere in evidence. Collins muddied the water, though, when he went on to locate the books in the nineteenth century and to add that because whites were quite active in the Yoruba world at the time, the works should in fact have included some (70). He did not help matters by observing that "in spite of this old-time pre-contact African setting of the folk novels, white man's customs institutions, techniques, and instruments make their appearance in the most interesting way" (78), and by proceeding to list Western, "postcontact" incidents and items (78–86).

Nor is Collins persuasive when he represented Tutuola as more favorably disposed toward traditional materials than to the Western. In his view, the Yoruba, being very "progressive," are caught in a headlong rush to modernize and Westernize. They are "a very 'progressive' people, anxious to be educated, to improve their conditions of life, and to accept the ways and works of the white man" (Collins 1969, 25).

> Too many Westerners fail to recognize the very considerable degree of Westernization that has taken place [in Africa] (the Mammy wagons, the Nigerian TV, the gas stations, etc.) and the widespread passionate desire for Western education, for industrialization. Their image of Africans entirely ignores all the dynamic desires driving Africans out of the bush and into some hitherto unimagined condition, some amalgam of Western technology and updated traditional politics, sociology, and religion. (Collins 1969, 90)

Already apparent is a meeting of minds between Tutuola and Collins—in their conception of what represents progressiveness and dynamism—pursuit of Western education, industrialization, flight from the "bush"—and in their subscription to the whiggism that assumes the necessary preferability of Westernism to Africanism. One begins to understand Collins's thinking, though, when one reads his ironic praise for Africans who are able to manage the level of achievement Tutuola has:

> Any reader who is inclined to feel superior to Africans should read George Kimble's account of the major diseases of tropical Africa, which include malaria, sleeping sickness, bilharsiasis, leprosy, tuberculosis, hookworm, filiariasis (including elephantiasis), pellagra, kwashiokor, ascariasis, yaws, amoebic and bacillary dysentery, pneumonia, ulcers, pneumonic, bubonic, and septicemis plague, typhus, yellow fever, relapsing fevers, smallpox, and meningitis. Considering the seriousness of these diseases and the very high incidence of them, we may wonder how Africans have been able to achieve anything at all. (Collins 1969, 92)

But Collins still left matters confused. If Africans manifest their progressiveness and dynamism in their headlong pursuit of Westernity, logically as a means of distancing themselves from diseased Africanity, how is one to take the suggestion that Tutuola is performing the creditable service of cultural reorientation, leading his compatriots out of their acculturating, Westernizing world, with its ready acceptance of Western technology, back into the old mythical world of heart's desire and heart's terror, or as though Tutuola were making the reader dream an old African nightmare and the technical figures were merely remnants of the mechanical paraphernalia of waking life"? (Collins 1969, 83–84)

Chapter Three

Sources

Inconsistent Stories

When asked how he came to create the characters and incidents in his stories, Tutuola has given the credit to different sources at different times. The account he gave to Arthur Calder-Marshall, which was published shortly after the appearance of *Drinkard*, reads like an episode from the book itself. Young Amos, it said, had gone to his father's farm one Sunday morning to visit a very old man. The old man served his visitor palm wine in a bamboo tumbler as deep as a glass tumbler and capable of holding half a bottle of the liquor. After about four drinks, Tutuola began to feel the effects of the palm wine: "My body was not at rest at all, it was intoxicating me as if I was dreaming." Noticing that his guest was becoming drunk, the old man suggested they go sit by a big river near the farm, where a "fresh breeze . . . was blowing here and there with strong power." At the bank of the river, they sat under a palm tree "which collected or spread as a tent," and Amos promptly fell asleep. The old man woke Amos after an hour, by which time he had come back to sobriety. "When he believed that I could enjoy what he wanted to tell me," Tutuola told Calder-Marshall, "he then told me the story of the Palm-Wine Drinkard."[1] Tutuola also claimed to have written the book in 15 hours, working 3 hours a day for five days.

Six months later, Eric Larrabee published the result of an interview he had conducted with Tutuola in Lagos. Larrabee was obviously dissatisfied with the interview, which he described as "uncomfortable and inconclusive" for both participants. He attributed the discomfort and inconclusiveness to the location of the exchange, the U.S. Consulate, which he thought made the "painfully shy" Tutuola ill at ease and perhaps suspicious of his interviewer's motives. Those conditions might account for the slight differences in the version of the sources for *Drinkard* Larrabee reported. In this case, the stories came from an old man who told stories on a palm plantation Tutuola frequented on Sundays. According to Larrabee's version of Tutuola's account, he "composed" the book in two days and wrote it in three months in 1950, "just playing with it" (Larrabee, 13).

The anonymous Nigerian correspondent for *West Africa* who gave an account of Tutuola's career in 1954, after the publication of *My Life,* had a much different story to tell. According to him, Tutuola learned all his stories from listening as a child to the "legends, and fairy tales with a moral" told by his mother and his aunt with whom he lived in the township of Iporo-Ake, Abeokuta. During his holidays, he habitually escaped to his father's farm, where in the darkness after the day's work, he exchanged the stories with his young friends. Years later, employed as an almost always idle messenger in the Labour Department in Lagos, he became "conscious of the weight of hours. To free his mind from the boredom of clock-watching he reverted to an almost forgotten childhood habit of story-telling." Because he could not tell his stories orally to an audience, he wrote them on scraps of paper instead. The correspondent reported that *Drinkard* had been "completed during forty-eight hours febrile work," and that Tutuola spent the next three months enlarging on the original (Lindfors 1975, 35–36).

The accounts fall neatly into a pattern of increasing plausibility, by which I mean that the third is, on its face, the most plausible, and the first the least. As the Nigerian correspondent observed, "Almost all children everywhere are told legends, and fairy tales with a moral, by their mothers" (Lindfors 1975, 35), and evening storytelling sessions are a pervasive fixture in Yoruba upbringing. Accordingly, like practically all Yoruba children, young Tutuola almost certainly grew up learning a number of folktales. Raised as he was as a Christian, though, it would be highly unlikely that his parents would have sent him to the farm to work on Sundays, usually observed as days of rest and worship. What is even more unlikely is that an old man wanting to tell him stories would first get him drunk. The usual Yoruba practice is to begin a storytelling session with riddles that must be solved, their solving being designed to hone the perceptive faculties the better to be able to draw the moral inferences from the tales to ensue. Moreover, the telling of tales is an evening activity, except in schools, where perforce it occurs during the school day.

Omission

A significant problem all three accounts share, though, is the glaring omission that clamorously calls attention to itself. One of the reasons for the widespread coolness to Tutuola's early works among Nigerian (and especially Yoruba) readers was the works' perceived derivativeness, the unoriginality of the constitutive tales. The objection was not so much that they were borrowed or adapted from the familiar folklore repertoire as that they were brazen "borrowings" from Fagunwa's published works, especially *Ogboju Ode Ninu Igbo Irunmale* (1938; *The Forest of a Thousand Daemons,* 1968)[2] and *Igbo Olodumare* (1949; *The Forest of the Almighty*). The Yoruba scholar Ayo Bamgbose, who was not one of Tutuola's early critics, pointed out Tutuola's dependence on Fagunwa, especially in *The Brave African Huntress* and *Feather Woman of the Jungle.* "In the latter," Bamgbose observed, "the narrator with his pipe, and the crowd of curious listeners to his tale are an elaborate extension of the interludes in the narration of Fagunwa's stories. Apart from the framework, several incidents and characters are taken directly from Fagunwa. For example, *The Brave African Huntress* makes use of a lot of material from *Igbo*."[3]

Another Yoruba scholar writing in 1971, long after the appearance of the novels in which Tutuola's reliance on Fagunwa is most pronounced, chose to minimize the inescapable. Afolabi Afolayan identified two channels through which Tutuola came by his material. The first is his exposure as a child to traditional storytelling, and also the regular folktale broadcasts on Radio Nigeria by D. O. Alabi, and later by Tunji Ojo. In addition, Afolayan pointed out that Tutuola undoubtedly read some of them from locally printed collections that were in circulation. Afolayan seemed less certain about the other channel: "Another source likely to have influenced Tutuola is Fagunwa in his novels," he wrote quite tentatively. "For example, the story of the half-bodied baby . . . *could have been influenced by Fagunwa's story of Ajantala* which has a similar type of hero and episodes" (italics mine).[4] Afolayan added that there was little doubt that Fagunwa "*may have influenced* the plot of Tutuola's later novels, particularly *Feather Woman of the Jungle.* But this question of Tutuola's indebtedness to Fagunwa should not be carried too far: both draw from the same source which has a traditional plot" (Afolayan, 205; italics mine).

Afolayan had most certainly read Fagunwa's works and, as a Yoruba language and literature scholar, is perhaps as knowledgeable as anyone about Yoruba folktales. Afolayan must therefore have known, as well as Bamgbose and Abiola Irele did, what Bernth Lindfors would later describe as "a strong kindred relationship between the texts [of Tutuola's books and Fagunwa's], possibly bordering on plagiarism."[5] He should, therefore, share some of the blame for not alerting the public to Tutuola's free borrowing. Afolayan's belief that one should not dwell on Tutuola's indebtedness arose perhaps out of generosity, but it placed him at variance with informed opinion on the matter, and also with demonstrable evidence. With regard to the Ajantala phenomenon, for example, there could be no doubt as to its provenance, since the abominable child first came into existence in Fagunwa's *Ogboju Ode.* Apart from using it as the basis for the half-bodied baby born to the Drinkard out of his wife's thumb in *Drinkard,* where the author calls the baby not Ajantala but ZURRJIR (*Drinkard,* 32), Tutuola retold his story (with some variations) in two entries in *Yoruba Folktales,* both elaborated from "Ajantala, the Noxious Guest," earlier published in Langston Hughes's collection *An African Treasury* (1960). The phenomenon reappears as a mature adult under his famous name in *Huntress* (122–28).

The most effective way to illustrate the extent to which Tutuola has relied on Fagunwa would be a synoptic comparison of the novels of both writers. Such a comparison is beyond the scope of this study, however, but enough instances of "borrowing" can be cited to make the point.

Both Bamgbose and Afolayan suggest that Fagunwa's influence is most pronounced in Tutuola's later novels, *Huntress* and *Feather Woman,* but a close look at *Drinkard* will show that the influence was considerable from the start. It should be remembered that *Wild Hunter,* which was the prototype for *My Life,* is referred to in *Drinkard* (40) and actually predates *Drinkard; Wild Hunter* also relied heavily on Fagunwa, perhaps even more so than the first published work.

The narration in *Drinkard* indeed begins with an encapsulation of the whole adventure, which demonstrates its close affinity with Fagunwa's novels. The Drinkard reports that he set out one fine morning with all his native juju and the juju his father had left him:

> But in those days, there were many wild animals and every place was covered by thick bushes and forests; again, towns and villages were not near each other as nowadays, and as I was travelling from bushes to bushes and from forests to forests and sleeping inside it for many days and months, I was sleeping on the branches of trees, because spirits etc. were just like partners, and to save my life from them. (*Drinkard,* 9)

Although the frame of the entire story itself is perhaps better attributed to folktale sources than to Fagunwa, one of its most important features does come from Fagunwa. When the Drinkard finally finds his dead tapster in the Deads' Town, we will recall, the tapster declines the

Drinkard's invitation to return with him to his town, "because a dead man could not live with alives and their characteristics would not be the same" (*Drinkard*, 100). Instead the tapster gives the Drinkard an egg. "He told me to keep it as safely as gold," the Drinkard narrates, "and said that if I reached my town, I should keep it inside my box and said that the use of the egg was to give me anything that I wanted in this world" (101). The egg later provides food in abundance for the Drinkard and his wife, and for his entire community. Similarly, in *Ogboju-Ode,* when Akara-Ogun is lost in the forest, he marries and lives with a ghommid for some time before stumbling onto the path home. When he goes back for his wife, intending to take her home with him, she declines to accompany him, saying, "A spirit like a ghommid cannot join with human beings to live together, for evil are their thoughts every day of their lives." She adds, "Take this little cloth, it is a gift for you; whenever you are hungry ask anything of it and the cloth shall provide it" (*Daemons,* 66–67). Fagunwa himself borrowed the idea from the tale of the all-providing ladle, a version of which is also to be found in Tutuola's *Feather Woman.*

In this connection, one might recall that Achebe was impressed by Tutuola's artistic and moralistic use of boundaries. Achebe referred first to the departure of the Drinkard and his wife from Wraith Island, when the friendly inhabitants walk them to the frontier and stop, and to the Drinkard's comment that "if it was in their power they would have led us to our destination, but they were forbidden to touch another creature's land or bush." Next Achebe cited their departure from the Faithful-Mother's White Tree, when the Mother would not grant their request that she lead them to their journey's end "because she must not go beyond their boundary." He noted that in several other instances, boundaries played a decisive role in the development of the plot, including boundaries between day and night.[6] In Fagunwa's *Ogboju Ode,* the pilgrims to Mount Langbodo also have to contend with a boundary. When they come to the road that leads to the dome of heaven, they encounter "two good-looking youths dressed in shining white." The youths give them directions to Mount Langbodo, which is a right turn just outside the gate of heaven. They warn the travelers "to be sure to turn at the right moment for Mount Langbodo because this turning was not far from the dome of heaven," whence heavenly hymns that might entice them to heaven can be heard. If the travelers allowed themselves to be so enticed, they would be met with harsh visitations (*Daemons,* 95).

One of their number who does not heed the warning wanders off to heaven, and his fate remains unknown (96).

Tutuola often resorts to the device of transformation to facilitate his hero's or heroine's achieving his or her objectives. When in *Drinkard* the old man sets the hero the initial three tasks of his quest, the Drinkard learns what the old man wishes him to retrieve from the blacksmith by transforming himself into a bird and eavesdropping when the man divulges the secret to his wife (*Drinkard*, 10–11). In his attempt to retrieve the lady who will later become his wife from the Skull, the Drinkard changes himself into a lizard, first to follow surreptitiously the complete gentleman from the market to his abode in the bush (26), and later to hear the Skull conveniently tell himself that to cure the woman's muteness, she must be given a certain leaf to eat (30). In the same episode, the Drinkard changes himself to "a very small bird which I could describe as a 'sparrow' in English language," into whose pocket he places the woman, now transformed into a kitten, to escape from the Skull and his cohorts (28).

Farther into the novel, after the couple have rid themselves of ZURRJIR and have made some money by ferrying people across a river, the Drinkard decides to make better speed toward the Deads' Town and avoid the dangers of the forest by taking to the air. He tells his wife to jump on his back with their loads, and with the aid of a juju that the "Water Spirit Woman" of the "Bush of the Ghosts" had given him earlier, he is able to become "a big bird like an aeroplane" and fly away with his wife (*Drinkard*, 40). In *Ogboju-Ode*, the hero Akara-Ogun once encounters a teary gnome with whom he exchanges insults. Afterward, though, a contrite Akara-Ogun seeks a boon from the gnome and is rewarded with pods of alligator pepper that will enable him to sprout wings and fly, and also to return to normal human form (*Daemons*, 19–20). The juju comes in handy on the journey to Mount Langbodo, when one of the emissaries angers the king of the town of birds, provoking attack on the whole company by the birds. Akara-Ogun distributes pepper seeds from the pods to his companions, and they sprout wings that enable them to take to the air, both better to fight their adversaries and later to escape from them and from land-bound dangers for a while (*Daemons*, 92).

Tutuola's episode also recalls a cluster of other events that occur during the journey to Mount Langbodo. When the travelers are hemmed in by a thicket that they can neither penetrate nor cut down, two birds alight on a tree nearby. Soon, Elegbede-Ode, one of the travelers, shoots and kills one of the birds. He understands the language of birds, and he had heard the bird say that unless it was killed and sacrificed, the imprisoned travelers would find no way out of their confinement. After they have sacrificed the bird, they do find a way out (*Daemons*, 82–83). When the intrepid pilgrims arrive at the city of birds, they find themselves in some trouble. The city, it turns out, is not the place to be for anyone who has ever needlessly killed a bird. On arrival without knowing of the interdiction against bird killers, the travelers are instantly arrested and taken to the king of the city, the Ostrich, but an ostrich of different feathers: he has a human head, the size of a normal human head, but the rest of him is ostrich. He greets their sight with "Who are these? Where did you come from? Where are you going? Doubtless you are thieves, and the mark of bandits is clearly branded on your foreheads. Therefore, prepare! Let loincloths be well secured and trousers belted tight, for I will show you a thing or two this day. I shall assign three tasks to you and, if you fail in them, most assuredly I shall slaughter you for food" (*Daemons*, 86). The tasks are (1) to fight a certain wild animal that lived in the king's father's shrine, (2) to fight the sand-elves, and (3) to rid the city of Were-Orun (Lunatic of Heaven). Failing in those tasks, the travelers will be killed, but if they succeed, they will be free to continue on their way (86–92). It is not difficult to see a connection between the episode and the three tasks the old man set the Drinkard at the start of his adventure.

Another clear case of borrowing is the partial burial of the couple by the wicked people of the "Unreturnable-Heaven's Town." They are taken to a field outside the town, where their tormentors dig two pits. In these they bury husband and wife up to their necks, packing the earth so hard that the victims can hardly breathe. Then they place food near the couple's mouths, knowing full well that they will not be able to reach it. Fortunately for the couple, after they have been subjected to a great deal of abuse and are left by themselves, a heavy downpour softens the earth enough to enable them to wiggle out (*Drinkard*, 61–62). This incident is copied from Akara-Ogun's plight after he has saved the king of the city of ghommids from assassination. The infuriated plotters apprehend him and take him to their market. There they order him into a hole they have prepared for him; it swallows him up to his neck. They fill it with earth, which they pound around his body. Then they shave off his hair and pour honey on his head to attract flies. Next they place all kinds of food around him, and also a signpost on which is inscribed,

"With your eyes behold this, but your lips will not touch." Thereafter they torment their victim "in every conceivable manner" before leaving him to his fate. Several hours later, the clouds gather and soon give way to a heavy downpour that softens the earth, enabling Akara-Ogun to extricate himself (*Daemons,* 56–57).

Besides episodes and incidents, other features of Fagunwa's first novel also surface in Tutuola's *Drinkard,* the following being only a few of them. Readers and critics have been impressed by Tutuola's personification of emotions, inanimate objects, and the like. Dylan Thomas remarked on the personified Drum, Song, and Dance performing on themselves (Thomas, 7–8). Along similar lines is Tutuola's treatment of such things as fear and death as material things that can be handled, lent, or sold. In the episode involving the Faithful-Mother and her white tree house, Tutuola writes that the hero sold his and his wife's death and lent their fear (*Drinkard,* 67); it is the earlier sale of his own death that kept him alive in his fight with the nine fearful creatures who are their coworkers on the farm of their captor, the huge creature (105–6). These will be familiar to readers of Fagunwa, who has Akara-Ogun say, after he has encountered some bad omens at the start of his second sojourn in the forest of a thousand daemons, "I simply bartered death away saying, 'What of it! Does a man die more than once? If death must take me then let me get on my way' " (*Daemons,* 37). Later Iragbeje addresses the brave pilgrims as "My good friends, strong ones, stout-hearted men, you fearless men who bartered death away in order to do your country good" (131). When Akara-Ogun weeps, he says, "I took hold of tears and began to weep them" (39); when he travels the forest with his companion Lamorin, they are accosted by Peril, who is the father of Loss, who lives in the home of Starvation (61); Lamorin will later be killed and eaten by Tembelekun (Conspiracy), junior brother of Bilisi (Devilry) and father of Chaos (65).

Thus far I have concentrated on Fagunwa's first novel and Tutuola's first published work to demonstrate that from the very start, Tutuola drew liberally from the earlier writer. When we expand our scope to take in other works by the two, the incidents of borrowing multiply, Fagunwa's second book, *Igbo Olodumare,* proving the richest vein for the prospecting Tutuola. The examples that follow are not intended to be exhaustive, but enough to establish that one can hardly make too much of Fagunwa's contribution to Tutuola's creativity.

The Smelling-Ghost of *My Life* is an obvious descendant of Egbin (Filth) in *Ogboju Ode.* Tutuola thus describes the Smelling-Ghost :

All kinds of snakes, centipedes and flies were living on every part of his body. Bees, wasps and uncountable mosquitoes were also flying round him and it was hard to see him plainly because of these flies and insects. But immediately this dreadful ghost came inside this house from heaven-knows-where his smell and also the smell of his body first drove us to a long distance before we came back after a few minutes, but still the smell did not let every one of the settlers stand still as all his body was full of excreta, urine, and also wet with the rotten blood of all the animals that he was killing for his food. . . . this "smelling-ghost" wore many scorpions on his fingers as rings and all were alive, many poisonous snakes were also on his neck as beads and he belted his leathern trousers with a very big and long boa constrictor which was still alive. (*My Life,* 29)

An excerpt from Fagunwa's description of Egbin follows for comparison:

Egbin never cleaned his anus when he excreted and crusts of excrement from some three years could be found at the entrance to his anus; . . . Egbin never bathed, it was taboo. The oozing from his eyes was like the vomit of a man who has eaten corn porridge, he stank worse than rotten meat and maggots filled his flesh. His hair was as the skin of a toad, grime from eternities was plastered on it, black he was as soap from palm oil. Earthworms, snakes, scorpions and every manner of crawly creatures came out from his mouth when he spoke. (*Daemons,* 94)

To the foregoing, Tutuola added details from other Fagunwa characters such as Fear (Èrù), and, of course, some of his own inventions.

One image that occurs repeatedly in Tutuola's novels is that of the hero or heroine being ridden like a horse by some ogreish captor. The hero of *My Life* falls into the hands of a boss in the seventh town of ghosts, who delights in changing the hero into different creatures. The boss once changes him into a horse and rides him about (37–39). Later on, in disclosing where a yam he wishes to roast and eat came from, the hero says it was given to him by a ghost who had "slapped my ears warmly ten times" (yams being very precious), and that having given him the yam, the ghost rode him about for three days and nights before releasing him (136). The hero of *Feather Woman* also suffers a similar indignity: the "senior chief of the savage people," into whose custody the hero was delivered after falling from a tree and landing on their king, rides him around his cave as part of his punishment (*Feather Woman,* 62–64).

Another image from Fagunwa that finds repeated use in Tutuola's work is one of strong winds that force the tops of trees to the forest floor. This phenomenon occurs in *Simbi*. The heroine has just eaten some pawpaws "when she noticed that all the living creatures were running helter-skelter. And within that moment a heavy wind started. The wind was so blowing with its full power that the topmosts of small and big trees were touching the ground and then getting up at once" (*Simbi,* 109–10). The image reappears in *Huntress,* announcing the approach of Odara. In Adebisi's words,

> I saw unexpectedly that more than one thousand bush animals, birds, snakes, etc., were running away as hastily as they could with closed eyes to every direction of this jungle. They were hiding themselves inside the holes, under the refuses, etc., and the snakes and birds were hiding on top of trees. As I was still wondering when I saw them that they were doing like that, a very strong wind came. This wind was so strong that the whole jungle was in disorder at the same moment. This wind was blowing to the trees so heavily that their tops or branches were touching the ground and all the dried leaves and refuses were blowing to the great height in the sky. (*Huntress,* 26–27)

She sees a similar phenomenon in the Jungle of the Pigmies:

> I saw that a very strong wind started to blow. In this wind there I saw that animals, big birds, pigmies, etc., of this jungle were running up and down and they were making fearful noises all over the jungle. As the wind was stronger it was so they were making more fearful noises and within five minutes the whole of the jungle was in disorder.
> After a while all the trees were blowing here and there, they were touching the ground with their tops. (*Huntress,* 57)

The scenes derive from a conflation of at least two events in Fagunwa's novels. The frantic scrambling of animals at the approach of a monster recalls the behavior of the animals in the forest of a thousand daemons at Agbako's approach, on Akara-Ogun's third day in the forest (*Daemons,* 22). The strong winds that bow treetops to the ground come from *Igbo Olodumare.* Six months into his sojourn in the palace of the forest as a guest of the king, Olowo-Aiye sets out to hunt game for his pregnant wife. He soon finds himself in a part of the forest where the trees have no roots but are nonetheless lushly green with foliage. "Soon," the hero recalls, "a wind began to blow, and all those rootless trees commenced to bow to the ground and rise up again."[7] Seeking to avoid being crushed by a tree limb, he hops atop a rather tall tree when its top is to the ground, and is duly raised to the sky when the tree resumes its upright

stance. Unfortunately he is stranded there for a while, because the wind
stops just as he is raised aloft. A passing rat later tells him that the earlier disturbance merely announced the assembly of all animals in the forest. At its conclusion, the rat tells him,

> you will hear a bell, following which you will see a strong wind begin to
> blow, stronger even than the earlier one. It is then you should find a way of
> getting yourself off the tree. But the wind will be extremely strong, for as
> trees bow to the ground, so again will they stand up erect. (*Igbo*, 59–60)

The rat proves correct, and Olowo-Aiye is able to get off the tree when
next it bows to the ground in the gale that marks the conclusion of the
animal congress.

One instance of Tutuola's borrowing from Fagunwa that critics have
often noted is the confrontational interrogation of each other by two
adversaries. In Simbi, when the Satyr comes face-to-face with the heroine
and her companion Rali, "he started to ask with his powerful voice, 'Who
are you? What are you? Where are you coming from? Where are you
going? Or don't you know where you are? Answer me! I say answer me
now!'" The two women being unable to answer, the Satyr continues:

> Certainly you have put yourselves into the mouth of "death"! You have
> climbed the tree above its leaves! You see me coming and you too are
> coming to me instead to run away for your lives!
>
> By the way, have you not been told of my terrible deeds? And that I
> have killed and eaten so many persons, etc. who were even bold more
> than you do?
>
> My house is near this Path of Death and it is in this Dark Jungle this
> Path of Death is ended. And the poverties, punishments, difficulties, cru-
> elties, etc. etc. are the rulers of this Jungle. Anybody who travels on Path
> of Death shall end his or her life in this Jungle. I am the Satyr who is
> guiding this jungle since from two thousand years!
>
> But this day that you bring yourselves to me! Hah! Having killed
> both of you, I shall enjoy your meat for a few days! (Simbi, 75)

The scene is repeated in an abbreviated form in *Huntress*. Adebisi comes
upon a gate whose keeper greets her with, "Who are you? Where are
you going?" (*Huntress*, 49–50).

The Simbi incident is a virtual reproduction of the meeting between
Esu-kekere-ode (Diminutive Outdoor Devil), the guardian of the gate
to Igbo Olodumare. I will quote the monster's tirade in full for reasons
that will be obvious:

Who are you? What are you? What are you worth? What is your significance? What is your relevance? What are you seeking? What do you want? What are you looking at? What are you seeing? What are you thinking? What is afflicting you? Where are you coming from? Where are you going? Where do you live? Where are you wandering? Answer me! You human, answer me in one word. Certainly you are in trouble today; you have climbed a tree beyond its leaves; you have fallen from a height into a well; you have swallowed unexpected poison; you saw an overgrown plot and planted peanuts in it. . . . You saw me, I saw you, I advanced, and you too advanced; you did not take to your heels, but you walk nonchalantly before me. Are you not terrified? Are you not afraid? Have you never heard of me? The skulls of people mightier than you sit in my stew-pot; their spine-bones line the corners of my room; the rib-cages of obstinate people are what I sit upon in my house.

I am the diminutive gnome of the anthills whose name is Esu-kekere-ode. . . . But today, as I have come upon you unexpectedly, I give thanks; my good fortune has brought a boon my way, because it has been quite a while since I tasted meat. After killing you I will savor you for three days. Your head I will cook in okra stew; your ribs will be assigned to vegetable stew, and your buttocks will ooze fat copiously into pepper-stew. Then I will save the remaining parts of you in my abode in the anthill. (*Igbo*, 14–16)

One more example and I will rest this case. It is the story of the Treacherous Queen of the Bush of Quietness, which constitutes the entertainment of the third night in *Feather Woman*. Tutuola's use of this material from Fagunwa offers an opportunity for a comparison of the artistic imagination of both writers. I offer first Tutuola's version.

The hero's search for wealth brings him to a not so big town some distance from his village, a town in which all the inhabitants are very rich. He is taken to the king, to whom the hero divulges the purpose of his travels. The king promises the hero much wealth if he can find his lost prince. The king explains that he had gone to the town where the prince lived one morning and had found emptiness; the people and the houses had simply disappeared, replaced by silence. At the hero's request, the king takes him to the site of the lost town and leaves him there. The hero wanders about until darkness forces him to stop, and he settles down to sleep, but before he dozes off, he wonders what had happened to "the prince and his wife, etc." (We must assume that the king had mentioned the detail about a wife, because there was no earlier mention of it.) In his sleep, the hero dreams that he is in a big town where he sees the prince and the people in great difficulties. He is so terrified of becoming one of them that he tries to escape, but one of the people grabs him to prevent his flight. He cries out and wakes up. It is midnight. He walks some distance and begins to hear a person groaning. His investigation brings him to the ruins of what must have been a resplendent palace, more beautiful even than that of the king who gave him his assignment.

The source of the groans is a handsome middle-aged man covered with sores, whose long beard and mustache indicate that he has lain there for a long time. His story is that he used to be the king of the missing town, and that he had a beautiful wife he loved very much. One midnight he lay on his armchair to rest, and four of his servants, believing that he was asleep, spoke of the wife's putting drugs into his drink so that he would sleep until cockcrow while in the meantime she went to meet her lover. Thus informed, the king pretended to take his drink as usual the next night but actually threw it away in the wife's absence. He pretended to sleep, and when the wife sneaked out, he followed. He saw her meeting a young man at the market; the man berated her for her lateness, which she blamed on her nuisance of a husband. They kissed and she proceeded to divulge the king's secrets to her lover, and later they enjoyed many jokes at his expense. Infuriated, the king drew his sword, advanced on the two, and slew the man. The woman escaped, the king took a shortcut back to the palace, and returned to bed before his wife arrived and climbed into bed also, as though nothing had happened.

The next morning, the king ordered that the corpses of all the men who had died the night before be brought to the palace. The order yielded six corpses, one being that of the queen's lover. When the king saw the queen make repeated trips to where the corpses lay, and devote particular attention to her lover's corpse only, he asked if he was a relative. No, she said, but she knew him before he died. Where from? The market? At that the woman became suspicious and evasive, whereupon the king produced his sword and told her he had killed the man the night before. The queen went to her cupboard then, and returned after a short while sobbing. She spat on the king and said loudly, "I command you to remain in one place until when my lover comes alive again" (*Feather Woman*, 46).

Since then the king has been unable to stand up, and the people of the town as well as all its houses were turned to the bush in which his palace alone stands. He lifts the cloth that covered his nether parts to disclose that he is half-man and half-snake. Finally, he reveals that his wife comes nightly to beat him with clubs, and later to visit the corpse of her lover, which she keeps in a grave in a room down the hall, at the "extreme end of the palace." The hero resolves to help. He goes to the grave, lies on the bones, and covers himself with a cloth he took down from a wall. From there, where he is hidden under a cloth in a room in that remote part of the palace, he is able to witness the following:

> When it was three o'clock in the morning, this woman entered the palace through the door of the premises. She held one mud lamp with left hand and one heavy cudgel with right hand. First, she went direct to the room in which her husband, the king, was. She beat him without mercy for about one hour. (*Feather Woman*, 49)

That done, she approaches the room where the remains of her lover lie. Again, before she enters, the hero is able to see that she is very beautiful, so beautiful, in fact, that he can not carry out his intention of shooting her immediately. On entering the room, she first takes care of the lamp so that it burns brighter, fully illuminating the room, then she stands by the grave, kneels down, "and saluted the skeleton as if it was still alive. After that she stood up and said loudly: 'My lover! My lover! My lover! When are you coming back to me? Have you forgotten me? Don't forget me! I am expecting you soon! For in respect of you, I had changed my husband, the king of a big town, into the form of a half-snake and I am beating him every midnight! Come! Come! Come back to me, my lover!' " (*Feather Woman*, 49).

The hero responds that he is her lover come back to life but will be able to stay with her only after she has restored the king to normal and brought back his city and people. She does as the hero asks, and she approaches the grave again. The hero then grabs her so roughly that she asks in fear if he is not her lover. In a "fearful voice," he replies, "I am not your lover at all but I am a man who come to take you to heaven now! Come inside the grave and let us go together!" (*Feather Woman*, 50). Her frantic struggles avail her nothing; he ties her up and forces her to surrender her supernatural powers to him, then he takes the rescued king (after giving him a haircut, a shave, and some grooming) and his treacherous wife back to the town. When the people see the man, they are so happy that "he was snatched with gladness . . . and was carried by head to his father's palace" (51–52). The king who commissioned the search orders the woman to be tied before the god of iron in front of the palace.

Fagunwa's original is told to Olowo-Aiye by his host Bàbá-Oníriùng-bòn-Yéúké (Old Sage of the Overflowing Beard). The host invites his guest to learn some wisdom from the tale of a king who once asked his wife to cook him some stew. She procured three fishes, one black, one red, and one white. She proceeded to cook the strange fishes, but when she made to stir the stew, a stout, sword-wielding woman emerged from the wall of the kitchen and upset the stew. The terrified queen fainted, and when she came to, she ran to tell the king of her experience. He resolved to see the sight for himself and asked the woman to repeat her purchase and cook the fishes in his presence. This time, when the wall split, it was a stout man who emerged, sword in hand, and again overturned the stew. The king fled but later ordered his chiefs to watch the strange phenomenon with him. The fisherman was sent to procure three more fishes, colored as before, and he was only too happy to do so, for each time he fulfilled the assignment he was paid very handsomely indeed. When the fishes arrived, the chiefs set to cooking them themselves, and when one of them stirred the stew, seven fierce stalwarts emerged from the wall and again knocked over the stew pot before putting king and chiefs to flight.

The king then asked the fisherman to show him and his chiefs the source of the fishes. The fisherman led them to a serene and clear lake that they had known nothing about, and in it they saw the colored fishes swimming about. The company settled by the lake for the night, but the king sneaked off to explore the area by himself in the moonlight. He soon came upon a palace even more beautiful than his own. He found the doors open and entered. He began looking around to see if there was an occupant, and soon he heard the sound of wailing from one of the rooms. He followed his ears and discovered a handsome man sitting in a chair. His story was that he was the king of a town, and married to a beautiful woman among others. One day, as he reclined with his eyes closed, two of his servants, thinking he was asleep, talked about how his wife regularly drugged his drink so that he would sleep soundly through the night, and then sneaked off, to return the next morning, when she would wake him.

That night, instead of drinking what his wife offered him, he threw it out of the window when she was not looking. He then went to bed and pretended to sleep. His wife, believing him to be asleep, placed an alligator peppercorn in her mouth, chewed it, and sprayed him with it, incanting, "When a rafter beam goes to sleep it never rises; you worthless being must not arise before my return" (*Igbo,* 124). That done, she got on her way, and the king got up to follow. To his surprise, the doors of the palace opened for her on their own as she approached them. He followed her until she came to a wide clearing. There, awaiting her, was a young man dressed in a voluminous, elaborately embroidered white *agbádá* garment. "You are much too late today," he said angrily. "If you could not make it why didn't you say so yesterday? I don't like people trifling with me. You must not repeat such behavior ever again!"

The woman knelt and pleaded that the king had not gone to sleep until late. The two embraced and fell to kissing, and the queen began divulging her husband's secrets to her lover. Both took to insulting the king and making fun of him. In his fury, the king drew his sword, advanced on the couple, and killed the man. The queen escaped, and the king returned to his palace.

The following morning, the queen came to her husband and showered him with flattery and praises, and then she sought his permission to bring the corpse of her older brother, who had just died on returning from a trip, and bury him in the palace. Not suspecting that she referred to her lover, the king consented, but when the corpse arrived, he discovered that he had been deceived. He went for his cutlass, sat on his chair, and summoned the queen. When she came to his presence, the look on her face was hostility itself; she had divined what her husband was up to, because she was a witch. "Welcome," he greeted her. "Is all well with your bogus brother?"

The woman turned on him then and doused him with some water she bore in her hands, saying,

> I command that a transformation befall you, man, who are making fun of my lover; that you become a rock from your feet to your hips; and that you sit where you are until the day I release you. When the yam is transformed it becomes pounded-yam; when corn is transformed it becomes corn gruel; and even though I too will reap the rewards of my ways at the hands of the heavenly hosts, yet I will not refrain from using the powers that the Creator has given to humans to the end of inflicting evil on you.
> (*Igbo*, 127)

He had remained in the condition the woman imposed on him since that day.

The unfortunate king further reveals that his evil wife transformed his entire town into the lake that the other king has seen, and that the three differently colored fishes are the three distinct religious groups in his town—Christians, Moslems, and unbelievers. The woman, he also discloses, had dug a shallow pit in the middle of the house and placed her lover's remains in it, but without covering them with earth. Every early dawn, at about five o'clock, she would come to the palace with a load of whips and deliver a hundred blows to her hapless husband before stopping. Then she would go to her lover's grave and lament, "My lover on earth, my lover in heaven, when will you return to me? For you I wiped out an entire town; for you I removed a ruler from his throne; my lover on earth, my lover in heaven, when will you return to me?" (*Igbo,* 129).

The visiting king resolves to help his benighted colleague. He places his pistol in the pocket of his trousers and goes to the lover's grave. After taking careful note of how the remains are wrapped, he removes the shroud and throws the skeleton away. He then wraps himself in the shroud and lies where the corpse used to be. When the wicked queen comes, he informs her that the day has arrived when he will return from heaven to rejoin her, but the gatekeeper in heaven will not permit his exit until she has released and restored her husband, as well as his town and its inhabitants. The woman eagerly complies, whereupon the concealed king calls to her: "Here I come! I have returned from heaven. My dear love, come to me in this pit and give me your hand so I may arise" (*Igbo,* 130). When she approaches and the king can see her clearly, he aims his gun at her chest and fires. Instantly, she falls down and dies.

Fagunwa did not derive the story from an existing folktale, even though the concept of the unfaithful wife who would go so far as to kill her husband in favor of her lover is not foreign to Yoruba imagination. There is no denying that Tutuola altered some details in his use of the material, or that he put his stamp on it in some measure. We might even concede that some of his alterations add something appealing, like the humorous detail in the hero's insistence that the treacherous queen accompany him back to heaven. On the whole, though, one can hardly argue that Tutuola's story improves on the original, or that it has the logical consistency of it. Fagunwa set up the situation astutely and resolved every mystery satisfactorily—why there were variously colored fishes, why they could not safely be cooked and eaten, why there was a sudden lake where none existed before, and so forth. The original avoids some of the troublesome details of Tutuola's version. Why does the missing prince (so called by his father, the king) turn out to be a king of another town? Such an arrangement is not impossible or unheard of in Yoruba history, but the prince was not so introduced. He also did not have a wife until the story required that he have one. Also, how was the hero, concealed in the grave, able to know and describe the queen, and how she was equipped on entering the premises (by which Tutuola apparently meant courtyard), and on her approach to the grave after clubbing her husband? And why did the punishment of the treacherous wife fall to the father-king and not to her husband-king, even if the hero's conducting both king and wife to the father-king in *his* town is explainable because he commissioned the search and had the reward to give?

One rare instance in which Tutuola uses Fagunwa creatively combines humor with some tongue-in-cheek commentary on the original. It is the episode in which the hero of *Feather Woman* attempts to soften the heart of the man riding him around like a horse by singing to him. We recall that when Fagunwa's hero, Olowo-Aiye of *Igbo*, realizes that nothing he tries in his fight with Esu-kekere-ode can ever defeat his opponent, or at least get him to give up the fight, he resorts to singing. His singing is so melodious and the words he sings so thoughtful and wise that Esu-kekere-ode lets him be (*Igbo*, 19–20). Tutuola registers his skepticism at the efficacy of music to soften a wicked heart when he has his hero thus describe his tormentor's response to his singing:

> I hardly started to sing that song when he took part in it. When I sang it in tenor, he sang it in bass. When I sang it in bass, he sang it in treble with great joy. But I blamed myself at last to form that song, because it added to my punishment instead of to lessen it. For as he was singing it with me, he was just doing as if he was crazy. He enjoyed it so much that he had lost all his senses at the same time and he was jumping up so highly that his head was striking the roof of that hole. And he rode me to the roughest part of the hole which he had avoided before. (*Feather Woman*, 63)

Fagunwa's inspiration is detectable in Tutuola's work not only in the incidents that make up his plots but also in the nature of his characters (human, ghostly, supernormal) and his descriptions of them. In the following description of Agbako, the first real peril Akara-Ogun encounters during his first sojourn in the forest of a thousand daemons, readers will find a representative prototype for Tutuola's weird creatures:

> He wore a cap of iron, a coat of brass, and on his loins were leather shorts. His knees right down to his feet appeared to be palm leaves; from his navel to the bulge of his buttocks, metal network; and there was no creature on earth which had not found a home in this netting which even embraced a live snake among its links, darting out its tongue as Agbako trod the earth.
>
> His head was long and large, the sixteen eyes being arranged around the base of his head, and there was no living man who could stare into those eyes without trembling, they rolled endlessly round like the face of

a clock. His head was matted with hair, black as the hearth and very long. Often swishing his hips as he swung his legs, Agbako held two clubs in his hand and three swords reposed in his sheath. (*Daemons*, 22)

Collins was certainly right when he said that any writer has a right to use materials from the folklore repertoire without acknowledgment (Collins 1969, 53). But the same is not true of material that has been published, and whose author we know.

Folktales as Sources

Knowledgeable readers of *Drinkard* were quick to recognize the many elements in it that are bequests of the rich folklore of the Yoruba. Afolayan has pointed out that aside from the major stories (or episodes) that came from that source, "the entire plot of the novel—the journey of the Drinkard to heaven to see his palm-wine tapster, and his return to his town—is itself built round the common story of an aggrieved person going to heaven to seek the help of a beloved dead relation and returning with a valuable possession" (Afolayan, 203). Toward the end of the book, Tutuola introduces two Yoruba dilemma tales in the form of difficult cases the Drinkard is asked to adjudicate in the town of mixed people. The first pits a "debitor" who never pays his debts against a "debit collector" who never fails to collect debts. They seek to protect their respective reputations, and a fight ensues. The "debitor," apparently sensing defeat, pulls out a knife and stabs himself to death. The "debit collector" is not about to let himself be cheated by such a gambit; if he cannot collect the debt on this earth, he decides, he will collect it in heaven. He too pulls out a knife and stabs himself to death. The two combatants happen to have an audience, a man so interested in the fighting that he vows to see its outcome even in heaven. Accordingly, "he jumped up and fell down at the same spot and died there as well so as to witness the end of the fight in heaven" (*Drinkard*, 112). The source tale is known as *Àwòdórun* (a spectacle one watches all the way to heaven). It is the most likely inspiration for Tutuola's idea of sending the Drinkard on a trip to heaven to retrieve someone he has lost. There are, of course, also myths that explain the distance separating heaven from earth as resulting from God's anger at humans' abuse of their easy access to heaven to lay complaints at his feet.

The novel incorporates several other characters and episodes based on Yoruba tales. The changeling who is a complete gentleman at the market but a skull in the bush is from the folk repertoire, Tutuola's innovation being the constitution of the captivated woman's recovery into a task for a hero. Give-and-Take is similarly adapted from a folktale designed to warn against obduracy. The one episode that I intend to compare in detail with its folktale original, to demonstrate the qualitative differences between the original and the adaptation, involves the killing of a king's son. After putting the incident of the red town behind them, the Drinkard and his wife continue on their way to Deads' Town and soon find a man sitting before a load in a sack. He promises to show the way to their destination if they will carry his load into the town for him. The Drinkard agrees to carry it, not knowing that it is the corpse of the prince of the town the owner of the load is headed for, the Wrong Town. The man had mistakenly killed the prince, and he wanted "somebody who would represent him as the killer of the prince," because he "knew that if the king realized who killed his son he (king) would kill the man instead" (*Drinkard,* 93).

When they enter the town, the killer excuses himself and goes to inform the king that his son has been killed, and that he has brought the killers to town. The king has the couple locked up for the night. Early the next morning, though, he asks that the two be groomed, dressed in the finest of clothes, and paraded on horseback around the town for seven days. The king, the Drinkard says, meant them "to enjoy our last life in the world for 7 days, after that he (king) should kill us as we killed his son" (*Drinkard,* 93). The real killer does not know the king's intentions and endures the parading, drumming, and feasting in honor of the couple until on the seventh day, unable to stand the spectacle any longer, he pushes the Drinkard and his wife off their mounts, gets on himself, and proclaims himself the real killer of the prince. He enjoys the ride for that last day, but in the evening, he is executed. A heading connected to the episode proclaims the king "wise," leading one to wonder what constitutes his wisdom, besides devising a clever scheme to expose innocent people like the Drinkard who might, for some reason, confess to murders they did not commit.

The original does not leave one wondering about motives and reasons. It is the story of lazy Tortoise and his friend Dog.[8] They own adjoining farms, but whereas Dog works diligently on his farm, Tortoise lets his farm become overgrown with weeds. After the harvest is in, Tortoise expects his friend to share it with him, but Dog refuses. To get back at him, Tortoise kills the king's daughter and leaves her body to be discovered on Dog's farm. When Dog is apprehended, he guesses correctly what has happened. He is able to convince the king, who is a just ruler, to stay his wrath awhile with the assurance that the true criminal will be exposed, failing which, Dog promises to submit to his fate. He then suggests a ruse—that he be paraded on horseback around town in the king's best robes, attended by drummers, dancers, and praise singers, and that the story be broadcast that Dog is being thus honored for ridding the king of a troublesome and unwanted burden. Tortoise falls for the ruse; he confesses to the murder and is grabbed and smashed to death on a rock. In this traditional version, the king's action is explained, and the sort of habits that the story's moral is directed against is clear.

Tutuola's conflation of two other folktales in one episode in *Pauper, Brawler, and Slanderer* can be argued as weakening their impact, even though the adaptation does not suffer from the illogicality one finds in some of his attempts. I refer to Pauper's enthronement in the town of women and his eventual forfeiture of his good fortune when he allows Slanderer, his deputy, to persuade him to enter a forbidden room (*Pauper,* 116–34). We learn that when Peace and Joy resided there, the town used to be known as the Town of Glory. However, since the two had departed—because they could not abide the "rebellion, confusion, chaos, brawls, poverty, wretchedness, restlessness of mind, etc." by which the menfolk died—the people of the surrounding area had imposed its new name on the town, but it had retained some of the glory for which it was named (*Pauper,* 119, 125). We must assume that despite the women's longing for men for several years, men from those other towns had no desire to take advantage of the their availability, and the royal reception they would have enjoyed there.

The Yoruba reader will recognize elements of two very similar stories, one in which an impoverished wanderer is taken from the bush into a town where he is heartily welcomed, groomed, and enthroned but warned never to enter a certain room in his palace. Much later, chafing at the restriction on his royal movement, which he considers insupportable, he enters the room and instantly finds himself at the very spot in the bush where he was found earlier. In the second version, the town is inhabited only by women, and here the interdiction is against climbing a certain palm tree. Again, much later, the king climbs the forbidden palm tree and cannot understand what the fuss and interdiction are all about, because he climbs and descends without incident. It does not take him long, though, to realize that there has indeed been some incident: he has lost the physical endowments of a man and taken on those of a woman. In consternation, he scrambles back up the tree and is relieved when he reaches the top that he is once again a man. But when he descends again, his predicament returns. It then dawns on him why all the inhabitants of the town are female.

In one adaptation, Tutuola not only alters a crucial detail but does so in a manner inconsistent with Yoruba practice. I refer to the episode in the chapter entitled "I Became the Private Barber for the King of Ibembe Town" in *Huntress* (41–46). After the heroine has killed the "semi-bird" that terrorized the people of the town, the admiring king asks her to remain in the town for some months, not only as his guest, but also as his barber. He will pay her handsomely each time she shaves his head, a pound to be exact, because he has a secret he wants kept from his citizens. His secret is the two short, thick horns on his head that, if they became public knowledge, might cause his people to exile him. The episode is for the most part faithful to the original story. The perturbed hunter, dying to divulge the secret but unable to breathe it to any human being, digs a hole and tells it the secret. A plant later sprouts from the hole, and a flute maker makes a flute out of the plant. When he puts it to his lips, the sound that emerges is the announcement that the king has two horns.

The departure that is problematic in Tutuola's version is the gender of the barber. The Yoruba are sticklers about details concerning the head, and even more so when the head in question is that of the *oba,* the king. Although Tutuola's whole book asks the reader willingly to suspend disbelief with regard to gender division of labor, by which a woman would not normally inherit her father's hunting profession and his hunting paraphernalia, the suspension can go only so far before disqualifying the proffered material as belonging to the Yoruba world. The other detail of a chief yanking the crown from the king's head when he sits in state in public is also beyond the pale, but the gender faux pas is the more serious.

Beyond establishing that Tutuola finds Yoruba tales useful for his creative purposes, and pointing out what is peculiar about his use of that quarry, I find no reason to dwell at any great length on the subject. Critics who suggested that the simple fact of his use of folktale material constituted a blemish on his artistry were simply misguided. His reliance on the folk imagination for frames for his adventures, for character or episode ideas, or for any purpose, is legitimate. Lindfors's argument about Tutuola's usage being "well within the conventions governing oral storytelling" (Lindfors 1986, 635) can be applied here—with the necessary modification, of course, for while Tutuola is using the folk tradition, he is not quite engaged in oral storytelling.

Collins's general defense of Tutuola included an assertion of freedom of access to folkloric materials for writers, as well as a suggestion of the imperative of making Yoruba tales available to the wider world. Tutuola himself, in a revision of what he had earlier said motivated him to write (to dispel boredom, that is), argued, "it seemed necessary to write down the tales of my country since they will soon all be forgotten," and "I wrote the *Palm-Wine Drinkard* for the people of the other countries to read the Yoruba folklores . . . . My purpose of writing is to make other people to understand more about Yoruba people and in fact they have already understood us more than ever before" (Lindfors 1975, 280). Collins was perhaps endorsing Tutuola's claim when he wrote:

> Anyone at all familiar with Yoruba folk tales will attest to their high value and their worth as a contribution to world culture. Their shrewd and realistic appraisal of human nature, their sharp social realism, their astonishing fancy, their wonderful unrestrained humor and high spirits, their level-headed celebration of such precious human virtues as prudence, good management, common sense, good-natured kindness, steady loyalty, and courage ought to be admired by readers the world over in some such sprightly, lively form as Tutuola's folk novels; they ought not to be buried in learned journals and specialized books. (Collins 1969, 54)

And there's the rub: the West African (or Yoruba) critics of Tutuola that Collins thinks are so wrong object to Tutuola exactly on that basis. They believe that his work does not do justice to those qualities Collins has cited; they are concerned that Tutuola sometimes mangles them and otherwise misrepresents the Yoruba imagination. They think Fagunwa, on the other hand, has more adequately celebrated those qualities that Tutuola sometimes corrupts. Certainly, if Tutuola has assumed the role of preserver and purveyor to the world of Yoruba cultural treasures, those who are concerned about those treasures have a legitimate reason to insist on some authenticity.

Collins sees Tutuola's departures from his sources as "contributions" (Collins 1969, 54–64). The "contributions" include the observation, with regard to the complete gentleman in *Drinkard,* that if he was in a town to be bombed, the assailants would refrain from the bombing because of his presence (55); the detail that the monstrous child incinerated by his father is resurrected as a half-bodied baby (55); the addition of a sacrifice to heaven to end the famine at the end of *Drinkard* (56); the dilemma tale about which of three wives should be regarded as most valuable (56); Super-Lady, the changeling deer a hunter marries in *My Life* (57); the king's wife whom her cowives wish to expose as an "amputy" (57); the story involving three separately named dogs (60); and the story in which a palm fruit drops into the ocean (60–61), among other incidents. But although one can concede that such details as describing starving people as "as thin as dried stick . . . upper and lower jaws . . . already dried up like a roasted meat," and so forth are original, Collins's list and comments only reveal his ignorance of the cultural context out of which Tutuola writes. Better knowledge would have prevented Collins from attributing to Tutuola's invention direct borrowings (such as the ones he listed) from Yoruba tales. One of the source stories, the inspiration for the Super-Lady episode, was in fact already familiar from Fagunwa's *Igbo* and Ogunde's folk opera *Half and Half* (1949).

Afolayan also credited Tutuola with more than he deserves, praising him for telling the stories his own way, even if he draws the material from traditional sources:

> In telling his individual stories Tutuola always paints the traditional scenes in detail. But the way he links these individual stories together to form a single super-story derives from his own imaginative genius, as can be seen from the summary of the story of the half-bodied baby given earlier. Thus Tutuola is to be seen not only as a man with "great visionary power and imaginative intensity" . . . but also a very keen and perceptive listener and an excellent reporter. Perhaps he is more of the latter and that is why some people fail to see the former in him. (Afolayan, 206)

Afolayan will most probably have some difficulty in persuading many Yoruba people familiar with the text and performance of Yoruba storytelling to his point of view.

Collins, for his part, would base his judgment regarding Tutuola's creativity on a comparison of his versions of folkloric materials with bare-plot summaries to be found in collections such as *West African Stories* by W. H. Barker and Cecilia Sinclair (Collins 1969, 62), apparently the only texts with which Collins was familiar. If he was familiar with the original stories in all their rich variance, he would probably be more cautious in his praise of Tutuola's contribution. Collins was right in observing that "there is no substitute for the real African storyteller in front of us, miming as well as speaking, changing his voice and his posture to fit the parts, singing the songs that go with the stories, punning

and making sly local references" (63). Donatus Nwoga's criticism of
Collins's book happens to be in part because Collins did not seem to be
mindful of his own observation.[9] I would differ with Collins, though, on
his addition: "But we do have in Tutuola a storyteller who embellishes
the fictional characters and situations as the native storyteller does, who
uses a language full of wit and word play and wild humor, not unlike
the traditional sort, who freely combines, varies, and rearranges the tales
in the manner of the traditional storyteller" (Collins 1969, 63–64).
Although Nwoga focused on the issues of plagiarism and originality,
concepts he pointed out "do exist in the storytelling tradition even if
they have to be differentiated in their application from the literary tradition" (Nwoga, 97), I believe that his point would apply equally to matters such as coherence, logic, didactic value, and artistry in general, areas
in which I believe Tutuola falls far short of the traditional storyteller's
art. What Collins demonstrates most of all is the incumbency for
Africanists to have a working knowledge of the languages of the peoples
and cultures on which they profess to be experts, and to be able to
research firsthand their cultural and linguistic resources.

Afolayan's postscript to his discussion of Tutuola's sources is nothing
if not dazzling. He suggests that "the Nigerian readers' failure to appreciate Tutuola largely arises from their own inadequate linguistic awareness and incompetent knowledge of the theory, principles and practice
of literary art" (Afolayan, 208). That being the case, he adds, the language and literature courses need to be overhauled to "give the African
students the opportunity to appreciate and enjoy literature at first
hand." Why a course in linguistics and literature should be a prerequi-
site for simply enjoying a fiction writer's work is difficult to understand.

Literary Sources

As Lindfors has pointed out, Tutuola's horizons widened somewhat after
the publication of *My Life* to embrace materials beyond the covers of
Fagunwa's books and those familiar to Tutuola from his personal experiences. After being interviewed by Eric Larrabee, Tutuola had requested
that he send him books such as *A Survey of Economic Education,* Aldous
Huxley's *The Devils of Loudun,* and "some other books which contain stories like that of the P.W.D. [*The Palm-Wine Drinkard*] which are written
by either West Africans, White men or Negroes, etc." Of the books
Larrabee sent him, Edith Hamilton's *Mythology* and Joyce Cary's *Mister
Johnson* reportedly impressed Tutuola most profoundly (Lindfors 1975,

291). He also read Bunyan's *The Pilgrim's Progress* and *The Arabian Nights.* Evidence of Tutuola's reading is plentiful in his subsequent stories: the satyr featured in the title and some episodes of *Simbi;* the goblins, gnome, imps, myrmidon, nymph, and phoenix in the same book; and the cyclopslike creature, demons, elves, genies, goblins, gnomes, imps, and, of course, pigmies in *Huntress.* The frame for *Feather Woman* is almost certainly copied from *The Arabian Nights,* and that of *Herbalist* would appear to be a conflation of the premise of the tale of Tortoise's sudden pregnancy[10] and the impetus in Bunyan's *The Pilgrim's Progress.*

To summarize, there can be no question that Tutuola was eclectic in his sources, the one to whom he is most heavily indebted being D. O. Fagunwa, whose first two books in particular served as the model for Tutuola's first books, from which his later works did not depart in any significant way. As a Yoruba man who grew up close to Yoruba social practices, it was inevitable that he would be familiar with Yoruba tales, and that he would resort to them for plot and character ideas, especially given the continuities between Fagunwa's literary practice and that of the traditional storyteller. Finally, once Tutuola's literary career got under way and he sensed the need to live up to his growing reputation, he ventured farther afield into European and other materials compatible with those he was already working with. Critics disagree regarding whether he improved on the originals he adapted, and the likelihood of any agreement on that issue must be adjudged extremely slight. On the question of plagiarism that his use of Fagunwa's ideas raises, critics are also divided, but as the perceived need (on the part of some) for partisan defense of every move Tutuola has made subsides, a judgment in keeping with literary conventions will very likely prevail.

Chapter Four

The Artist and His Mission

Tutuola's Choice of Themes

Two perspectives jostle each other in critical discussions of Amos Tutuola. One represents him as a highly contemplative and philosophical writer who by means of his creative fiction offers his readers a sophisticated reading of the universe and human nature, a reading, moreover, that is informed by his profound inside knowledge of the Yoruba ethos, and one that is also deeply moral and deeply human. The other, by contrast, portrays him as a freewheeling, fun-loving writer out for little more than giving free rein to a playful and eclectic imagination for the entertainment of his readers. Any attempt to arrive at an understanding of Tutuola the man, and his work, is doomed to flounder if it fails correctly to determine which perspective better applies to him, and if, for that reason, it is predicated on inapplicable assumptions and expectations. It is with the foregoing in mind that this discussion of Tutuola now turns to an exploration of the relative merits of these two perspectives.

Discussion of Tutuola's career and output has been bedeviled from the start by many critics' ignorance of the quarries he mines for his stories. He has, most are able to tell, borrowed liberally from the Yoruba oral repertoire, and he has also drawn with considerable frequency on the Yoruba literary texts popular when he began to write. These include the works of writers such as A. K. Ajisafe (*Aiyé Àkámarà,* 1929), Adekanmbi Oyedele (*Aiyé rèé,* 1947), but most especially D. O. Fagunwa, who is the real inspiration for Tutuola, and whose creativity Tutuola's only poorly reflects. After he became successful internationally, of course, he set about expanding his horizon to include materials from Western traditions.

Even when his readers are aware that what they are reading is adapted from existing materials, those of them who have no access to the sources have no means of comparing him with his originals. They also have no reliable means of arriving at any informed judgment on his

originality or his fidelity to the *integrity* of his sources, by which I do not
mean his faithful reproduction of their details, but rather of their coherence. Further difficulties derive from critics' insistence on imputing to
him intentions that he did not have, that he has in fact explicitly dis-
claimed, and on attributing to him structures that he would find befud-
dling. Parrinder is an early example. He reported that when he asked
Tutuola his reason for the apparently haphazard ordering of the towns in
his second book, he "replied, quite simply, 'That is the order in which I
came to them.' "[1] What Tutuola meant, of course, was in fact precisely
what he said—that he set them down in the order in which they
occurred to him. Parrinder chose, however, to take the answer as an
indication of "how deeply he lived in his own narrative." Tutuola made
substantially the same point he had earlier made to Parrinder when he
told Eric Larrabee in 1953 that he "composed" *The Palm-Wine Drinkard*
in two days and wrote it in three months, " 'just playing with it' . . . for
lack of anything better to do" (Larrabee, 13). Tutuola did not work
according to any plan or blueprint; he was simply playing around, setting materials down as they popped into his head.

The champions of Tutuola who laud him as an exemplar of Yoruba storytelling and compare his products favorably with the sources he uses mis-
construe Yoruba folk artistry. Yoruba storytellers (and the same goes for
African storytellers in general) do not simply play with their materials,
and do not engage in storytelling for lack of meaningful employment.
One of the best known facts about African creativity, in fact, is that it is
almost invariably directed at some utilitarian purpose. That is not to say
that Africans do not customarily engage in creativity for pleasure, but
only that in most cases the activity is directed to some useful end.

Stories as Vehicles for Moralization: Achebe on Tutuola

The critic S.D.D., writing in the August 1962 issue of *West African
Review* about *Feather Woman,* called attention to its "childlike innocence,"
a quality, the critic thought, that characterized Tutuola's earlier books
also, and that made him unique. In the critic's view, the quality was contrived by an author who without doubt understood the meaning and
symbolism of his tales. S.D.D. was of the opinion that Tutuola, like
Achebe, consciously and deliberately chose to move away from the "man
of two worlds" theme that had marred much of early African literature
in order to concentrate on "life and problems among Nigerians" (Lind-

fors 1975, 93). A fruitful approach to deciphering the validity of such claims, to determining what Tutuola's intention might be and assessing it, is to conduct a thematic investigation, that is, to examine the premises and rationales for the major actions in his novels, and how they relate to the denouements. What, for example, are the initial circumstances of the principals? What set them off on their adventures? And what did the adventures accomplish?

Growing up as a Yoruba who was undoubtedly exposed to storytelling and, one assumes, told stories himself, Tutuola certainly experienced and thought of stories as vehicles that combined entertainment with didacticism based on close observation of human nature. If for some reason that quality of traditional narratives was submerged in his mind, his reading of Fagunwa would certainly have called it to the surface. One admiring critic who has argued that Tutuola did in fact intend didacticism and has in fact excelled in employing his fiction as a medium for moralizing is Chinua Achebe. So impressed was he with Tutuola's moralizing genius that he declared him the most moralistic of African writers. Achebe's thesis and supporting argument bear close attention.

Numerous candidates would do as exponents of the opposing view, but Tutuola himself will fill the role, in view of his statement to Parrinder (quoted earlier). Unlike most other celebrated African writers, though, Tutuola has not been prolific or talkative in bolstering with lectures and nonfiction writing whatever views his fiction purveys. For that reason, in addition to the few statements he has made to interviewers, his fiction will do practically all his speaking for him. Moreover, because his reputation was substantially made with his first published work, *Drinkard,* which most critics agreed he has merely repeated in his subsequent writings (with some innovations, to be sure), and because there is very little of substance in the later works (by way of plotting or characterization) that is essentially new, that first work will receive considerably more attention in the ensuing pages than the later writings. Fortunately, Achebe arrived at his opinion of Tutuola's moral purpose and artistic astuteness on the basis of a brief passage and an episode in the same work. I will of course draw instances from the later works for corroboration as necessary.

Achebe was so impressed by what he read in *Drinkard* that he devoted the august occasion of the First Equiano Memorial Lecture that he delivered at the University of Ibadan in 1977 to praising the author and the book in superlatives. The opinion Achebe elaborated in the lecture was a drastic revision of his earlier thinking on his subject; 13 years earlier (in a 1964 paper entitled "The African Writer and the English Language"), he had contrasted Tutuola, whom he characterized as "a natural," with "conscious" writers like himself, in effect disagreeing with S.D.D.[2] In the 1977, lecture Achebe hailed Tutuola as "the most moralistic of all Nigerian writers," one who had "a richer imagination and a more soundly based moralism" than the Onitsha Market chapbook authors (Achebe 1989, 101). His earlier description of Tutuola as a "natural" and his contrasting him with "conscious" artists clearly indicated that in Achebe's opinion at the time, Tutuola wrote without premeditation or perhaps even meditation, that he had no preconceived grand design that his fiction unfolded, elaborated, and executed. His evolution in the intervening years to become a consummate craftsman and artificer must be considered nothing short of momentous. Also significant is that Achebe's revised opinion was not prompted by Tutuola's later publications; rather, Achebe went back to revisit Tutuola's pioneering novel and came away with a revelation that he must have missed earlier: Tutuola's art "conceals—or rather clothes—his purpose, as all good art must do." Anybody who asked what *Drinkard* was about, Achebe declared, could hardly have read him (101).

The two sentences in which the Drinkard briefly introduces himself make up the material that occasioned Achebe's change of mind: "I was a palm-wine drinkard since I was a boy of ten years of age. I had no other work more than to drink palm-wine in my life." According to Achebe's reading, these statements hold clues to an impressive moral system. Tutuola, Achebe argued, was in fact exploring the question "What happens when a man immerses himself in pleasure to the exclusion of all work; when he raises pleasure to the status of work and occupation and says in effect: 'Pleasure be thou my work!'?" (Achebe 1989, 102). If that was the case, the reader should expect to be led through a fictive experience in the course of which characters would be confronted with choices to work or not to work, whose consequences would be fraught with weighty moral implications. The reader would further expect a close articulation of context, character, and conflict, and a plot progression in which the successive stages in the movement toward the denouement would result from rational choices by the characters that determine the trajectory of the action. In none of these particulars does Tutuola's work justify Achebe's suggestion.

Achebe must have realized the necessity of explaining why the work on which he based his assertion fails to fulfill the foregoing expectations, for he went on to construe that failure as a coup, praising Tutuola for not wasting time "exploring or elaborating on the offense itself" (Achebe 1989, 102). The reason Achebe offered for the almost complete absence of exposition and of any suggestion (by the author) of the Drinkard's culpability is far from convincing:

> This disposition of emphases might appear somewhat uneven to the "modern" reader brought up on lengthy psychological interpretations of guilt. But Tutuola belongs primarily to humanity's earlier tradition which could say simply: "Thou shalt not commit murder," without necessarily having to explore what motivations might lurk in murky prenatal experience! (Achebe 1989, 102)

The information that the Drinkard's father procured an expert tapster for him because he could not work is, said Achebe, Tutuola's gesture to "the moderns," for he "knows perhaps instinctively what they are about" (Achebe 1989, 102). In this construction, "unconscious" Tutuola, who belongs to an earlier tradition that divorced action from motivation, environment, and (one assumes) other sorts of conditioning, nonetheless is sophisticated enough to know that the "moderns" are hung up on such considerations, and calculating enough to offer them a palliative. Moreover, Achebe advanced the proposition that we can reasonably pass moral judgments on fictional characters by concentrating on their actions to the exclusion of all other factors—upbringing, environment, circumstance, motivation, and the like.

One major problem with Achebe's explanations, as I have noted, is that there is no hint in the work that Tutuola considers the Drinkard an offender. All indications are that the author is not particularly interested in an elaborate exposition and a sound moral grounding for the Drinkard's character, that he is rather more concerned with devising a formula, *any* formula, to set his hero off on his adventure. The formula Tutuola settles on for the purpose is this: the Drinkard is incurably and insatiably addicted; an indulgent father has accommodated and furthered his addiction by providing him with a palm tree farm and a tapster to keep him and his hangers-on supplied; the irreplaceable tapster has suddenly died; and the Drinkard will go to the abode of the dead to bring him back. The ensuing string of episodes depicting marvelous encounters with assorted creatures, both benign and bizarre, in wildly extraordinary situations constitutes the raison d'être of the work; it is not, as Achebe suggests, to moralize on "the punishments [the Drinkard] undergoes in atonement for his offence and . . . a fairly brief coda on his restoration" (Achebe 1989, 102).

The thesis Achebe deduced from *Drinkard* would lead us to conclude that the author subscribed to the socialist realism that was popular among Nigerian academics at the time of Achebe's revised opinion.[3] The thesis goes as follows:

> A man who will not work can only stay alive if he can somehow commandeer to his own use the labor of other people either by becoming a common thief or a slave-owner. Thanks to the affluence of his father . . . the Drinkard is enabled to buy a slave and to press him into a daily round of exploitative and socially useless work. The point is made quite clearly—lest we be tempted to dismiss the Drinkard's love of palm-wine as a personal drinking problem—that refusal to work cannot be simply a "self-regarding act" but is a social and moral offence of colossal consequence. (Achebe 1989, 70)

Later he described the appetitive and pyromaniacal child born to the Drinkard and his wife as a smaller version of his father, with "the same insatiable appetite, the same lack of self-control, and moderation, the same readiness to victimize and enslave others" (Achebe 1989, 73–74). Yet no evidence exists that before he embarked on his quest for his tapster the Drinkard ever commandeered other people's labor for his own use, that he was a thief, or that he was a slave owner. Nor is there any instance of his victimizing or enslaving others. In his self-introduction the Drinkard says, "my father . . . *engaged* an expert palm-wine tapster for me," (*Drinkard*, 7; italics mine), not that he or even his father "bought" a "slave" and impressed him into daily labor, useless or otherwise.

The Evidence of Give and Take

It is to bolster the ascription of a moral message—a version of the Puritan work ethic—to Tutuola and his work that Achebe invoked the episodes involving Give and Take, the "Invisible Pawn." The weird creature approaches the Drinkard in the town of the (no longer) red people with the plea that he wishes to know poverty, for he has hitherto only heard the word "poor" without knowing its meaning. The latter obliges by hiring him as a farmhand and general odd-jobs person. Such is his overzealousness, though, that not only can he not discriminate between the Drinkard's property and that of the rest of the community, but he and his cohorts are also incapable of halting any activity until their helpfulness has become utter destructiveness. When the incensed townspeo-

ple raise an army to expel the Drinkard and his wife from their midst, he
calls on his troublemaking helper, who, with his own army, wipes out
the entire population of the town.

Tutuola constructed the episode, Achebe argued, "to make the point
that those whose personal circumstances shield them from the necessity
of work are really unfortunate and deprived and must do something to
remedy their lack" (Achebe 1989, 70). If the message applies to Give
and Take, how does it apply to the Drinkard? one might ask. Also difficult to accept is Achebe's assertion that Tutuola employs Give and Take
to demonstrate the duality of promise and fulfillment: "Tutuola never
allows a broken promise to go unpunished," Achebe contended. The
creature in search of poverty

> got the experience he seeks but in the process establishes the principle
> behind his name: that a community which lets some invisible hand do its
> work for it will sooner or later forfeit the harvest. Give and Take proves a
> merciless extractor; for the labor he gives he takes not only the people's
> crops but, in the conflict that ensues, their lives as well. (Achebe 1989, 75)

Let us review the events and their consequences to see if they can support such a deduction.

Give and Take pawns himself to the Drinkard, not to the people;
therefore, if engaging a pawn (letting some invisible hand do one's
work) constitutes a moral offense, the Drinkard and his wife are at fault,
and according to the scheme Achebe proffered, they are the ones who
must forfeit their harvest. The people did not engage Give and Take;
they did not *let* an invisible hand do their work and are therefore blame-
less. Furthermore, with the exception of the instance when Give and
Take provides meat in overabundance for everybody in the town, all his
activities are annoyances or disasters for the people, not favors in any
sense of that word. Moreover, when the destruction of their crops by the
creature and his helpers provokes the people of the town to rise up in
anger against the Drinkard, Give and Take and his cohorts come to *his*
aid and destroy *them*. The Drinkard and his wife, the beneficiaries of the
pawn's labors, are left alive. The evidence from the episode therefore
cannot support the morality Achebe suggested.

The Imperative of Clarity

Afolabi Afolayan posited the subject matter of *Drinkard* to be Yoruba
oral literature set in a contemporary Yoruba community (Afolayan,

202). He broke down the elements in the stories into three categories, the first of which he placed in "an earlier, though partly contemporary, Yoruba rural agricultural economy where money is in the form of cowries, where palm-tapping is an industry for men, where gourds (kegs) serve as measurement standards, and where credit facilities could be based on a system of domestic and agricultural service (pawn)." The second, he said, "points to the contemporary emergence of a more modern, though in this instance greatly exaggerated, economy of the Yoruba community which could be symbolized by the organizational setup of the Faithful Mother's household." The third set "represents the religious and magical sentiments and beliefs of the Yoruba world (real and imaginary) of gods and people with an all pervading belief in myths, mysteries, and spirits" (Afolayan, 202). The point I wish to make is that Afolayan invites us to see an underlying Yoruba quality in Tutuola's novel, that quality being its consistency with Yoruba storytelling practice.

Bernth Lindfors has cited the formulaic endings of the episodes in Tutuola's books as evidence that he was operating in the arena of the oral storyteller, specifically the Yoruba storyteller. "Indeed," Lindfors observed, "the fact that the story [of *Drinkard*] consists entirely of a series of short, separable episodes immediately arouses a suspicion that it is little more than a collection of traditional tales strung together on the lifeline of a common hero" (Lindfors 1975, 283). It is against that standard, therefore, that Tutuola must be judged. Comparison with Fagunwa is legitimate here also, not only because he is an important presence in Tutuola's work, and not because Fagunwa also operates within the Yoruba story tradition, but especially because a number of critics, having compared the two, have placed Tutuola closer to the heart of Yoruba creativity and ethos.

Yoruba storytelling, to reiterate, has a definite didactic (moralizing) purpose, which explains the (almost) mandatory statement of a moral at the end, introduced with words such as *ìtàn yí kó wa pé* (this story teaches us that); alternatively, if the audience consists of children, the storyteller might invite them with the question *kí ni ìtàn yí kó wa?* (what does this story teach us?) to take a shot at deducing the moral.

Moreover, the moralization that is an important aspect of storytelling is not encrypted or hidden as Achebe said Tutuola's is. Indeed, as I have already noted, so concerned are the Yoruba that the message get across that they precede their storytelling sessions with riddle solving to sharpen the intellect. To that same end, the storyteller creates characters and constructs plots that will clearly convey the message. For example,

Character A is confronted with situation B, he or she takes action X, and the result is Y. Ergo, when one finds oneself in a situation such as B, one should (or should not) do X; in other words, Character A is either a good model to emulate or a bad one.

Because of this imperative of clear communication and the insistence that the audience receive the tale's message ungarbled, the storyteller often explicitly states the moral at the end, as I have indicated, and occasionally digresses during the telling of the tale to moralize.[4] A traditional African text readily available to American readers is *The Mwindo Epic,* which ends with the moral:

> Heroism be hailed! But excessive callousness either pushes a man into a great crime or brings him a great one, which (normally) he would not have experienced. So, whosoever in a country is not advised will one day carry excrements—and to experience that is terrible.
>
> Mutual agreement brings about kinship solidarity; the one who will save his companion is unknown; it is like the chief and his subordinates. So, the world is but made of mutual aid. So, then, may the chief safeguard (his) subordinates and the subordinates safeguard the chief. Kinship is the stamping (of feet); it is the tremor of people.
>
> Even if a man becomes a hero (so as) to surpass the others, he will not fail one day to encounter someone else who could crush him, who could turn against him what he was looking for.[5]

With the foregoing in mind, let us compare some of the episodes in *Drinkard* with the originals that inspired them (Yoruba folktales and Fagunwa's creations) to determine the moralization to which they lend themselves.

Tutuola and Sources Compared: Give and Take, the Invisible Pawn

The story of the Invisible Pawn, or Give and Take, retells (in a fashion) a Yoruba folktale about an obdurate man who, newly arrived in a strange town, is warned against farming a certain invitingly lush bush nearby. The newcomer heeds the warning for a while but eventually yields to the lure of the seemingly incredible fertility of the plot. He begins to rationalize that the long-term inhabitants of the town must be capital fools to believe whatever superstition made them leave their best farmland unexploited and advise others to follow suit. He discards the advice and resolves to farm the land. The first task he undertakes is to clear bush, and the moment he takes the first swing at some brush, number-less unseen hands magically take up the task, and in no time the entire vicinity is bare of foliage. After he has mastered his astonishment, he begins to make heaps to plant seeds in, and the same invisible hands instantly convert the whole field into rows of heaps for him. His happiness is boundless, for he is convinced that his skepticism in the face of the excessive credulity of the townsfolk is paying off. So it continues, mysterious helpers completing in a trice every task on which he embarks, including planting the seeds and periodically removing the weeds. In time, the crops mature and ripen, and the fortunate farmer thinks of harvesting just enough of them to feed himself for a few days. But the moment he commences that task, his invisible helpers pluck and hew every fruit and tuber on the farm. Usually when a Yoruba person is visited with sudden disaster, he or she smacks his or her head with both hands and exclaims, "Oh, my head!" The farmer does just that, and as soon as he does, a million invisible hands rain blows on his head until he falls down dead. No intelligent reader will have any difficulty deciphering the message of the tale, even if the teller omits explicitly stating it at its conclusion. One does not need the mediation of a moral sleuth for the purpose.

ZURRJIR

One of the numerous materials Tutuola appropriated from Fagunwa is the figure of the extraordinary child that the Drinkard and his wife have so much trouble ridding themselves of. He is featured in different guises in several of Tutuola's works. In this particular case, he appears under the improbable name of ZURRJIR, "which means a son who would change himself into another thing very soon" (*Drinkard*, 32). He is based on Ajantala, one of Fagunwa's most brilliant creations in *Ògbójú ode*. Fagunwa features him in the edifying tale with which Iragbeje enter-tains and instructs his august guests, Akara-Ogun and company, on the first day of their visit to Oke Langbodo.

In Fagunwa's original, Iragbeje's parable begins:

Once a woman gave birth to a child, a very beautiful child, but no sooner was the child born than he began speaking out loud in these words, "Ha! Is this how the world is? Why did I ever come here? I had no idea it was such a rotten place. I thought the world would be as spotless as heaven! Ha! Just look at the pit and look at the mound! Look at the cow-dung in the middle of town! Look at the dirt in the open!" (*Daemons*, 106)

The abnormal child got to his feet, gave himself a thorough scrubbing with sponge and soap, and demanded some food. When it came, the morsel he stuffed into his mouth each time was enough food for a grown man, and he stopped eating only because there was no more food in the house. On the seventh day of his birth, he was to be named according to custom, but he forestalled his parents and announced that his name was Ajantala.

His parents laid on a feast in honor of the new birth, as was expected of them; but impatient with the slow progress of those preparing the feast, Ajantala pushed them aside and took over the task. When the horrified guests exclaimed that the child was something of an abomination, he gave them all a good thrashing, including even the stalwarts who attempted to restrain him. The ill-used guests fled at the earliest opening with Ajantala in hot pursuit and indiscriminately belaboring every person he caught up with. Eventually his alarmed parents sought out a renowned *babaláwo* to either control or get rid of the child, but when the *babaláwo* showed up at the house, he too suffered the same fate as the guests at the child's naming. In the end, the mother took him into the bush and contrived to abandon him there.

Iragbeje's story continues:

> As Ajantala wandered around in this bush he arrived at a place where lived five creatures in perfect amity—the first was Elephant, the second Lion, the third Leopard, the fourth Hyena, and the fifth Goat. Ajantala pleaded to let him live with them, that he would be a servant to them, and they readily agreed. (*Daemons,* 111)

The five creatures customarily took turns foraging for food for the whole company. On the day following Ajantala's arrival, the duty fell to Goat, the least of the five, and the new servant was assigned to accompany Goat and be generally helpful to him. But Ajantala, apart from not helping Goat in the least, subjected him to merciless beating. Badly bruised and thoroughly subdued, Goat did all the work and carried the load of food nearly all the way home. When the two were within sight of their abode, however, Ajantala transferred the load to his own head and assumed the mien of the dutiful servant, having warned Goat on pain of further beating against revealing any of his traumatic experience to the others. Accordingly, to all inquiries about his bruises, lacerations, and swollen eyelids, Goat responded by blaming bees whose hive he had upset, and wasps whose nests he had disturbed as he sought to escape the bees.

When on the next day Hyena, whose turn it was to find food, returned from foraging with Ajantala in much the same condition as Goat, Hyena explained that he too had run afoul of bees and wasps. All five similarly suffered in turn at the hands of their servant. They counseled together thereafter that their best course was to flee their home while their troublesome guest still slept. They made preparations, which included packing, on the eve of their intended departure, enough food to last them awhile into a bundle before they retired for the night. But unknown to them, Ajantala had overheard their plot, and while they slept, he crawled into their package of provisions.

At what they thought was an opportune moment, the five sneaked out of their home and got under way, Goat carrying the food bundle. Some distance along the way, his gluttonous nature got the better of him, and he told the others he had to empty his bowel. They needn't wait for him, he urged them, but should walk on ahead instead; he would catch up with them as soon as he was done. Once by himself, he set the bundle down and untied it, intending to cheat his companions out of some food. To his discomfiture, Ajantala emerged from the bundle and again gave him a severe beating. Satisfied, Ajantala ordered Goat to retie him into the bundle, join the others as though nothing had happened, and transfer the load to Hyena. Goat was only too happy to comply.

Hyena, and after him Leopard, Lion, and finally Elephant, were every bit as devious as Goat; the same cheating idea occurred to each in turn, and in turn each suffered the same visitation from Ajantala. Elephant, the last to be thus abused, managed to free himself before the diminutive bully was quite done with him and took flight in the direction of his companions. When they heard the frantic pounding of his feet they knew what had happened, and they too took to their heels. They made what they thought was good speed for a while and, believing that they had shaken off their nemesis, paused under a tree to recover their breath.

Rest and the assurance that they were at last rid of the pestilence named Ajantala disposed them to the idea of assigning blame for his intrusion into their peaceful existence. Not surprisingly, the blame fell on Goat, who, of course, protested his innocence vigorously, even invoking an oath proper to their present circumstances: May the earth open and swallow him, Goat swore, if he was guilty, but if not, may Ajantala descend again among them and punish his accusers. The oath was barely out of Goat's mouth when Ajantala dropped into their midst from the branches above; he had taken a shortcut and climbed before their arrival into the branches of the very same tree under which they were resting. The five resumed their flight, but this time in different directions. Goat eventually wound up among humans, Elephant in forests in the countries of the black people and the Indians (in Fagunwa's world a creature apparently can wind up in several different places at once), Leopard and Hyena in the jungle, and Lion in the plains. As for Ajantala, the Creator, seeing that the child was out of place among humans, removed him from earth and confined him to the out-skirts of heaven.

Tutuola's Version

Tutuola's first story, "Ajantala, the Noxious Guest Is Born,"[6] ends at the point of Ajantala's expulsion: after the terrible child had beaten more than 100 people to death on the day he was to have been named, the college of *babaláwo* in the town pooled their special spells for expelling just such a child. Although Tutuola's version departs in some regards from Fagunwa's and shows the sort of logical and plot permissiveness typical of Tutuola, we can ignore them for our present purposes and concentrate on the rest of the story as he tells it in "Ajantala and the Three Brothers."[7]

In this version, the creatures Ajantala found in the forest were three brothers, the lion, the tiger, and the he-goat, "who were in those days human beings and were born of the same father and mother" (*Folktales,* 7). The order in which Ajantala beat them up is not ascending as in Fagunwa's. It responds to no apparent scheme: first was the tiger, second was the lion, and last was the he-goat. When the he-goat sought to cheat his companions of some of the food he carried, he succeeded in eating to his satisfaction while Ajantala remained in hiding in the food basket. Not until the entire brotherhood sat down to eat and the depletion of their food became apparent to all, when first the tiger and after him the lion accused the he-goat of the theft, did Ajantala emerge from the bottom of the basket. He did so in response to the he-goat's false plea that he did not steal their food, and his swearing, "If I did, then let something bring Ajantala to us now and judge the case for us!" (*Folktales,* 13). When the three finally fled and scattered, the lion wound up in a far country, the tiger in a faraway forest, and the he-goat in the town; "and thus he has been one of the domestic animals since that day" (14).

Of the significant differences between the story as told by the two narrators, I will dwell on only those crucial for my present purpose, an investigation of the extent to which one can impute a moral purpose to Tutuola, and a determination of the complexion of his morality, if any. When one considers that in Fagunwa's original Ajantala emerged from the bundle and meted out well-deserved punishment to Goat at the moment he commenced to cheat his colleagues, and that his emergence to similarly beat the others was also in the immediate wake of their contriving to cheat the others, one has little difficulty in grasping the author's message: misappropriating communal property is a culpable offense. In Tutuola's retelling, the he-goat implausibly succeeded in eating his fill of the food and rejoined the group without mishap while Ajantala, for some reason, remained hidden in the basket. Not until the culprit invoked Ajantala's name in dishonest self-vindication did he rouse himself, not to punish the cheating and lying he-goat but to belabor and disperse the three indiscriminately.

Furthermore, the moral, ethical, and logical consistency of Fagunwa's story is demonstrable in the prompting for Ajantala's final intrusion into the company. Goat's companions charged him with responsibility for introducing the abominable child into their midst in the first place, a false and unjust accusation. Goat invoked Ajantala's name, *unaware of his presence in the branches above,* in his effort to vindicate himself. Ajantala's sudden materialization was, in effect, an affirmation of the traditional Yoruba faith in a moral order controlling the universe. In Tutuola's story, Ajantala reappeared in response to his invocation by the he-goat, who *was* guilty of the accusation against him. The he-goat's oath was a cynical and deceptive stratagem consistent with his devious nature, and a display of contempt for, or defiance of, the god of oaths. He was certain (erroneously, it turned out) that Ajantala was nowhere around, and he sought to befuddle his companions by making a show of swearing a genuine oath, but one he knew was a sham and thought was safe. True, Ajantala did surprise him by jumping out of the basket and scattering the three, and thus, one might say, restoring one's faith in a just order; but the offender suffered no worse fate than the others, who were innocent. On the contrary, as a result of their dispersal, the he-goat came off best, since he became a domesticated companion of humans in their towns. The he-goat's fate thus being the most fortunate,[8] one would be hard-pressed to argue for more than chance or amorality on the authority of Tutuola's story, but not so of Fagunwa's.

The Importance of Morals

The fictive context of the Ajantala story is important as an indication of the important place moralization occupies in the Yoruba scheme. In Fagunwa's novel, Akara-Ogun and his illustrious companions undertook their perilous pilgrimage on behalf of humankind to the king of Oke Langbodo, a place located hard by the boundary between earth and heaven. Their charge was to seek from the king the wisdom necessary to order affairs in the pilgrims' society for the greatest benefit of all. Iragbeje, the king's designated sage, employed the story as his vehicle for instructing his guests on the importance of inculcating in children the reverence for their parents and elders. Children thus raised are, according to his instruction, a boon to their parents and the community, whereas those who are raised otherwise are a veritable pestilence. Iragbeje's choice of theme and his organization of details for educating his visitors on their first day attest to the great value the Yoruba attach to children, *and* their insistence, nevertheless, that a child in whom proper regard for the norms and values of the society is not imprinted is not worth having. Although Tutuola's story offers his reader an entertaining sequence of events featuring an abnormal birth, its detachment from its original purpose robs it of its ethnographic import. In addition, whereas even if detached from its original context, Fagunwa's story would still serve as an instructive dramatization of the inevitability of retribution for unnatural or antisocial behavior, the indifference of Tutuola's version to the sequence of incidents, and its disregard of Fagunwa's carefully contrived elements of causality, render it valueless as a record of Yoruba morality and values. Put differently, Tutuola's tale lacks a recognizable moral purpose and the sort of logic that makes possible the deduction of a coherent statement or worldview from a tale.

In the Matter of the Murdered Prince

The episode involving the murder of a prince in *Drinkard* is another case in point. The Drinkard, we will recall, is tricked into carrying into a town a bundle that turns out to be the corpse of the king's murdered son. The bereaved king, believing the Drinkard to be the murderer, arranges to give him a week of earthly delights before executing him. The real murderer sees the Drinkard being feted and paraded in all luxury through the town (without knowing what awaits him on the seventh day) and comes forward to confess that he is the real culprit. Thereupon he is substituted for the Drinkard and is regaled until he is duly dispatched. Tutuola offers no explanation for the king's strange reaction to the murder of his son, feasting and honoring the murderer before punishing him. The story that serves as Tutuola's source in this instance clearly indicates why the king behaves as he does, and also what the moral to be drawn from the story is.

The Case of Antere

Comparison of another tale from the later *Folktales* with its folktale original further illustrates both the difficulty of deriving useful didactic values from Tutuola's stories and the persistence of the problem in his career. I have in mind the story "Antere, the Child of the Goddess of the River."[9]

A couple, long frustrated in their quest for a child, consult a diviner to discover the cause of their misfortune. The diviner informs them that they were "born barren" (*Folktales*, 15), but touched by their desperation, and their declaration that they do not care if they have a child one day and it dies the next, just so long as they can be parents for a brief spell, he undertakes to aid their cause. He will employ his powers to make them parents, he says. He warns them, though, that the child to be born to them will bring them much sorrow, because she is the last offspring of the goddess of the river. The medicine man says he will have to kidnap her, but she will eventually return to her mother. The would-be parents accept the terms. The diviner then instructs them that after the child is born, she must not be permitted to go to the river until after she is married and raises a child of her own. The supplicants consent to that stipulation as well and are sent home to await the happy event.

In due time, the woman conceives and gives birth to a baby girl, who grows to be a most beautiful maiden. She is courted and betrothed, and the day nears when she is to be married. The parents "did not forget the warning of the medicine man who had told them that they must not allow her to go and fetch water from the stream until she was married and had got a child," Tutuola informs his readers (*Folktales*, 17). But only five days before her wedding, when every preparation has been made for the occasion, when the praise singers and flatterers are already busily at work singing the praises of the bride-to-be, she seeks her parents' permission to go to the stream to wash her clothes. Inexplicably they agree, "for they thought she was at this time old enough and that she was free to go to the stream or anywhere else." When the maiden arrives at the stream, the river goddess reclaims her.

The parents soon miss their daughter and go to the stream looking for her, but they search in vain. They report her loss to the king, and he sends his messengers to take up the search, but it yields only the calabash she took to the stream. When they call her name, though, an unearthly voice answers, singing a song that causes them to dance uncontrollably in spite of themselves. They dance and dance, all the way to the palace, there to report their experience to the king. Incredulous, he summons all his counselors, and they troop in a procession to the stream, accompanied by the entire town. The unearthly voice responds as earlier to the call on Antere, and the effect on king, counselors, and multitude is no different. In the general dancing that ensues, the horses of the king and his counselors (which they had insisted on riding, against the advice of the messengers) trample many children to death, thus sobering the multitude.

The bereaved parents of the trampled children turn in fury on the king and his counselors and lay into them with sticks. Several counselors lose their lives, but not the king, who along with the more fortunate counselors is only beaten senseless. "When the king, his remaining counselors and the people became conscious," Tutuola's story concludes, "the enchanting music stopped suddenly. They all returned to the town with grief for missing Antere" (*Folktales,* 19).

The story of Antere is familiar fare in Yoruba storytelling; it follows a more or less standard formula whereby the violation of a taboo abruptly ends some good fortune that is conditional on the beneficiary's continued observance of the taboo. The violation invariably results, however, from a plausible eventuality or logical rationalization: the person forgets the interdiction, he or she is tricked into violating it, or he is so confident in his own wiles that he is convinced that he can finesse the prohibition and outwit its enforcing powers (as is often the case when the trickster is the subject). In no event would the person simply and casually ignore the taboo, or dismiss it with the sort of cavalier rationalization Antere's parents use in this case.

Screenplay writers in the Hollywood tradition have a term for stories that require characters to behave like idiots in order for the plot to arrive at the denouement the writer desires: "idiot plots." Such plots have practically no utility as thematic vehicles, for few people take films based on them seriously, and few serious writers believe in any case that they are writing for idiots. In the Yoruba original, Antere goes to the stream either because she does not know of the interdiction (her doting parents having kept it from her for their own reasons) or because they are guilty of an inadvertent lapse after so many years of hawkishly watching her every move in order to counter her natural impulsion toward the stream. They do not simply permit her to make the trip, so close to the time when all restrictions on her movement in that regard are to lapse, even though they "did not forget the warning of the medicine man." To reiterate, the plots of Yoruba folktales make sense and have their impact because they are predicated on the principle that people deliberately make choices and are, therefore, accountable for them. If the actions of folktale characters are not based on conscious choices but on happenstance, or if they follow no acceptable logic, the thematic or exemplary usefulness of the tales becomes severely attenuated.

There are other ways of demonstrating on the basis of *The Palm-Wine Drinkard* and later novels by Tutuola the considerable risk taken by any analyst who attempts to assign a coherent and consistent moral purpose to him and his fiction.

Non Sequitur Extrapolations in *Drinkard*

In his review of Collins's book on Tutuola, Donatus Nwoga stressed the a priori necessity of establishing what would substitute, beyond the three main stages demanded by the quest romance, for "the natural expectation for causative as distinct from sequential continuity" (Nwoga, 96). I have briefly cited Lindfors's observation on the randomness of Tutuola's plots, but I will cite it again, more fully this time. With particular reference to the plot of *Drinkard,* he wrote:

> Like boxcars on a freight train, they are independent units joined with a minimum of apparatus and set in a seemingly random and interchangeable order. There is no foreshadowing of events, no dramatic irony, no evidence of any kind that the sequence of events was carefully thought out. Tutuola appears to be improvising as he goes along and employing the techniques and materials of oral narrative art in his improvisations.
>
> To search for an orderly system or well-developed artistic pattern in the succession of disjointed episodes in *The Palm-Wine Drinkard* is to search for symmetry in chaos, for deliberate design in chance. (Lindfors 1975, 283)

"Some critics," he added, "have risen to the challenge with bold imagination."

Another commentator (in the *Times Literary Supplement* of May 25, 1962), while specifically focusing on the problem of symbolism in

Feather Woman, was in fact addressing the difficulty of finding thematic coherence in Tutuola's stories. Looking for exact symbolism in it was pointless, the commentator wrote, "though occasionally one glimpses something meaningful in the same way as one follows the coils of the snake in the darkness of the tree in Douanier Rousseau. But increasingly one's reaction is irritation, a desire to say 'So what?' in quite the rudest way, and to protest against what is dangerously near a cult of the *faux-naïf*" (Lindfors 1975, 92).

It is the general absence of causative continuity in most of Tutuola's novels that bedevils efforts to derive coherent themes and morals from them and lends support to the conclusion that, at least at the start of his career, Tutuola was less interested in didacticism than in entertaining. Because the emphasis of *Drinkard* is clearly on adventure and the excitement attendant on it, Tutuola addresses himself to thinking up the most frightful possible adversaries, the most daunting obstacles, and the most challenging situations for his hero. So intent is he on the frightening and entertaining purpose that moralization, when it intrudes at all, seems somewhat forced. Lindfors's observation on the formulaic tags at the conclusion of the discrete episodes in the book is consistent with this argument. They do not seem to have been at the back of the author's mind during the development of the episodes; they appear to be afterthoughts that argue against any suggestion of organic or thematic unity among the episodes.

Moreover, because an emergency in the Drinkard's universe—the loss of his tapster—necessitated his departure from home, and because the action of the entire book is the discovery and return of the dead tapster, one would expect that the ending of the narration, when taken together with the opening premise, would reveal some coherent and consistent message. Some argument that such a message does in fact exist might have been possible (or plausible), tenuous though it would be, had the series of episodes concluded with the regluing of the broken egg and the punishment of the Drinkard's fickle friends and neighbors. But it ends with the plight of the hapless slave who bore a sacrifice to Heaven to put an end to the famine that was plaguing the land, an extraneous, superfluous, and quite gratuitous graft that drastically weakens the ending of the book.

Lindfors has suggested a reading of this ending that, if accepted, would defuse the objection I have just raised. He portrays the returned Drinkard as having achieved moral and ethical growth as a result of his adventures, such that instead of being an indolent, palm-wine-addicted parasite, he has been transformed into a practical and benevolent savior of his community (Lindfors 1975, 282). I suggest that such a reading is unconvincing, and at variance with the typically inorganic randomness of the episodes that constitute the book. Let us consider the evidence.

The Drinkard reports that after he returned to his town with his wife, he celebrated the event by hosting his old drinking friends with 200 kegs of palm wine. All the trials and difficulties he and his wife had endured, he remarks somewhat ruefully, "brought only an egg or resulted in an egg," which he hid in a box in his room. On the third day after his arrival, he continues, he went with his wife to visit her father in his town, returning home finally after spending three days with his father-in-law. "That was how the story of the palm-wine Drinkard and his dead palm-wine tapster went," the account concludes (*Drinkard*, 118). The switch from the first-person "I" to a third-person point of view gives the impression of the termination of the Drinkard's presence and animation in narrative. He becomes at that point, it seems, what I would describe as a perfected nonpresence, a shade now devoid of the capacity to act, with only the capacity to exist as a silent reminder of a completed life. In other words, at that point, the creator of the Drinkard seems to retire him to a shelf, like a statue that can no longer speak but can only be spoken about. What comes after this point, then, cannot properly be regarded as part of the Drinkard's story but is more like a gratuitous graft, a somewhat irrelevant postscript.

Even if one were to grant that the quoted statement does not denote the withdrawal of the Drinkard as an agent, but is only a rhetorical ploy on his part (he is reanimated in first-person voice for the concluding episode), the appended account would still ill suit Lindfors's suggested reading. It revises the earlier account of the Drinkard's activities on his return home. To recapitulate, he first backtracks to say that for six years his town had suffered from a famine so severe that it forced the people to cannibalism, the cause being a quarrel between Land and Heaven over a mouse they had killed in a joint hunting venture. When the Drinkard arrived and found famine raging, the account continues, he went to his room, put water in a bowl, and commanded the egg to produce food, which it did in abundance. After he, his wife, and his parents (his father had apparently returned from the dead) had eaten their fill, the Drinkard sent for his old friends and gave them the rest of the food and drinks. Dancing ensued, and when the friends asked for more palm wine, he commanded the egg to produce more. The friends told him that they had not found water or palm wine to drink in the past six

years, and he informed them that he brought the palm wine from the
Deads' Town (*Drinkard,* 120). This is of course inconsistent with the
earlier account that on his arrival in town he "sent for 200 kegs of palm-
wine and drank it together with [his] old friends as before" (117–18).

The news of free food and drink spread throughout the surrounding
area, and multitudes converged on his house at all hours demanding
food, so much so that he could hardly open his door for the press of the
crowd and could also hardly sleep at night. Eventually he set the egg
and bowl out in the open among the crowd, with the inevitable result
that it was soon shattered. "When these people had waited for four days
without eating and drinking anything," the Drinkard continues, "then
they were returning to their towns etc. one by one, but they were abus-
ing me as they were leaving" (*Drinkard,* 122). A short while later, he
glued the egg back together and discovered that it had regained its
powers, but with a difference: instead of food, drinks, or money, now it
would only produce whips. He asked the king to summon all the people
with a promise of more food and drinks from the restored egg, and
when they had assembled, he had the egg unleash whips on them, men,
women, and children.

> Many of them ran into the bush and many of them died there, especially
> old people and children and many of my friends died as well, and it was
> hard for the rest to find his or her way back home, and within an hour
> none of them remained at the front of my house. (*Drinkard,* 124)

The Drinkard's action was vindictive, deliberately murderous, and indiscriminate in its victims—which included old people and children. It can
hardly qualify as the sort of boon the returned hero customarily delivers
to his people, nor is the behavior that of a universal savior. He cannot,
therefore, be "the savior and benefactor of all mankind" (Lindfors 1975,
282).

The later episode that ends the famine is also unsatisfactory, in addition to being adventitious. First, the hero, who had lately engineered the
death of numerous people, seeing that many more people (among the
survivors of his vengeance) continue to die from the famine, summons
an assembly of the populace and tells them how to end it. Because no
new knowledge or information revealed the solution to him before he
convenes the meeting, we are at liberty to assume that he knew the way
out all along, or could have thought of it had he addressed himself to
the task. In any case, he prescribes a sacrifice, which must be carried "to
Heaven in heaven." The king's attendant, who is the first to be nomi-

nated for the role of bearer, will have none of it, nor will the poorest person around, who is tabbed next. The duty then falls on one of the king's slaves, who apparently has no option of refusal. Consistent with the Yoruba tale that is the source for the episode, on the slave's return from his successful mission, he is caught in the deluge that signals the end of the famine. The unfortunate messenger seeks shelter from the beneficiaries of his mission, but none will offer it. What finally happens to him, the narrator does not say. All we know is that after three months of regular rainfall, the famine ends. (In the traditional tale, in which the sacrifice-bearing emissary is the vulture, the consequence of his beneficiaries' denial of shelter to him is his bedraggled appearance. And there, one might say, hangs another tale, or moral, namely, that altruism does not always pay.)

A noteworthy detail in Tutuola's version of the folktale is that Earth, whose quarrel with Heaven caused the famine, has absolutely no part in the settlement of the dispute. Heaven was piqued because Earth would not acknowledge his seniority, we must remember, for which reason he withheld rain from Earth. The sacrifice the slave carries to Heaven, according to Tutuola, "meant that Land surrendered, that he was junior to Heaven" (*Drinkard,* 125). But the surrender is in effect arranged and enforced without Earth's consent, input, or even awareness; it was by the Drinkard's fiat. The nature of the relationship between Earth and humans, at least according to Yoruba ethos, and the implied harmonious, reciprocative mutuality between earth and heaven are here fundamentally fractured. The edifying quality Lindfors suggests for the conclusion of the Drinkard's adventures therefore fails for a number of reasons.

Non Sequitur Extrapolations in *My Life*

My Life specifically gives a nod to the didactic intention in Yoruba storytelling with its concluding sentence, "This is what hatred did." In this case, the armature is that of any number of Yoruba tales in which a jealous woman comes to eventual grief when the death she had plotted for her cowife's child recoils on her. For example, a woman dies, leaving her beloved daughter, who is also her father's favorite, in the care of her (jealous and wicked) cowife. This cowife oppresses the poor orphan child with impossible chores that she will not ask her own pampered child to do. The orphan fouls up so badly while carrying out one of those tasks that she dares not return home to face certain abuse at the hands of her stepmother. In her peregrinations, the orphan comes across a grotesque, wizened old woman who takes her in but also gives her the most odious assignments. The child carries them out without complaint, even cheerfully, and the woman ultimately sends her back home with inexhaustible riches. She offers to share these with her half sister, but her stepmother shuns her generosity. She will have her daughter retrace her half sister's steps and garner her own riches. But the daughter is so spoiled that she will not carry out the tasks the wizened creature assigns to her. What she returns with, therefore, spells certain death for both mother and daughter. That, in this case, is what hatred (or wickedness) does—it visits both mother and daughter with horrific deaths.

The familial environment at the start of *My Life* repeats that of the paradigmatic Yoruba tale. The hero's mother was the last married of his father's three wives. She had two sons whereas the other two wives had only daughters. "So by that the two wives who had only daughters hated my mother, brother and myself to excess as they believed no doubt my brother and myself would be the rulers of our father's house and all his properties after his death" (*My Life*, 17). His mother, a petty trader who sometimes went on overnight trading trips, was absent on one such trip when one of the "slave-wars [that] were causing dead luck to both young and old in those days" forced both brothers to flee. The other two wives had fled with their daughters on hearing the commotion announcing the approach of the "slave-war," but the two brothers, "too young to know the meaning of 'bad' and 'good,' . . . were dancing to the noises of the enemies' guns which were reverberating into the room" (18) where they were eating the yams their mother had hidden there for them. Knowledgeable readers will recognize details from the Èrò-tí-ńrÒjéje story, which etiologically explains women's longer hairs in comparison to men's, at least in the Yoruba experience.

The perfidy of the cowives in leaving the two youngsters behind when they fled with their own children is the "bad" into which the young children are initiated, and it sets the adventure in the bush of ghosts in motion. None of the book's episodes (many of which represent quite audacious corralling of materials from Fagunwa) refer to the hero's life before the bush, to his family situation, or to any members of his family until close to the end. Even after he finally returns to his earthly town, is recognized by his brother, and is reunited with his mother, there is no mention of the wickedness or hatred of the cowives or the disaster they caused for the hero. Rather, a discussion ensues as to whether the returned ghost-bush wanderer would go back for the

" 'SECRET-SOCIETY OF GHOSTS' which is celebrated once in every century" (*My Life,* 174). Naturally, when the hero broaches the notion of returning to the bush for the celebration, his mother and brother will hear nothing of it. But the hero informs the reader that he has dreamed his attendance at the event, and since the hero's dreams never fail, the reader will read about it in a future work. "This," the hero concludes, "is what hatred did."

The sense of incongruousness, or irrelevance, of such a conclusion to the rest of the narrative is only heightened by its close proximity to the hero's desire to return to the site of his adventures, and the promise to furnish news of his return at a later date. If at the end of all he has been through he harbors enough nostalgia for the bush of ghosts (for whatever reason) that he can contemplate returning there for some sort of reunion, then hatred did nothing unbearable to him. Quite the contrary. Furthermore, because we learn nothing of the fate of the perfidious cowives, we can consequently conclude that their hatred caused them no ill either. What then, one might ask, is it that hatred did? The tale, even when it appears to bring the narrative in compliance with Yoruba storytelling ethics, winds up confirming its violation of Yoruba moralistic sensibilities.

Non Sequitur Extrapolations in *Simbi*

Simbi also promises an initiation for its heroine. The singing, irrepressibly happy daughter of a wealthy woman lost her inseparable friends Rali and Sala to the kidnapper Dogo. The loss stopped Simbi's singing and killed her appetite for a while, and although her appetite soon returned, she "did not happy, except to see her two friends." She soon despaired of enjoying her mother's wealth and "became entirely tired to be in happiness, etc. that which her mother's wealths were giving to her." Because she had never experienced hardship, she said to herself, "merriments are now too much for me than what I can bear longer than this time. But the only things that I prefer most to know and experience their difficulties now are the 'Poverty' and the 'Punishment' " (*Simbi,* 8).

Her experiences after she falls into Dogo's hands amply satisfy her desire to know poverty and punishment. Her captor sells her into slavery in a town that forbids singing, which is an addiction for her. There she is fattened and abused by "myrmidon." Inadvertently, she violates the taboo against singing, and her master dies in his attempt to stop her. The infuriated family members reject the option of beating or stabbing her to death, because "to stab her to death does not severe enough" (*Simbi,* 28). They instead seal her in a coffin and set her adrift on a river. The fishermen who later find and rescue her offer her as a slave to their king, fortunately for her, because among the slaves already in the king's service are the people Dogo had earlier kidnapped from her town.

As her adventures continue, she escapes being beheaded as a sacrifice to the king's gods, herself beheading the king and his attendants instead and leading the other slaves into fugitive freedom; she also escapes execution in the town of the "multi-coloured people," fights an inconclusive battle with the Satyr of the dark jungle, is abducted by an eagle, and is almost swallowed by a boa. A woodcutter rescues and marries her, but she is compelled to flee him and his town after her two sons are sacrificed shortly after their birth. Eventually, after battling the Satyr a second time and vanquishing the creature with the aid of the three gods she had acquired in the meantime, she finds her way back home, accompanied by her friend Rali and other captives she had released from Dogo's captivity. (Her other friend Bako, who had become a "cockish lady" after stealing a cock in the town of the multicolored people, had been carried off by a phoenix, the Satyr's ally.) Back in her town, Simbi after a few days' rest goes from house to house "warning all the children that it was a great mistake to a girl who did not obey her parents," and to her mother she vows, "Hah, my mother, I shall not disobey you again!" (*Simbi,* 136).

Given that Simbi's objective was to become acquainted with punishment and suffering, to undergo some sort of flagellation supposedly as a sacrifice or penance and a means of moral redemption, her mission would seem to have been accomplished by the end. Her vindication would also seem to be signaled by her successes in defeating the Satyr, reforming Dogo and rescuing his victims, and, of course, by her safe return home. Her community itself would seem to have benefited from her return with the three gods she had acquired from an old woman in the bush. Within six months, the author tells us, "Simbi had become well known to all people in all villages and towns, in respect of the three gods which were given her by the old woman. The gods were helping all the people of her village etc. whenever they needed their helps" (*Simbi,* 136). In its totality, therefore, the adventure was worthwhile and fortunate. Simbi returns, no longer the easy-living, pampered, and socially useless child she was, but a tried, tested, seasoned, experienced, and worldly-wise woman, whose actions are instrumental in ridding the community of different types of menaces and also greatly improve the fortunes and circumstances of her community. Again, there is an obvious disjunction in the articulation of the premise, the unfolded action, and the conclusion on the one hand, and the lesson proffered on the other.

Ajaiyi as an Exception

One work by Tutuola stands out as a spectacular exception to the observations I have made about *Drinkard, My Life,* and *Simbi,* observations that I contend apply in general to Tutuola's novels. The exception is *Ajaiyi.* In this work, Ajaiyi, first with his sister Aina and later on his own (with occasional company he picks up for a while along the way), embarks on a quest to rid himself and his sister of the poverty they have inherited from their father. The quest takes him to the abode of the Creator, the town of the god of Iron, the country of the witches, and the home of the Devil, among other places, before he returns disappointed to his town. Although the quest is for riches that would put an end to their poverty, Tutuola consistently preaches the lesson that the love of money is the root of all evil, and in several episodes he demonstrates the evil that results from valuing money above all things.

In the town of the Creator, the head drummer conducts Ajaiyi and his two companions, Ojo and Alabi, on a tour during which they see tableaux that recall those presented in Fagunwa's Igbo to Olowo-Aiye and his host, Bàbá Onírùgbòn-yéúké, when they pay a courtesy visit to Death, the host's neighbor. One of the tableaux in *Ajaiyi* is of people burning in a huge fire. The head drummer explains to his guests that the people were "lawyers, judges, etc. who had committed these offences [of partiality] when they were alives in their respective countries" (*Ajaiyi,* 99). The hero continues:

> Some of the people that I knew before they died in my village and who were in the big flame, were judges who were not honest in judging cases, except when bribery was offered. The murderers, liars, thieves, deceivers, etc. etc., and many politicians who had embezzled the states' money, lands, etc. (*Ajaiyi,* 104)

After showing the visitors the scene, the head drummer advises them to be righteous in all things when they return to their villages (104).

Tutuola reinforces the message with the response the holy man who serves as their emissary brings back from the Creator:

The Creator Almighty said that since the three of you have not asked for the heavenly things but money. And since money is the father of all evils and the creator of all insincerities of the world. Therefore, if you don't want something from this town of the Creator which can bring you out of your sins but only money which rules the world. You should go back to your town or village to seek for the Devil, the ruler of the world. He will certainly give you the money that which you require! Please go to the Devil, the enemy of Truth. (*Ajaiyi*, 109)

Even the wizard who conducts them to Devil warns, "I want you to understand that money is the father of all evils and the creator of all sins of this world" (*Ajaiyi*, 179–80). Devil accedes to Ojo's and Alabi's request for wealth, granting them £200,000 and £400,000 respectively, but only at the cost of their sisters' lives and the shortening of their own remaining life spans from 66 to 6 years (188–89). Ajaiyi rejects the bargain; he remains consistently virtuous in the story, pointedly opting to continue in his affliction rather than "to spare the life of [his] sister to Devil and be his follower in respect of money" (190).

Even in what could be considered the teaser to the main adventure, the account of the parents' death, Tutuola purveys a moral lesson that is relevant to that of the main event. The father always warned his children to "remember The Day After Tomorrow." Inexplicably, the children, ages 15 and 12, construe what they are supposed to remember as a person, a relative, thus making a kidnapping adventure possible.[10] After the parents die in their crippling poverty, the children are able to give the father an elaborate funeral because people offer them all they need for free, citing as their reason the dead man's great kindness to all in spite of his poverty. After the obsequies, Ajaiyi remarks:

Now, my father's warning before he died that we should remember "The Day After Tomorrow" came to the truth because almost everything which we used for his burial and funeral ceremony were given to us for free of charge in respect of his kindnesses to his neighbours and other people. (*Ajaiyi*, 30)

Later, after their escape from the slaver to whom their kidnapper had sold them, Ajaiyi adds: "And it was in this town [into which they were sold] Aina and I had understood the meaning of 'Remember The Day After Tomorrow.' The meaning of it was also—'One will reap what he sows.' So if we sow a bad thing we must reap a bad thing in future" (40).

Another instance of effective, well-handled moralization from the same book is the episode in the chapter "Don't Pay Bad for Bad" (*Ajaiyi*, 76–84), which is based on another traditional tale. Aina had borrowed a pitcher with a hole in its bottom from her friend Babi to protect a kola nut seedling from goats. When the mature kola tree becomes a source of wealth for its owner, the jealous Babi demands the pot back, unbroken. Aina must cut down her tree to comply. Later Babi has a child to whom Aina gives a necklace. When her head has outgrown the circumference of the necklace, Aina demands it back, unbroken. When Babi refuses, the case goes to the king, who finds in Aina's favor. "In the judgement, the judge added that the head of Babi's daughter should be cut off in the palace of the king and in the presence of the whole of the village, so that everyone might learn that jealousy was bad" (81). At the last moment, Aina forgives her friend and stays the execution. In the traditional tale, the child's head is severed; Tutuola's modification achieves the moralizing purpose without the distasteful detail of the execution of an innocent child for its mother's sins.

Another View of Moralization

I should note at this point that the perception that Tutuola's customary inattention to moralization is a flaw in his work is by no means universal. Comparing Fagunwa and Tutuola in this regard, Ulli Beier wrote:

> Tutuola differs from Fagunwa in two major points: Tutuola does not moralise and he is never sentimental. Fagunwa is a much more Christian writer. As we have already seen, he loses no opportunity to moralise and to improve his reader. He can also be sentimental and even sloppy. There is nothing very Yoruba about Fagunwa's naïve, somewhat tearful sentimentality.[11]

He later added, "Fagunwa does not attempt to solve any problems in his books. He has two simple aims as a writer: he tries to delight and to entertain; he also tries—alas—to instruct and to improve his reader. But he succeeds so excellently well in his first aim that we willingly forgive him the second" (Beier 1979, 205).

For Beier, then, moralization is a flaw in Fagunwa that Tutuola happily does not share. Beier is quite correct about Fagunwa's tearful sentimentality, which can sometimes be difficult to take, especially when intrepid, battle-tested hunters become maudlin. Also, Fagunwa is undoubtedly a devout Christian: the Christian God's presence, and his surrogates' as well (for example, Iragbeje of *Daemons* and Bàbá-Onírùngbòn-Yéúké of *Igbo*), weave in and out of his plots. Beier's judgment on the writer's comparative proneness to moralization is also unassailable. As he indicated, Fagunwa can be faulted for being somewhat long-winded in that respect. He never misses an opportunity to call his readers' attention to the edifying import of his story. From the first, Akara-Ogun insists that his scribe draw the right lesson from his account about his mother the wicked witch:

> Look on me, my friend, if you are not yet married I implore you to consider the matter well before you do. True, your wife ought to be beautiful lest you tire of each other quickly; and a lack of brains is not to be recommended since you must needs hold converse with each other, but this is not the heart of the matter. The important requisite is that your wife should not be prone to evil, for it is your wife who gives you meat and gives you drink and is admitted most to your secrets. (*Daemons*, 9)

The lecture Akara-Ogun receives from the tearful gnome he had berated is also a piece of didacticism, as is the explanation Iwapele gives him for the scourge of the silent city of the blind (*Daemons*, 30–31). Another example is Akara-Ogun's account of how he finally bested the creature who rode him around like a horse and tied him down when he was not so employed. Akara-Ogun was near despair after all his efforts to free himself had failed. Then:

> Much later, however, I began to understand where I had erred. I realized that I indulged in magical arts but had failed to reckon with God. I forgot that He created the leaf and created the bark of the tree. Before daylight broke on my third day I cried to God and prayed. (*Daemons*, 41)

The final pages of the book are given over to extended passages of moralization—I mean the sermons Iragbeje delivers to the pilgrims during their seven-day sojourn with him. It is as part of the first day's lecture on children and how they should be reared that he tells the Ajantala story to illustrate his point (106–15). As a final touch, Iragbeje concludes the story with the prayer:

> And that is how the story goes, may your heads save you from a home-disrupting child, may your shoulders save you from the type also who sells off the home lest he sell you with your roof. May your legs and arms keep wreckers of life away from you that they do not harm or ruin your lives for you. (*Daemons*, 115)

Tutuola's Relation to African Thought

Apart from exemplary moralizing, one of the accolades critics have bestowed on Tutuola is in recognition of what they regard as his service to the Yoruba ethos in faithfully representing it to the world. They also applaud his service to the world in making available an insider's personal experience of, and deep insight into, the Yoruba experience. In a 1970 article reassessing his career, Omolara Leslie praised Tutuola's accurate representation of an African (and a Yoruba) consciousness. In spite of his handicaps, she wrote,

> he is able to "tell it as it is." He writes genuinely about a real world, about a world which has validity for some men. The consciousness of the Drinkard is probably an African consciousness and certainly a Yoruba one. Death is not a thing of horror and the worlds of the living and the dead are co-extensive, yet different, as Tutuola poignantly shows in the scenes of the Drinkard with his dead Tapster.[12]

But the first influential reviewer of Tutuola's work to cite the significant extent to which elements of the Yoruba experience permeate his work was Ulli Beier. Later critics who have elaborated on his discovery have been prepared to go much farther than he did.

Beier's opinion came in the context of his discussion of D. O. Fagunwa and, specifically, his commentary on *Igbo*. Saying that the plot of the saga was rambling and somewhat disorganized, Beier pointed out the presence of elements from Yoruba folktales but concluded, "Fagunwa does not draw as heavily on Yoruba folklore as Tutuola. Most of the stories are invented, many of them are also taken from European tradition. The true Yoruba flavour of Fagunwa's work lies not in the material he used, but in the language, in the manner and the tone of his story-telling" (Beier 1979, 199). Later he added:

> His plot, of course, is fantastic, and so are many of his characters, but Fagunwa is extremely realistic in much of his detail. He knows how they speak. He knows how they laugh, how they flirt and how they flatter. In his description of people's manners and mannerisms, of their greed, their weaknesses, their humor, Fagunwa is more realistic than many "modern" Yoruba novelists. As an observer of the Yoruba mind at work Fagunwa is still unsurpassed. This is also where he surpasses Tutuola. It is true that Tutuola rivals him as a story-teller, that the stories he tells are in fact more authentically Yoruba and traditional. (Beier 1979, 204)

Beier's point, obviously, is that whereas Fagunwa invents most of his stories and draws on non-Yoruba resources, such as the European tradition, Tutuola borrows more heavily from the Yoruba folktale repertoire. Significantly, Beier credited Fagunwa with being unsurpassed as a reader of the Yoruba mind, and, one can deduce, in his understanding of that mind and the world it creates and that forms it.

If Leslie's declaration that the Drinkard's (and by implication his creator's) consciousness is "an African consciousness and certainly a Yoruba one" is not much different from Beier's observation, what Abiola Irele later made of it effects a significant transformation. "What I personally consider to be the achievement of Amos Tutuola, for instance," Irele has written, "despite his obvious limitations, is the extension he has given to the traditional fantasy in Yoruba folk tales, and to the mythical novel in Yoruba created by Fagunwa, purely by the poetic quality of his own individual evocations."[13] With regard to the comparative authenticity of the two writers, Irele, relying on evidence supplied this time by Gerald Moore, followed Beier in rating Tutuola as the more authentically Yoruba, but in more ways than Beier suggested, and different ones as well. Harold Collins, for his part, argued that although we might agree that Fagunwa surpasses Tutuola as an observer of the Yoruba mind at work, "we might prefer Tutuola's more authentic Yoruba materials" (Collins 1969, 68).

Moore's discovery of an "Orphic significance" in Tutuola's *Drinkard* was important, Irele noted, especially as it lay at "the high road of myth" that Tutuola's imagination (which is here at one with that of his culture) "traverses with such zest and assurance" (Irele 1981, 185). In this regard, Tutuola was superior to Fagunwa, Irele added, the Orphic being "the dominant element in the individual apprehension of Tutuola the artist and not, as is the case with Fagunwa, in the individual expression of a collective consciousness" (185). Irele helpfully provided the following explication:

> Where Fagunwa achieves a personal reorganization of the traditional material, and is thus able to put his stamp on this material in his own writings—aided especially by his gift of language—one feels that with Tutuola, there is a total reliving of the collective myth within the individual consciousness. The artist is here at the very center of his material and of the experience that it communicates. It is not so much a matter of authenticity, of a literal fidelity to the details of the tradition, as of *the degree to which the artist has assumed the tradition and so interiorized its ele-*

ments, its very spirit, as to bring to it, in his own work, a new and original dimension. (Irele 1981, 185; italics mine)

In other words, Fagunwa, whom Irele had earlier described as "nothing less than a complete artist and indeed a master in his own full and independent right" (Irele 1981, 177), merely expresses a collective consciousness; he is merely the individual conduit for something that already exists; his significant contribution is limited to the language he uses. Tutuola, on the other hand, is completely immersed in the material and experience he communicates. He knows and lives the experience more than Fagunwa does. This is, of course, an elaboration (and complication) of Moore's translation of Tutuola's answer to Parrinder's question about the haphazardness of the order of the towns of ghosts in *My Life:* "He has *lived* through his material before ever he sets it down; the many fragments of folklore, ritual and belief embedded in it are not just things remembered (whether from individual or racial knowledge), but things already experienced; they have all passed through the transmuting fire of an individual imagination and been shaped for its ends" (quoted in Irele 1981, 192).[14] Quite obviously, more is being made here by Irele of Moore's deduction, which means little more than that the author identifies rather closely with his hero and the hero's experiences, *whatever those experiences might be.*

If Tutuola is so much closer to the Yoruba experience than Fagunwa, one might wonder why Yoruba readers would identify so closely with Fagunwa and his work while Tutuola has nothing like the earlier writer's following. Irele himself, recalling Haitian writers who won acclaim in France but were not remembered *anywhere* in the world, had asked, "can [Tutuola's] acclaim in Europe be sustained if he hasn't got roots at home?" (Irele 1981, 40). Even Beier conceded that Fagunwa spoke to the Yoruba, and they responded, "for Fagunwa has the humor, the rhetoric, the word play, the bizarre imagery that Yorubas like and appreciate in their language. He impresses his reader with his knowledge of classical Yoruba ('deep Yoruba' as the phrase goes) and he is as knowledgeable in proverbial expressions as an old oracle priest. Yet he is not content with that: he uses the language creatively and inventively, constantly adding to the traditional stock of imagery and enriching the language" (Beier 1979, 199). By contrast, Tutuola has not published in Yoruba.[15]

Irele's essay provides hardly any specific examples of the imaginative powers or "evocations" he so admired in Tutuola, which mark his work as authentically African and specifically Yoruba. One of the few Irele did offer is from the Give and Take episode of *Drinkard*. He was impressed by "the constant recurrence of images built upon the play of light through the entire range of the color spectrum." Tutuola's imagination, Irele commented, "can indeed be qualified as being characteristically luminous, for his visual imagery constantly communicates a brilliant intensity for which the only parallels one can think of in modern African literature belong to the work of Senghor and Okigbo." But the passage Irele quoted for illustration does not cover the color spectrum:

> She was the Red-smaller-tree who was at the front of the bigger Red-tree, and the bigger Red-tree was the Red-king of the Red-people of Red-town and the Red-bush and also the Red-leaves on the bigger Red-tree were the Red-people of the Red-town in the Red-bush. (Irele 1981, 185)

If it is the pervasive redness of the description that lends it luminousness, we might compare Fagunwa's description of red-eyed, red-toothed death as quoted by Beier (Beier 1979, 201).

It is, of course, possible to take the same passage as an example of Tutuola's sensationalistic manner of achieving effects, this time expressed in his insistent resort to redness. His expectation, obviously that the intensification of the image through accumulation will maximize its impact on the audience, is consistent with his penchant for piling on detail after gross and grotesque detail in his description of situations and figures intended to frighten. The extended description of the God of the State in *Herbalist* (12–13) is a good example. Irele saw this tendency as another argument for Tutuola's African genius. He described it as Tutuola's "unrestricted play of the imagination." The imagination, Irele explained, is "outsize":

> It tends towards a constant comprehensiveness; it seizes with energy upon any aspect of experience within its range in order to integrate it into the particular tenacity of feeling determined by its own mode of apprehension. There is a cumulative effect in Tutuola's way with imagery which is akin to the manner of much of African music, which often progresses by an insistent building up of tension. (Irele 1981, 186)

African music does indeed build from the expression of a motif by a single instrument to a cumulation of variations on that motif by the entire ensemble of instruments, but always detectable in the music is the discipline and restraint imposed on each instrument or voice by the need to acknowledge and respond to the others. The difficulty with Tutuola's unrestricted imagination is that it often lacks discipline, because writing for him, as he himself admitted, is "just playing" with materials.

In any case, one might ask with regard to the lurid redness of Tutuola's imagination, how representative it is of the Yoruba "collective myth," experience, or imagination. Europeans, for example, who live much of their lives in the grayness of autumns and the whiteness of winters while the sun hibernates in the southern hemisphere, are noted for their sun- and color-worshiping propensities. The long absence of both natural phenomena for sometimes more than half of the year impresses them on the people's minds and places them at the center of their desire. By contrast, the Yoruba live with the sun and color almost year-round: there are only brief spells when the sun is in hiding, and hardly any time of the year when flowers, fruits, and especially foliage do not add color to the landscape. Furthermore, any one who knows the Yoruba associates them with the color indigo primarily, and then with the rich purples of camwood (osùn) and beads (sègi, iyùn). William Bascom, writing about Yoruba dyeing, notes, "The most popular dye is indigo, which produces varying shades ranging from a light sky blue to a purplish blue-black, depending upon the number of batches of dye used. . . . There [are] also red and yellow dyes, a tan dye to imitate the more expensive wild silk, and the natural white and tan colors of light and dark cotton."[16] Sányán, the much sought-after fabric woven from the silk of the silkworm, is rich brown. In fact, the Yoruba ridicule people who are impressed by, or attracted to, glittering or lurid things, which they dub sàgbèlójúyòyò (something that bedazzles the farmer's eyes).

One more word on this issue. If Irele is correct that when one reads Tutuola, one feels that he is the hero of his own stories, that the stories "relate to his own immediate sense of humanity and proceed from his own immeasurable appetite for experience rather than from a more general social and moral awareness" (Irele 1981, 187), then that quality of his writing calls into question the claim that he is a great moralist, inasmuch as what Irele is saying here amounts to an imputation of a vacation of reflection. In the face of complete immersion in experience and an absence of a general social and moral awareness, one is hard put to see how there can be "a contemplative quality that is implicit and immediate in Tutuola's evocations, and which goes deeper into the spirit of the mythical language which he employs than the works of Fagunwa" (187). Of Fagunwa, on the other hand, Irele had written that in all his stories, "a distance seems to separate the characters and events that he represents from the deepest feelings of the author himself. This impression of a dissociation between the narrative content and the writer's response is reinforced by Fagunwa's habit of didactic reflections and constant asides to his audience" (186–87). Because contemplation and reflection are customarily conceived of in the context of liminality and subjunctivity, not of submersion in immediate experience, the conclusion would have to be that Fagunwa is far better placed to contemplate, to reflect, to moralize, than Tutuola. That, indeed, happens to be Beier's point.

On Man and Society

Gerald Moore has observed that Tutuola is concerned in his work with "man alone, suffering and growing amid the images thrown forth by his own mind and by the imagination of the race," rather than with "man in society" (Moore 1962, 42). Yet critics such as Beier and Irele have claimed that Tutuola embodies the Yoruba ethos, which he has lived (or lives) profoundly. The two views are clearly inconsistent and incompatible. The Yoruba concept of the individual is consistent with what prevails in most African cultures. The individual is fundamentally bound with others in cohesive groups. V. Y. Mudimbe paraphrases Henri Maurier's dissertation on the African mode of thought (*forme de pensée*) as follows:

> This "form" is . . . characterized by three factors. First, an anthropocentrism affirms the centrality of the human, while defining everything else in terms of this human locus. Second, this anthropocentrism would be community-oriented insofar as the African individual is always perceived as a member of a specific community, that is to say, his or her being-for-itself can only be linked to his or her being-with-others. Thus, a third factor: *this individual is essentially a relational being who gets significance and pertinence by his or her integration in a given human community.* Maurier thinks one could deduce that the form of thinking in Africa is relational.[17]

A preoccupation with "man alone" rather than with "man in society" is obviously contrary to the relational habit of the mind that Maurier describes. If he is correct—and the preponderance of knowledgeable opinion and experience suggests that he is—then it would seem that either Irele is wrong, or Moore is wrong. In fact, though, Moore is quite right. Tutuola's heroes and heroines seem to answer to no law beyond themselves, and they seem to be bound by no group's ethos, further arguments against the suggestion that Tutuola in his works espouses a (or *the*) Yoruba worldview.

The Ethnographic Value of Tutuola's Writing

One of the great appeals of the early works of Achebe for Europeans was its anthropological quality, its exposure of the workings of African traditional institutions to the European reading public. Especially attractive to them was his liberal sprinkling of proverbs throughout the texts of *Things Fall Apart, No Longer at Ease,* and *Arrow of God.* Achebe's practice in this regard bears testimony to the great importance his Igbo culture attaches to the use of proverbs. What is true for the Igbo is perhaps even more so for the Yoruba. Proverbs, they assert, are the horses of communication, the means by which one retrieves lost or broken connections. The Yoruba child grows up hearing proverbs at every turn, especially in the speeches of the elders and particularly on formal occasions. Being ever intent on remaining true to the way that the wisdom of the ages has sanctioned, whenever a person in a position to instruct others does so, he or she appeals to the authority of proverbs for authentication. And because storytelling is partly for instruction, a measure of the Yorubaness of a storyteller would be the extent to which he or she employs proverbs.

Tutuola's Use of Proverbs

Unlike Achebe, Tutuola did not take advantage of his culture's rich stock of proverbs in his early writing career and did not do so until *Huntress.* Here Tutuola employs proverbs (as well as nonproverbial sayings) as epigraphs at the heads of some chapters, the events in which are supposed to illustrate the purport of the proverbs. He dropped the practice in *Feather Woman* but took it up again in *Ajaiyi,* beginning with the fourth chapter, "The Spirit of Fire," and omitting it in some chapters thereafter. Indeed, the earlier books are so devoid of proverbs that their sudden appearance in *Huntress* commands considerable attention. In that work (and to a degree in *Ajaiyi*), the applicability of the proverbs (and sayings) is sometimes forced. As an example, the chapter in the earlier book with the title "The Kind Gorilla Saved Me from the Debris" has the following for its epigraph:

The Farm always sees the end of the farmer
He is as ugly as the devil's cross
The pen always sees the end of the clerk
Never you protect another person's head until the hawk carries your
     own away

                                                                                    (Huntress, 100)

One recognizes the echoes of the Yoruba proverbs *"Àhéré ni yóò kéhìn oko;
àrò ni yóò kéhìn ilé"* [It is the hut that will survive the demise of the farm;
it is the cooking hearth that will survive the collapse of the house] and
"A kìí du orí olórí kàwòdì gbé teni lo" [One does not scramble to protect
another person's head and leave one's own for the chicken hawk to make
off with]. "He is as ugly as the devil's cross" is certainly not a Yoruba
saying, nor is "The pen always sees the end of the clerk."

The reviewer Akanji (Ulli Beier) also found Tutuola's use of proverbs
in this work unsatisfactory. It was, Beier suggested, Tutuola's attempt to
make up for the lack of imagination, invention, and humor in the work.
The attempt was, Beier claimed, "quite a charming innovation. Unfortunately the proverbs are not always very meaningful to non-Yorubas in
Tutuola's translation" (Lindfors 1975, 84). As I have observed, although
the proverbs have meaning for the Yoruba, they are not always apt. More
important, however, are the rather tenuous rationales for the sayings.
The events in the chapter in question come immediately after Adebisi has
destroyed the town containing the "custody" where she was imprisoned
and has killed all its inhabitants. Her survival of her captors justifies the
sayings about who (or what) sees the end of whom (or what). The heroine
explains the other recognizable Yoruba proverb by saying that her difficulties in finding an exit from the town arose from her helping others: "It
was right as this thing happened to me because I had protected another
person's head (all the captives) until when the hawk was going to carry
my own head away now" (*Huntress,* 100). One can of course see a connection between the events and the proverb. But its logic is to warn against
imprudent actions whose outcome might be disastrous, and its application is either to enjoin reconsideration *before* an action, or as a you-should-
have-known-better comment after the fact. In this case, though, the
proverb comes after the event, whose outcome was happy and desirable.
By the time he came to write *Pauper,* Tutuola had become more adept at
proverb usage. He did not employ them as epigraphs, but they occur
with some profusion and aptness throughout the text.

Fagunwa's use of proverbs, by contrast, is pervasive, and his mastery of it exemplary. Akara-Ogun, the hero of *Daemons,* begins his narration with the proverb "Like the sonorous proverb do we drum the *agidigbo;* it is the wise who dance to it, and the learned who understand its language" (*Daemons,* 7), and equally astute proverbs are sprinkled liberally through the narrative. When, for example, the travelers to Mount Langbodo encounter Fear (incidentally, one of the models for Tutuola's fearsome monsters),[18] they try all their weapons and charms on him, but nothing prevails against the terrible and formidable creature. Eventually an unlikely idea suggests itself to them, and they ask Olohun-iyo (He of the Mellifluous Voice) to sing. The ploy succeeds: they are able to overcome Fear by song. Apropos of the event the narrator observes, "Thus did we overcome by mere song a foe who was impervious to guns and bows, for whatever it is that man attempts by gentleness does not come to grief, but that which we handle by violence rebounds on us with equal toughness" (85). The concluding observation is a well-known Yoruba proverb *"Ohun tí a bá fowó líle mú líle ní ńle kórókóró; ohun tí a bá fowó èlè mú rírò ní ńrò gbèdègbèdè."*

Human Scruples

On another point, susceptibility to scruples, Tutuola's work cannot be a reliable guide to the Yoruba habit. ZURRJIR, we have already seen, is a version of Fagunwa's creation Ajantala, even though his name in this particular incarnation is changed. Tutuola's manner of ridding the parents of the scourge is somewhat typical:

> One night, when it was one o'clock in the mid-night, when I noticed that he slept inside the room I put oil around the house and roof, but as it was thatched with leaves and also it was in the dry season, I lighted the house with fire and closed the rest of the windows and doors which he did not close before he slept. Before he woke up, there was a great fire around the house and roof, smoke did not allow him to help himself, so he burnt together with the house to ashes. (*Drinkard,* 34)

The cool, calculated incineration even of an animal is not part of the Yoruba way. A Yoruba proverb says *"Ògèdè dúdú ò séé bù sán; omo burúkú ò séé lù pa"* [A green plantain is nothing to take a bite of; an evil child is not to be beaten to death]. No matter how horrible a child might be, the Yoruba would still frown on infanticide, let alone the cruel manner in which the Drinkard accomplishes his end. The resurrection of the child as a half-bodied baby does not minimize the enormity of the crime.

The sensibility Tutuola displays in the elimination of the problem child surfaces in *Ajaiyi* in a slightly different fashion. Ajaiyi is desperate and disappointed in his expectation that his (supposed) father will grant him wealth in exchange for the rams Ajaiyi has sacrificed to him as he asked. The hero vows to his wife that he will go to his dead father in his grave, confront him with the demands he had made through the Witch Doctor (for a sacrifice of nine rams), and express his puzzlement at why his father would make such demands knowing what poverty he had bequeathed to his children. Ajaiyi will also demand an explanation for his father's insistence on receiving all nine rams before he will grant the promised wealth, even though Ajaiyi has already provided six and promised the rest later. He continues, "I explained further to my wife that if my dead father confirmed all what the Witch Doctor had told me to do then I would behead him (my dead father) before I would come out of his grave" (*Ajaiyi,* 229). We must grant his desperation and extreme anger, but even a desperate, angry, and disappointed son does not behead a father, even a cheating father, at least not in the Yoruba scheme of things. Tutuola, his defenders might object, is writing nonrealistic fiction in which everything and anything goes, and with regard to which we must suspend the usual standards of judgment. If that is the case, then we must desist from holding him up as a mirror of the Yoruba world.

Fagunwa, by contrast, has something to teach about the wanton murder of even someone to whom one is not related by blood. I refer to the killing of Akara-Ogun's mother by his father. Under orders from the Almighty that he must dispatch her because of her wicked witching, he makes his way homeward, his gun primed to accomplish the grisly task. Along the way, though, he accosts an antelope eating okro. He shoots it and is astonished to hear the animal cry out in a human voice and escape with its gunshot wound. When the hunter arrives home, he finds his wife dead from a gunshot; her top half is human, but her nether half is antelope (*Daemons,* 12–13). Wife killing is not the sort of thing the Yoruba approve of. Another instance is Kako's killing of his wife. Anxious to answer the summons that he join the pilgrims to Mount Langbodo, Kako prepares to abandon his innocent, loving, and newly wedded wife without so much as informing her. "It was most unbecoming behavior," Akara-Ogun comments (75). When she learns of Kako's intention and clings to him to prevent his departure, he cleaves her nearly in two with his machete. Akara-Ogun is horrified (77).

Later, when the pilgrims are on their way to Mount Langbodo, the forest unaccountably closes on them, halting their progress. Elegbede Ode (who understands the languages of birds and animals) overhears a bird explain that Kako is the cause of their predicament because the innocent wife he killed had petitioned heaven for redress. The bird also says that the trapped travelers will be able to escape and proceed on their mission only if they kill it (the bird) as a sacrifice of propitiation. They do, whereupon Helpmeet (who had once saved Akara-Ogun from almost certain death) materializes to lead them out (*Daemons*, 83). In these incidents, the points are made that a man does not treat his wife as though her wishes do not matter, that wanton killing is an unacceptable offense, and that the offender pays sooner or later.

When one compares such interdictions against killing with Tutuola's heroes' and heroines' seeming delight in such acts (the wanton killing of animals at the start of *Herbalist*, the relish at the genocidal destruction of the pigmies in *Huntress*, even the hero's pride in carrying the grisly two-headed trophy around in *Herbalist*), one can assert that Tutuola as a writer is not overly concerned with illustrating the Yoruba way, and that ethnologists interested in synthesizing a Yoruba ethos look in his work at great risk. Fagunwa is far more reliable. Take for another example the description of the gifts the king of Mount Langbodo sends back to the king of Akara-Ogun's town: "Six diamond rings, six gold chains, six beaded crowns, six velvet cushions, six household ornaments, and six bibles in different language" (*Daemons*, 137). Why six? The king explains in the accompanying letter: "I send you some small gifts in sixes, as is the custom of the Yoruba in days gone by and at other times even in the present age; I do this as a king who, with the symbol of six, seeks to draw you closer in my affection" (137). The Yoruba word for six is *eéfà;* because it incorporates the syllable *fà* (draw [something] close), it is pressed into service as a sign indicating a desire for closeness.

Even the geographical locations of Fagunwa's two sages, Iragbeje and Bàbá-Onírùngbòn-Yéúké, illustrate the Yoruba conception of sagacious-ness and its conditions. Both have their homes at the boundary demar-cating heaven from earth. Bàbá-Onírùngbòn-Yéúké, in fact, reveals that he is only half human, his other half being spirit; and the songs of heaven are easily audible from Iragbeje's abode. The physical situation of the two (near heaven) is a symbolic expression of their nearness to heaven, or to death, in the normal course of human life, and therefore of their access to wisdom. Age equates to experience in the Yoruba scheme, and experience equals wisdom. Nearness to heaven, therefore, is a condition for sagaciousness.

Tutuola does make some effort in some of his later works to incorporate Yoruba elements, to infuse his narratives with authentic Yoruba cultural resources. Thus in *Pauper* he makes a point of using the Yoruba names for the days of the week, and of making the events that happen on those days suggest, in accordance with Yoruba belief, that the names somehow determine the nature of the occurrences (*Pauper*, 3, 41, 90, 107). In *Ajaiyi*, in the course of reporting the troubles the three seekers had with the "terrible active lumps of the iron" that were chasing them, Tutuola writes that when they arrived unexpectedly in a certain country, "we hid behind a house, we thought that we were safe like 'the hawk in the sky which does not realise that the people in the land are seeing it.' It was so for us this day which was 'The Day of Trouble' (Friday)" (*Ajaiyi*, 129).

In *Pauper*, Tutuola provides a correct hierarchy for the royal council, the *oba* followed by the *òtún* and then the *òsì*. He also notes that the *oba* consulted a *babaláwo* on the third day of his child's birth to determine his *esè 'nt'ayé*, giving his reader a capsule description of the paraphernalia and procedure for *Ifá* divination, and of court etiquette (*Pauper*, 2–4). An author's note that explains Yoruba expressions, lists the hierarchy of chiefs, and explains the *esè 'nt'ayé* ceremony forms the preface to the book. The book also includes a description of the rock at the entrance to Laketu town, at the bottom of which is a hole whence comes "a fearful voice" that shakes the forest and frightens young and old into believing that it leads to the home of the Creator. A "pond of antiquity" is also located nearby, containing "horrible" water that scares the people (1–2). The description recalls a phenomenon that legend locates somewhere near Ile-Ife, which myth identifies as the origin of the world. In addition, Tutuola uses a number of identifiable Yoruba proper names, and game songs (99, 100), although he also dubs a member of the *alágemo* cult "chameleon worshipper" (19) as only a novice about Yoruba mysteries would. Similarly, in *Ajaiyi*, the popular Yoruba game *ayò* becomes the "native game (warry)" (*Ajaiyi*, 175), again as though the author knew no Yoruba.

Collins, who is an enthusiastic admirer of Tutuola, apparently considers it meritorious that he purveys sentiments and attitudes at variance with those that characterize the Yoruba. So much one can deduce from the following assessment of his greatest merit:

Tutuola's most important literary virtue is what we must call, for lack of a better term, his humanity—his compassionate view of human beings and his dramatizing and offering for his readers' admiration some of the saving traits of humanity: courage, resolution, persistence, ingenuity, resourcefulness, tolerance, kindness, and forbearance. His main characters, untrammeled by the usual human modes of moral bondage, are free from such idolatries as the devotion to slogans and fanatical ideals, to a domineering god or gods, to social standards, to war, to tribal traditions, to class mores, to sexual demands. (Collins 1969, 126–27)

I am not concerned here with the long list of qualities, a few (at least) of which are debatable, but with the purported nature of his characters. Characters who consider human modes of morality as some kind of bondage with which they would not wish to be trammeled, who believe in no "domineering" god or gods, who shun social standards, "tribal" traditions, and class mores, are decidedly alien to the Yoruba spirit. But perhaps Collins's intention was indeed to demonstrate Tutuola's distance from Yoruba ethos, for he approvingly quoted Beier's comment, "To a Christian and half-educated man, Yoruba tradition would obviously look more frightening, monstrous, and grotesque than to somebody in that culture" (Collins 1969, 78). Collins accepted Beier's explanation, which in effect positions Tutuola outside Yoruba culture in his attitude to Yoruba cultural artifacts, as "plausible." Collins would have no difficulty with Tutuola's description of Yoruba cultural practices as "primitive" (*Pauper*, 3), and his characterization of the gods of the Yoruba pantheon as "false gods" (*Ajaiyi*, 11).

Like Collins, Michael Thelwell offers opinions that depict Tutuola's cosmology as varying from that of the Yoruba, although in his case the depiction is clearly unintended. In Thelwell's introduction to the 1984 edition of *Drinkard*, he has the following to say of Yoruba mythology, intending his description to coincide with what can be deduced from that book:

The central Yoruba tradition—that of the sacred myth describing the creation, evolution, and jurisdiction of the deities and historical heroes— represents a remarkably rigorous cosmology of intellectual coherence and elegance. It is a universe of elemental forces both natural and social which find metamorphic expression in a pantheon of deities, whose complicated interrelationships, jurisdictions, and necessities are rationalized into an architectonic system of knowledge. The sophisticated worldview embodied in this myth has as its central value the balancing and harmonizing of powerful forces—natural, numinous, and social.[19]

Society became possible, Thelwell says, as a result of the accommodation these forces established through language, rituals, mutual obligations, and traditions. But beyond this stable society lay "terra incognita: the evil forest, the bad bush. Here was the home of chaos, where random spirits without name or history, or bizarre forms and malignant intent were to be found. This was the domain of the deformed, the unnatural, and the abominable" (Thelwell, 189).

Much of what Thelwell says is true enough, but his conception of the bush is a projection of European prejudices onto the Yoruba mind. The forest can of course be evil and the bush bad, but they are not necessarily so, nor are they necessarily the home of chaos and random spirits with no name or history. There is no randomness in the Yoruba scheme, where everything has a name, a history, and a purpose, which may not be generally known, but is knowable and known to the few who have access to deep mysteries. As Fagunwa demonstrates, even supposedly evil creatures such as Esu-kekere-ode can be good-natured, just as the god Esu (erroneously equated with the Christian Devil) after whom he is named can be either malevolent or benevolent, depending on the circumstance. Subscription to the European (or Christian) tendency to pathologize the different explains Tutuola's attitude to the creatures of the bush, bizarre and malignant in intent and therefore deserving of indiscriminate slaughter. That is another point of difference between him and Fagunwa, and between his and the Yoruba's spirits.

Although characters that can be described as bizarre and malignant creatures of the bush appear in Fagunwa's novels, their construction is by no means simply whimsical. The famous Agbako of *Daemons* and Ojola-ibinu of *Igbo* (to pick just two examples) serve specific purposes in their respective novels. Agbako is a figure in the Yoruba moral universe who embodies unexpected misfortune. Fagunwa was obviously giving objective form to what is essentially an abstract idea, in much the same way as he would personify and objectify Fear and a host of other concepts.[20] To reiterate, in the Yoruba scheme, nothing is random; to say that a misfortune is unexpected, or even inexplicable, is not to say that it is random. A consultation with a *babaláwo* is all it would take to divine the cause.

Ojola-ibinu was also not being hostile to Olowo-Aiye and his companions for no reason. The manner and words with which he greeted them speak for themselves:

> Humans! Humans! Humans! You have sought me out even here! You human beings! Ah! Ah! Ah! Only God the Most Glorious can end the enmity between us. Poisonous snakes are hated by humans; harmless

snakes are hated by humans. If a human sees a snake in the open the
human kills it; if a human sees a snake in a nook the human kills it.
There is no enmity like the one that prevails between humans and snakes
save the one that obtains between the children of the Devil and those of
God the King. (*Igbo,* 145)

The ultimate reason for the Ojola-ibinu character is, therefore, similar to
that of the Ostrich in *Daemons,* who gave the hunters trouble because
they were all guilty of having mistreated birds in the past. The moral is
that we should learn to see animals as beings deserving of life, and not
regard any species as collectively (and automatically) evil and dangerous, with the result that we condemn them to indiscriminate extermina-
tion. It deplores the sort of behavior the hero of *Herbalist* boasts of at the
beginning of his hunting career, behavior that appalled even the people
of his community, at least for a while:

> As I continued to kill many of the wild animals every day for some
> months all of my friends deserted me, because they thought that sooner
> or later I might kill them as I was killing the wild animals in the jungle.
> (*Herbalist,* 15)

We cannot take the revelation as indicating any sort of remorse, for it
did not lead to a change of heart, as the events on his journey to the
remote town demonstrate.

The sum of the foregoing discussion is to suggest that Tutuola's imagination is, for the most part, subordinated to a sense of fun that places a
premium on the sensation of the moment and whatever might maximize
it in preference for a grand design from which a moral purpose could be
detected. Critics who have imputed such purposes to him have had to
make allowances for him and bend facts in his favor to an extent they
would hardly consider were the author not Tutuola. Moreover, for all the
fact that he had as his model the consummate (admittedly sometimes
tedious) moralizer Fagunwa, whose novels have been an irresistible quarry
for Tutuola, he has not consistently followed his material benefactor in this
regard, even though morals are an integral part of Yoruba storytelling.
Nor has he, like Fagunwa, demonstrated much facility with proverbs, the
cornerstone of Yoruba verbal artistry. And in certain other significant
regards, Tutuola has evinced attitudes that contrast with characteristic
Yoruba preferences. For these reasons, among others, I suggest that
Tutuola could hardly serve as a guide to the Yoruba world or the Yoruba
mind, and that those critics who hail him as an exemplary Yoruba storyteller, more Yoruba than even Fagunwa, have a difficult case to prove.

Chapter Five •

The Critics' Amos Tutuola

Colonial Tendencies in African Criticism

In Camara Laye's *The Radiance of the King,* Clarence, the derelict French hero of the novel, finds himself in sudden need of employment in one of his country's West African colonies and proposes to petition the king for help. On being told that the king does not receive just anybody, Clarence retorts, "I am not 'just anybody,' I am a white man."[1] He must eventually settle for being represented before the king by a local beggar. When the beggar returns to inform him that the king has no job for him, Clarence pleads, "But I would have accepted any post whatsoever! . . . I could have been a simple drummer boy" (Laye, 48). Whereupon the beggar lectures him:

> That is not a simple occupation. . . . The drummers are drawn from a noble caste and their employment is hereditary. Even if you had been allowed to beat a drum, your drumming would have had no meaning. You have to know how . . . You see, you're a white man! (Laye, 48)

The notion that whiteness is not all-empowering must have come as a shock to Clarence, whose expectations are in accordance with the assumptions of Europeans vis-à-vis their African colonies.

During the colonial period, European colonial governments established the tradition of dumping superfluous and expendable personnel into their African colonies as administrators and white-collar functionaries. In numerous instances, wellborn profligates were packed off to some colony to live down a scandal, learn some discipline, or simply grow up. After both world wars, these territories also provided employment opportunities for thousands of demobilized soldiers whose only qualifications were whatever they had learned during the wars, their proven patriotism in having risked their lives for their countries, and, of course, their whiteness. Many such colonial officers occupied positions for which in other contexts some expertise would have been mandated, but the assumption of their governments was that the colonies mattered so little that their affairs could be entrusted to just about any person, or, more specifically, any white person. Whatever special skills a colonial administrator required, he could acquire on the job, and whatever damage he caused during his on-the-job training would be inconsequential.

The colonial mentality at work in that administrative practice was also operative in other regards, in the acquisition and dissemination of knowledge about the colonies, for example. One measure of its persistence is that even today, a major complaint about the discipline of African studies seizes on one important feature that differentiates it from other area studies: the discipline seemingly beckons all comers and imposes no prerequisites other than a dilettantish curiosity or adventuresomeness. I refer in this particular case to the assumption that, unlike in the case of other parts of the world (Europe, China, or Russia, for example), the requirements for certification as an expert on Africa do not include a knowledge of pertinent African languages, let alone fluency in them. Even when the subject in question has everything to do with language and its use, as in the people's various forms of verbal artistry, the European "expert" is assumed to be capable of learning all there is to learn simply by applying knowledge gained from his or her upbringing in a supposedly more sophisticated and more complex civilization to the presumedly much simpler formations characteristic of African societies. All the so-called expert needs is minimal help from an interpreter, whose bilingualism is most often imperfect.

The same mentality, assumptions, and practice were of course prevalent when Tutuola first came to the attention of European readers and critics, and they have exerted a lasting determinate influence on the scholarship on the writer and his work.

Problems of Tutuola Criticism

Tutuola has, to put it mildly, always posed a considerable problem for critics, simply because he scored his initial acclaim in spite of what would normally be considered fatal flaws in a writer. On reading *Drinkard,* instead of being put off by its bad English, Dylan Thomas was captivated by its "brief, thronged, grisly and bewitching story, or series of stories," and by the language itself, which he described as "Young English." He singled out for special notice phrases such as "did not satisfy with water as with palm-wine," and the description of the half-bodied child who talked with a "lower voice like a telephone" (Lindfors 1975, 7), all of which makes the writing, in Thomas's opinion, "nearly always terse and direct, strong, wry, flat and savoury" (8). At the time of *Drinkard*'s publication there was not much African literature to speak of, and most European readers and critics had little or no exposure to the little there was. But if they were initially uncertain about what to make of the work, which seemed to thumb its nose at all the conventions of literature as they knew it, Dylan Thomas's enthusiastic review dispelled the uncertainty, and Tutuola's success as a literary artist was assured. Foreign (non-Nigerian) and some non-Yoruba critics in particular have tended to praise him, as Abiola Irele has noted, for the wrong reasons. Sometimes, indeed, critics have praised Tutuola for reasons that defy reason. The following are only a few representative examples.

Eric Larrabee, one of Tutuola's earliest interviewers, found in his travels through West Africa that Tutuola was the only original writer in that part of the world. Whereas "the enterprising African is much more likely to go to work for the government, where he can put on glasses and necktie and safely harass the white man with the white man's own weapons of legalism, bombast, and chicane," Larrabee found that Tutuola "had by-passed this adolescent stage in the growth of Africa into modern society and gone on to something entirely different" (Lindfors 1975, 11). With regard to the language of *Drinkard,* Larrabee said that it was "written in English but not an English of this world. The style is unschooled but oddly expressive" (11); and when he discovered that the "British Intellectuals" at the University (then University College) of Ibadan did not think much of the book (although they felt compelled to read it), he attributed their coolness to the fact that Tutuola had written to ask the bookstore to keep his book in stock.

Kingsley Amis added his plaudits for Tutuola after reading *My Life,* which quite took Amis's breath away. In his effusive praise for the book, which he said was "written in a completely new English idiom, for, presumably, a native audience" (Lindfors 1975, 25), he declared, "this book clearly needs repeated readings before its extraordinariness can be fully noted, let alone mastered, and then there is no doubt of the size of Mr. Tutuola's talent, which makes the average 'modern novel' look jejune and vapid" (26).

The Effects of European Assault

The initial challenges to the clamorous approbation of Tutuola's writing came mostly from Nigeria after his work had already earned enthusiastic praises such as the foregoing from abroad. Some Yoruba readers (especially but not exclusively) dismissed his materials as unoriginal and overindulgent; they were unimpressed by his craftsmanship and were bewildered by Europeans' applause for bad grammar and vocabulary. Some were affronted by the implications of the publishers' acceptance and publication of *Drinkard*. Knowing the author, they knew that his English was neither an experiment nor, as some thought, a West African dialect. Babasola Johnson made these critics' point when he rejected European rationalizations for what he referred to as "Mr. Tutuola's strange lingo (or, shall I say, the language of the 'Deads'?)," and suggestions that it was some sort of West African patois. "Patois does not contain such words as 'unreturnable,' 'weird' or such expressions as 'the really road,' " he declared (Lindfors 1975, 32). Had the book been written in West African patois, Johnson observed, "then Mr. Tutuola's literary tactics would have been exposed," the tactic being, as he went on to indicate, an unacknowledged raid on D. O. Fagunwa's *Ogboju Ode*. Moreover, the critics recognized the episodes that made up the plot as amateurish rerenderings of materials from Yoruba folktales, when they were not equally inept reworkings of the published inventions of Fagunwa.

It is important to stress that the hostility to Tutuola, in Nigeria or West Africa, was never unanimous. On June 5, 1954, Ade Sodipo wrote to *West Africa* to disagree with Johnson and proclaim that both *Drinkard* and *My Life* had literary merit. Sodipo did not think the language of the first book was strange, and he believed that Tutuola had successfully met the difficult challenge of writing "folk tales," a task that demanded that the style be attuned to the subject matter. "Mr. Tutuola has, in my opinion, achieved this," Sodipo averred; "the style is romantic" (Lindfors 1975, 39). But opinions like Sodipo's remained rather muted in comparison with negative ones.

Suspicious Praises

The obvious uncertainty of Tutuola's command of English, his maladroit handling of plot and structure, and his lack of originality were not the only factors that caused his compatriots to suspect a hidden agenda behind the praises non-African critics showered on him. They were also suspicious of observations like Selden Rodman's that "Amos Tutuola is not a revolutionist of the word, not a mathematician, not a surrealist. He is a true primitive" (Lindfors 1975, 15). One might also point to a passage in Larrabee's interview in which, after describing Tutuola as "an author who (1) probably has never met another author, (2) owns no books, (3) is not known to his daily acquaintances as an author, (4) has no personal contact with his publisher, (5) is not certain where his book is on sale, and (6) does not think of himself as an author" (Lindfors 1975, 13), Larrabee quoted Tutuola verbatim as telling him, "I think, when you reach there, the U.S.A., you write a letter to me." Asked why he wanted a letter, Larrabee reported, Tutuola explained, "So I know you not forget me" (14).

Larrabee's management of that brief exchange, especially his care to preserve Tutuola's ungrammatical English, to some betrayed a particular, perhaps even perverse, fascination with "quaintness" and offers an explanation for the suspicion many Nigerians harbored about the foreign acclaim for the writer. I. Adeagbo Akinjogbin voiced his misgivings in this connection in a letter to *West Africa* on June 5, 1954, two months after V. S. Pritchett had commented in *New Statesman and Nation* that Tutuola conjured up for readers "a fantasy life as barbarous, bloody and frightening as the masks of the tribal ceremonies" (Lindfors 1975, 21). Akinjogbin was startled by the news that *Drinkard* had already been translated into French, for he could not believe that the lively European interest in the book resulted from Europeans' assessment of its literary value, but from their love to "believe all sorts of fantastic tales about Africa, a continent of which they are profoundly ignorant" (41). After Tutuola had got his money, Akinjogbin complained, the ones who would suffer the consequences of the images of Africa Tutuola had propagated would be "the unfortunate ones who have cause to come to England or Europe" (41).

Nigerians and other West Africans were confounded for yet another reason, namely, that the praises being showered on Tutuola were inconsistent with what they had been taught—often by the same westerners whose selected authors included the likes of Aeschylus, Shakespeare, Milton, Molière, Dostoyevsky, and Arthur Miller—about what constituted good literature. They had been led to believe that creative writing required a mastery of language, adeptness at plotting, ability to create believable characters, and a clear idea of the theme(s) the work will convey. Now they were being told that with regard to Tutuola (perhaps with regard to African creativity), none of that mattered. Furthermore, some of the arguments in support of the new thesis were downright disingenuous.

European Recalcitrance

Many of the foreign critics arrived at their sometimes worshipful endorsement of Tutuola in some ignorance about his background and circumstances. However, when the challenges surfaced from several incredulous Nigerian (and other African) readers, often armed with quite persuasive information that should have indicated some need for reassessment, these critics tended stubbornly to reassert their earlier positions rather than reconsider them in the light of better information. They adopted a tactic that was a mix of what amounted to inventive and often daring manipulation of the evidence to show Tutuola in the best of lights, rather condescending attacks on those of Tutuola's compatriots who failed to concede his genius, and the imputation of ulterior motives to them. In addition to touting Tutuola's powerful imagination and defending his use of substandard English, these critics also proposed most indulgent rationalizations for what they would have cited as damaging flaws in any other writer while also comparing him with legendary artists from Homer to Blake. Prominent among such critics are Harold Collins (whose monograph on Tutuola is distinguished for its unconditional commitment to the writer), Robert Plant Armstrong, O. R. Dathorne, Vladimir Klima, Charles Larson, Gerald Moore, and Adrian Roscoe, all of whom included either chapters on Tutuola or substantial segments on him in their books on different aspects of African literatures.

Collins was genuinely and thoroughly persuaded that Tutuola was at the forefront of African literary development, perhaps even of African intellectual thought:

> Tutuola must have some sense that he is bringing the riches of his oral tradition to the world; his updating, Westernizing, adapting of [Yoruba] tales suggests that he knows what he is doing. By now, probably, most educated Nigerians have gotten over the shock of Tutuola's crudity and backwardness, and understand that since something has to be done with the oral tradition, his use of it is in many ways quite admirable. (Collins 1969, 54)

One comes away from that passage with the impression that Collins believed "something had to be done with the oral tradition," because, being crude and backward, it needed "updating" through Westernization. Only after such purification, it seems, would it be worthy of pre-

sentation to the world, and Tutuola was the self-appointed Westernizing
agent. Yet just before that statement, Collins had written:

> Anyone at all familiar with Yoruba folk tales will attest to their high value
> and their worth as a contribution to world culture. Their shrewd and real-
> istic appraisal of human nature, their sharp social realism, their astonish-
> ing fancy, their wonderful unrestrained humor and high spirits, their
> level-headed celebration of such human virtues as prudence, good man-
> agement, common sense, good-natured kindness, steady loyalty, and
> courage ought to be admired by readers the world over. (Collins 1969, 54)

Collins thought, however, that these qualities could be better enjoyed in
the form of Tutuola's "folk novels," and not in "learned journals and specialized books."

Collins's contention that Tutuola knew what he was doing was obviously meant to undercut those who imputed some naïveté or innocence
to the writer. In Collins's view, Tutuola was quite deliberate in his plan-
ning and execution. On this point, Collins would seem to be contra-
dicted by Gerald Moore, who found the most remarkable feature of
Tutuola's first three books to be "his apparently *intuitive* grasp of the
basic literary forms" (italics mine), since, as Moore revealed, all Tutuola's
heroes' and heroines' careers followed the heroic monomythical cycle,
Departure–Initiation–Return.[2] Moore also applauded "the naivety and
directness" of *Drinkard,* which he described as "a journey into the racial
imagination, into the subconscious," a journey in which the adventurer
was "descending, like Gilgamesh, Orpheus, Heracles or Aeneas before
him into the Underworld, there to confront death itself and attempt to
carry off some trophy to the living as a symbol of his mastery over the
two worlds" (Moore 1979, 189).

The instances in which his admirers sought to explain away Tutuola's
errors give the unfortunate impression that they thought him infallible.
For example, Moore was able to impose a design on the shift at the end
of *Drinkard* from the quest for the tapster and its outcome to the quarrel
between Heaven and Earth. "In this way," he argued, "the resolution of
the Drinkard's individual development as a hero is linked with the
restoration of harmony between man and his gods, for it is the
Drinkard's new understanding, won by the hard way of adventure,
which enables him to settle the cosmic quarrel through which man is
suffering" (Moore 1979, 191). Unity and consistency of theme and
action are thus rendered inconsequential. Yet Moore added that Tutuola
managed by means of the same episode to "impose an extraordinary

unity upon his apparently random collection of traditional material. The unity is that of intense vision, for Tutuola is a visionary writer and must be seen as such if he is to be understood or effectively judged" (191). Critics have erred in judging his work as novels, Moore continued, betraying "an astounding lack of literary education." Finally, he pointed out that "Tutuola's affinities are with Bunyan, Dante and Blake rather than with the Western novel" (191).

What sometimes appears like a compulsion to exonerate Tutuola at all costs leads the defenders themselves into some careless errors. Explaining Tutuola's terminology in his second book, Moore had the following to say:

> To the uninitiated European reader the word "ghost" is likely to be rather misleading, for the ghosts of this book are not the individual spirits of those who once lived on earth; they are the permanent inhabitants of the Other World, who have never lived as mortals, but who have intimate knowledge of that life and are in constant intercourse with it. (Moore 1979, 193)

Although conceding that none of the foregoing "is worked out with theological exactitude," Moore nevertheless excused the inexactitude by contending that "Tutuola assumes this kind of knowledge" (Moore 1979, 193). How a writer whose cosmography is so uniquely idiosyncratic can or should (be allowed to) assume a knowledge of it in the reader is a pertinent question. It is also highly unlikely that the failure to work it out with exactitude would be tolerated on the part of any other creator of a unique world. In any case, what Moore claims with regard to "ghosts" is incorrect. The hero's cousin and his wife were once mortals (as was Victoria Juliana of *Wild Hunter*). The hero also provides an address to which mortals wishing to inquire about their dead relatives now living in the towns of ghosts should send their inquiry.

Larson was also most inventive and accommodating in explicating *Drinkard*. Going to quite some lengths to make virtue out of an obvious shortcoming, he cited two episodes. In the first, the Drinkard refers to the complete gentleman as "only a Skull," anticipating the discovery that the creature is in fact a skull. In the second (a later incident in the same episode), the Drinkard gives the captive woman a curative leaf, which she eats and is cured, even though the Drinkard had earlier pointed out that her affliction derived from a cowrie shell tied around her neck, preventing her from talking and eating. Larson thus explains away the inconsistencies:

I do not attribute these two incidents to errors in Tutuola's thinking or inconsistencies in the text (the average reader probably would not even notice their existence). Rather, it seems to me that they typify the protean nature of Tutuola's work, reminiscent of Strindberg's *Dream Play;* for in Tutuola, too, characters merge into one another, change sex, the dead return to life, time is frequently ignored, slowed down, or speeded up, and only the dream or nightmare pervades. (Larson 1972, 99–100)

The first proffered rationalization, that the reader would probably not notice, seems a rather curious ground for arguing excellence. As for the others, the Drinkard nowhere claims clairvoyance for himself, although he does attribute that power to the woman later, after she has become his wife and joined him in his quest.

Larson could have added several other examples of narrative details that at first glance seem logical but on reflection prove otherwise, and whose illogicality inattentive readers would miss. One such is the information that the eagle meant to pluck out the eyes of the Drinkard and his wife while they are buried up to their necks in the field outside the Unreturnable-Heaven's Town does not carry out the assignment because the Drinkard had tamed such a bird in his town before he embarked on his adventures (*Drinkard,* 61). If one wonders how the eagle knew of the Drinkard's earlier experience with another eagle, apologists such as Larson would most probably answer that the Drinkard must have communicated the information to the bird somehow. Thus, where the narrator does not supply pertinent information, his champions obligingly fill in the gaps and chide those who notice them with punctiliousness.

Finally, responding to the insistence by Yoruba-reading critics that much of Tutuola was tepid, warmed-over Fagunwa, Bernth Lindfors reasoned that in helping himself so liberally to Fagunwa's earlier published materials, Tutuola was "working well within the conventions governing oral storytelling" and that "even when he follows Fagunwa most slavishly he does so from memory rather than from a printed text. . . . instead of actually plagiarizing he vividly recreates what he best remembers from Fagunwa's books, knitting the spirit if not the substance of the most suitable material into the loose fibers of his yarn" (Lindfors 1986, 635). Lindfors was being too generous, of course, for Tutuola was not engaged in oral storytelling. Robert Plant Armstrong similarly minimized the author's unattributed borrowing in the general defense of his art. Armstrong complained that "numerous of Tutuola's contemporaries, notably young writers," who should have been first in line to praise *The Palm-Wine Drinkard* had instead maligned it. He continued:

> Not only have they slighted the work on the basis of the normative considerations of grammar . . . but they have also suggested that *The Palm-Wine Drinkard* is derivative. By such an observation, I suppose the intent has been somehow to demean the stature of the work. The sophisticated reader, however, jealously defends those works he values, and he is not to be put off by such observations. He knows there is much to be encountered in world literature that is borrowed. The envy or embarrassment of his contemporaries cannot hide the fact that Tutuola's work is rich with imagination. (Armstrong, 152)

Moore was at least more knowledgeable about Tutuola and the literary context in which he wrote, and even when Moore pronounced debatable judgments on the author's literary merit, he did not blunder into the realm of the ludicrous. Collins was not so fortunate. That much is evident in his speculation on Tutuola's "adaptation" of *Drinkard* for the stage. Collins noted that the structure of the staged version was tighter than that of the fiction and wrote, "It would be interesting to know how Tutuola's prolific multiplicity came to be curbed. Did the translator and producer Ogunmola cut and revise, or did Tutuola himself, with the advice of Professor Collis of the University of Ibadan, 'neaten' the exuberant plenty?" (Collins 1969, 52). The facts of the production were, of course, that Kola Ogunmola, a consummate creative dramatist, was entrusted with extracting a Yoruba drama out of Tutuola's fiction, and that he worked closely with Geoffrey Axworthy, the director of the School of Drama, and Demas Nwoko, an artist and set designer. The tighter structure of the drama thus owed nothing to Tutuola. Adrian Roscoe would fall into a similar error by crediting Tutuola with the popularity of Ogunmola's play (or opera) among the Nigerian intelligentsia (see hereafter).

Collins's wish to attribute the play's success to his adopted charge is understandable, though, considering his highly inflated opinion of Tutuola's talent and standing. After all, did he not rate Tutuola over Achebe, Ekwensi, and Nzekwu? One wonders to what extent Achebe would agree with the following assessment by Collins:

> By now the realistic [African] novels have had a chance to show their mettle—and, in the opinion of this critic, they have not driven the fantastic romance off the field. Consider the work of Cyprian Ekwensi and

Chinua Achebe, the leading Nigerian novelists. Ekwensi's novels *(People of the City, Jagua Nana, Beautiful Feathers* and *Iska)* are lively and graphic evocations of the new Westernized life in Lagos, but they are uncertain in their positive values, as we shall notice when we discuss the attitudes of Nigerian writers towards the old African past. Achebe's novels *(Things Fall Apart, No Longer at Ease, Arrow of Gold* [*sic*] and *A Man of the People)* are so nostalgic about the lost old Ibo culture and so discouraged and fainthearted about the new Nigeria that we may perhaps be forgiven for remembering Tutuola's exuberant good cheer. And at any rate, after we have read Ekwensi, Achebe, Nzekwu and the other Nigerian novelists, Tutuola's strange tales still linger bright and splendid in the memory. (Collins 1969, 65)

The extent of Collins's commitment is evident in his declaration at the end of an essay in which he presented his "theory of creative mistakes and the mistaking style of Amos Tutuola." "Even if Tutuola's romances are absolutely without literary merit," he vowed, "we Tutuola freaks will die rather than admit [it]" (Collins 1969, 170).

At the 1994 National Endowment for the Humanities (NEH) summer seminar, during which I was invited to make a presentation on Tutuola, I cited the Drinkard's account of his and his wife's arrival at the Deads' Town as another example of Tutuola's (il)logic. As they approach it, the town keeps receding from them; they do not know that "anybody who had not died could not enter into that town by day time." Once his wife "knew the secret" (he does not say how), they make their approach at night, but then they stop at the outskirts and "did not enter into it until the dawn, because it was an unknown town to us" *(Drinkard,* 95). If the town will not permit their entry "by day time," I asked, why would it permit it at dawn? My generally negative valuation of Tutuola sat ill with the seminar director, whose lead a well-regarded professor of African philosophy and literatures attending the seminar followed. He saw no lack of logic in Tutuola's account, because, he said, the dawn was not part of "day time." He had read the book, of course, and was therefore aware of Tutuola's elaboration: "When it was 8 o'clock in the morning, then we entered the town and asked for my palm-wine tapster" (96). In the Yoruba world (which critics agree is reflected in Tutuola's works), it is daylight by eight o'clock in the morning, regardless of the season of the year, and that fact is underscored by the presence of people (or ghosts) about, from whom the Drinkard could inquire about his tapster.

Tutuola's account acknowledges the Yoruba belief that one should not enter a strange town at night because, as a proverb puts it, *"alé tí kò ti ojú eni lé, a kì í mo okùnkùnun èé rìn"* [one never knows how to negotiate the darkness of a night that did not fall in one's presence]. The other reason is a matter of etiquette. In the words of another proverb, *"àlejò tó fòru wòlú, igídá ni yó je"* [a visitor who enters a town at night will have only "Alas!" to eat]. Tutuola obviously had some difficulty in combining the town's stricture against a night entry, which he wanted, with compliance with Yoruba belief and practice, which he also wanted.

European Attacks

Unwilling to concede superior knowledge to Nigerian readers about Tutuola's circumstances and the most likely explications for his unusual narratives, Western critics preferred to dismiss their negative assessments as evidence of incompetence, impaired perception, or worse. We are already familiar with Moore's charge that those who did not read the author's work the same way he did displayed an astounding lack of literary education. Collins attributed such disagreements to blindness on the part of the dissenting Nigerians (Collins 1969, 67). He also speculated that it might be "a result of their shame about the observances of the traditional religions, especially human sacrifice, the political atrocities of the old order, including slaving, and most important, the traditional belief in spirits, magic, and witchcraft" (89). Given the generally Afrophobic tone of Collins's study, one is hardly surprised that he attributed the atrocities of the slave trade to Africans and not to Europeans. So little did he think of his Nigerian (especially Yoruba) targets that he cavalierly dismissed one of their most serious gripes—the charge that the writer plagiarized Fagunwa and his admirers did not seem to care. "Without knowing Yoruba," Collins declared airily, "we cannot tell whether Fagunwa was more successful than Tutuola in adapting folktales for extended romances, though we may distrust the educated Yoruba critics' judgment somewhat because of their blindness to Tutuola's merit" (67). A more cautious critic would probably have been more concerned with defending his credentials to engage in the debate on the subject despite his handicap with regard to Yoruba, but not Collins.

Adrian Roscoe, for his part, was so incensed by the lack of esteem for Tutuola at home that he concluded that all of Africa, black Africa one presumes, must be psychologically afflicted:

> There are probably psychological reasons, too, for Tutuola's isolation and lack of followers and there is enough evidence that Africa's psychological

problems are acute. It might not go wide of the mark to suggest that he is ignored by other Africans because he has committed the grave sin of ungrammatically describing their inner lives for readers in the western world, a western world where respect for a clinically clean, ghost-free, inner life holds sway. He has opened a window onto a part of the African soul which for the moment most of his westernized compatriots prefer to keep hidden. . . . How else can we explain the attitude of a country which gives its first international writer the exalted post of a storekeeper at a radio station? How else can we interpret recent reports that Tutuola in translation, that is in the vernaculars, has become very popular? Enjoy him in the protective secrecy of the vernacular, but heavens forbid that he should appear in an international language![3]

Roscoe was himself writing with some handicap, for he did not have the correct information on which to base his accusations. There was, for example, no such thing as Tutuola in translation; no one had bothered to translate him into Yoruba or any other Nigerian language. What was popular, to repeat, was the Ogunmola-Nwoko collaborative production of the Yoruba adaptation of *Drinkard*.

Some of the European (and American) rationalizations of Tutuola's English are worth citing at this point. The first is by Dathorne, who argued that those who found Tutuola's English "wrong" failed to consider two factors:

One is that they forget that the story is written in the first person and is about a palmwine drinker. Were he to speak standard English this would be ludicrous to anyone acquainted with the realities of West African speech. Secondly, Tutuola's English is a sensible compromise, between raw pidgin (which would be unintelligible to European readers) and standard English. (Dathorne, 72)

Typically, Dathorne considered it incumbent on an African writer to ensure that his work is intelligible to European readers. More objectionable, though, is his own failure to consider that although *Drinkard* was written in English, we are to assume that the characters involved are in fact speaking in their native language. We have no reason to believe otherwise. That being the case, it matters nothing whether the speaker is a palm-wine Drinkard or a teetotaler. And even if one were to admit that excessive imbibing could result in a slur in the speech of a person under the influence, one still must bear in mind that the Drinkard, for the duration of the story, was without the services of his tapster, the very object of the search, and that he was not in a permanent state of intoxi-cation.

Various admirers have taken the very incorrectness of Tutuola's Eng-lish as one of the many qualities that argue for his greatness. Proceeding from the premise that a language gains in vitality to the extent that enterprising users force it to new possibilities of expression, they have hailed his deviations as a service to English. Armstrong quoted Achebe as follows to support that stance: "The English language will be able to carry the weight of my African experience. But it will have to be a new English, still in full communion with its ancestral home but altered to suit its new African surroundings." Armstrong went on to say:

> This, clearly, shows Tutuola's attitude toward and use of the English language. Yet his diction, which is that of the proletariat rather than that of the university graduate, has undoubtedly caused some among his con-temporaries to deny him the great esteem he deserves as a major literary artist. Such persons have perhaps been "embarrassed" by his "illiteracies." (Armstrong, 150)

I believe that what Achebe intended by the alteration of the English lan-guage to suit African surroundings can best be illustrated by his own use of the language. I cannot be entirely sure of what he meant by saying that the English still had to be "in full communion with its ancestral home," but here is the same man speaking: "I submit that those who can do the work of extending the frontiers of English so as to accommo-date African thought patterns must do it through their mastery of Eng-lish and not out of innocence."[4] I do not believe that Achebe was wor-ried by competition from Tutuola, or angry that Tutuola was violating the sanctity of the adopted language of the "university graduate." Nor do I think it fair that any statement of Achebe's should be used to pro-mote "illiteracies." The fact is that most reasonable people have come to regard experimentation as something that is consciously done by intel-lectual explorers who are well equipped for the task.

Of course, Professor Armstrong has suggested that Tutuola's lan-guage is in fact a "popular" language, and he made the following com-parison:

> Chaucer wrote in English rather than in the French of the Court; Dante, in Italian rather than in Latin; and Tutuola, in a marked English dialect rather than in Yoruba or in the standard "literary" English his contempo-raries learned in their colleges and universities. (Armstrong, 150)

But were the comparison to the use of English by Chaucer and Italian by Dante to be taken to its logical conclusion, we would have Tutuola writing in Yoruba, not in Yoruba-flavored English, not even in "pidgin English."

Larson, for his part, placed Tutuola at the vanguard of West African linguistic experimentation. Said he,

> In Tutuola, West African "experimentation" in prose fiction reaches its zenith, for the oral tradition which he uses is more specifically a private mythology where daring tricks and innovations in time, space, and description—no doubt at times unintentionally—attain a level which makes them almost pure examples of surrealism. (Larson, 95)

Tutuola perhaps has as much capacity as anybody for experimentation as far as time, space, and description are concerned. He could well be a master even with regard to inventiveness in situations, but for the unfortunate fact that he allowed himself to borrow too freely from previous works. It is difficult, though, to accept the theory of art implied in Larson's statement. Without in any way dismissing the possibility of intuition in art, I believe that acquired skill, conscious study, and purposiveness are more pertinent. The issues of serendipity and happenstance may at times be very happy, but in such cases, we have to give our thanks to chance rather than to the midwives attendant on it.

Collins's tack was to pooh-pooh the notion that a creative writer should be expected to be a competent user of the language in which he or she chooses to write. He argued his thesis in "A Theory of Creative Mistakes and the Mistaking Style of Amos Tutuola," in which he attributed one of the chief obstacles to "a proper appreciation of Tutuola's great style" to "the lingering influence of the doctrine of correctness in language study." He explained the "simplistic doctrine" as requiring every spoken or written linguistic form to be "either correct, and permitted, or incorrect, and proscribed with passionate exhortation." The doctrine, according to him, "takes no account of varying situations, the varying personalities of persons using the language, the varying kinds of subject matter; all commands and proscriptions are absolute; contingencies count for nothing."[5] He further contended that the doctrine was useless in literary criticism: "A literary work may be utterly perfect in its correctness and yet be worthless as literature; and it can be as full of 'errors' as Shakespeare's plays and have impressive value as literature" (Collins 1974, 156).

Collins went on to paraphrase Mercedes McKay's opinion that West Africans' resentment of Tutuola was based on the fact that they had labored on, and won prizes for, their correct English and therefore regarded his bad English as shocking. Then he commented:

> Educated West Africans were hypersensitive about westerners' opinions on their ability to speak and write unexceptionable standard English. They must have felt that they needed to prove that they had all the language skill required to qualify as civilized persons, "incorrect" being accounted "uncivilized." The genuine flourishing of West African literature in English since the fifties, indeed the work of Achebe and Soyinka by themselves, should have quieted this particular jangled nerve. (Collins 1974, 157)

It is of interest to add that Collins preceded his explication of his interesting theory with the revelation that he and fellow Tutuola freaks "write passages of Tutuolese in their letters to each other" (Collins 1974, 155). It is also of interest that for all his belief in incorrectness, he wrote his article in perfectly correct English. One might justifiably conclude that the adoption of Tutuolese by Collins and his fellow Tutuola freaks amounts to nothing short of literary slumming, a playful indulgence in the "subnormal" or "abnormal" by dilettantes who are secure in the place and jobs their correct English has won them and can afford to patronize and mimic the exotic on the sly. Their Tutuolese, typically and revealingly, is for secret use only, when only cult members are present, listening or reading. So much for their commitment to incorrectness.

What Collins alleged about absolute insistence on correctness in writing, especially creative writing, is incorrect, of course, for teachers of the subject teach their students that dialogue must be true to life, and must match the occasion, the social and academic levels of the speaker, and the subject matter. And with regard to the reference to Shakespeare, one would ask whether Collins was placing Tutuola's English usage alongside Shakespeare's. Was he contending that the reasons for the "errors" in Shakespeare's plays are the same for the errors in Tutuola's novels? And why did he place "errors" in Shakespeare in quotes?

In his adoption of McKay's speculation on the reasons for Tutuola's unpopularity among educated West Africans, Collins failed to see the logic of his own comments. If Achebe and Soyinka had by themselves demonstrated the ability of West Africans to write correct English, might that fact not suggest that West Africans had satisfied themselves that Achebe's and Soyinka's success would offset whatever testimony to their competence Tutuola might have given the world earlier? Would they not, therefore, have ceased worrying about being tainted by Tutuola's English, if they ever did worry?

Whatever the case, Collins's theory of creative mistakes proposed nothing new. According to it, if a large number of users of English make the same sort of mistake, then it should no longer be considered a mistake but a new variety of English; Tutuola's English should be considered the "vulgate English of Southwestern Nigeria"; his theory would "also take notice of the fact that novelty and eccentricity of language, as the poetry critics long ago discovered, aroused the readers' interest, and tend to make for slower, more deliberate, more alert reading" (Collins 1974, 158).

Linguists have long acknowledged the existence of variants of languages and therefore write about "Englishes" and not simply "English." Collins is characteristically wrong in his understanding of evidence and in his deductions from it. Tutuola's language cannot be "the vulgate English of Southwestern Nigeria" for the simple reason that it is not typical of the English spoken by competent users of the language in that part of the world. If incompetent and uneducated usage (by however large a number of users) were to enjoy the legitimacy Collins proposed, then courses in composition (that teach correct standard usage) would have to be eliminated from American schools and colleges. As for his invocation of the concept of poetic license, the response would be the same as to his invocation of Shakespeare: deliberate artistic use of "errors" for effect, and taking advantage of poetic license, are quite different from stylistic blunders that result from ignorance. With regard to language use at least, Raoul Granqvist was quite mistaken in his "realization that Tutuola was a literary craftsman who roamed within the framework of the tale with an exuberance and licence that no known story teller had done before."[6]

Given that Tutuola expressed his embarrassment about his incorrect language to Larrabee, that he obviously thought he was using correct English, and that he cared enough about acquiring correctness in the language that he took measures for that purpose, one must judge as strange the phenomenon by which Collins and company were fighting on Tutuola's behalf for a privilege he wanted no part of. He did not think his language was as forceful as his admirers thought, or he wanted no part of the type of forcefulness his admirers saw in his work. He hankered for the dull "schoolmarmish" language writers such as Achebe used. Tutuola did not revel in the role of the unspoiled primitive (linguistically speaking), of the literary noble savage. To that extent, Tutuola was in tune with his Yoruba heritage.

Martin Tucker was on to something crucial when he observed that "Tutuola has had little influence on Nigerian writers principally because he has relied on a personal mythology and because many Nigerians feel he has been playing the court jester to the European literary kingmakers."[7] Nigerian readers, especially Yoruba readers, would have been more put off, though, by their perception of him as a "court jester" than by his use of private mythology. They do not believe that self-respecting people, especially adults, should demean themselves for any sort of gain. (The crisis that led to Toundi's leaving home in Ferdinand Oyono's *Houseboy* arose because his father regarded his chasing lumps of sugar thrown at children by a Catholic priest as a disgrace for himself and for his family. In this case, the Ewondo and Yoruba sentiments coincide.) In the Yoruba world, a person who, for any sort of consideration, is willing to "dance the dance of wretched ridicule for others to see" (*jó jó ìyà ká wò ó*) would be considered beneath contempt. Knowing that, Tutuola would not have deliberately opted for incorrectness, which Simon Raven dismissed as deliberate childishness, another unstomachable insult for any self-respecting Yoruba person.[8]

Finally, as recently as 1987, Mark Axelrod was favorably comparing Tutuola's mastery of fictional English to that of Daniel Kunene. Reviewing Kunene's collection of short stories *From the Pit of Hell to the Spring of Life,* Axelrod faulted the author for not distinguishing between the speech styles of his characters: "No attempt is made to alter the prose," he observed, "as Amos Tutuola does, for example, to make it sound less Anglicized and more African."[9]

Time has exploded the claims of Tutuola's supposedly wide appeal and exposed the untenableness of assessments of him as a writer superior to Ekwensi or Achebe. If one were to measure appeal in terms of recognition, then available evidence must lead us to the conclusion that Tutuola has very little at home. When the Ibadan University Press published *Folktales,* his collection of short stories, they expressed their gratitude to Robert Wren in an acknowledgment for "putting us in contact with Amos Tutuola, and for some editorial work" on the manuscript, and to the Ford Foundation for subsidizing the publication (*Folktales,* v). Robert Wren was an American scholar who specialized in Nigerian literatures and made periodic visits to Nigeria to do research. He interested the press in Tutuola's collection while he was resident on the campus of the university during one of those visits. Tutuola was himself resident in Ibadan at the time, and it would seem a little curious that it took a visiting American professor to interest the press in him, or put them in contact with him. One cannot imagine Ekwensi or Achebe requiring such intervention.

Moore's Revision

In the early going, dissenting views among non-Nigerians were hard to come by, one of the few belonging, predictably, to V. S. Naipaul, who asked in seeming disbelief, "in what other age could bad grammar have been a literary asset?" (Lindfors 1975, 87). Moore is something of an exception among Tutuola's early admirers, for he proved able and willing to reverse himself when he perceived that the object of his admiration no longer deserved it. His positive assessment of Tutuola's first two books included his granting the author the intention to offer his reader "an extended vision of Initiation and Purgatory," because Moore saw in the last sentence of *My Life*, "This is what hatred did," a connection with the book's opening pages. But he conceded that in *Simbi*, as in *My Life*, "Tutuola seems to be only fitfully aware of his overall theme and he does not succeed in relating Simbi's adventures to it in any significant way" (Moore 1962, 51). In his view, Tutuola's talent seemed to decline with each publication: Moore was almost unreserved in his praise for *Drinkard*; he found a certain degree of thematic disengagement in *My Life*, a disengagement that worsened in *Simbi*; but he also saw in both *Simbi* and the earlier *My Life* "a decline of power compared with the *Drinkard*" (54), adding that "a much more definite decline is evident in *The Brave African Huntress*," the last of Tutuola's publications at the time. "The magic has all leaked away," he observed. "The catalogue of creatures with their European names straight out of Grimm's Fairy Tales—'gnomes,' 'goblins' and so forth—is a terrible letdown. Even the word 'jungle' reads like a concession to European taste, for it is seldom used by West Africans, who always speak of 'the bush,' as Tutuola did in his first books" (55).

Africans' Transformation and Retreat: Liyong, Anozie, Leslie, Irele, and Chinweizu

The trend that critical reactions to Tutuola's career have followed also has its ironies. The initially clamorous approbation abroad had by the

1970s become overtaken by a palpable cooling of enthusiasm, but as though to make up for that reversal, Nigerian scholars, in the face (and perhaps because) of attacks by foreign critics on their intelligence, rationality, and motives, increasingly warmed toward Tutuola. As the already cited example of Achebe illustrates, Nigerian scholars discovered hidden, hitherto unnoticed merit in Tutuola and succeeded—albeit often with some mental gymnastics—in aligning themselves with their foreign counterparts. For instance, (Ogundipe) Leslie, in addition to praising Tutuola's accurate representation of the Yoruba world, commended him for forcing English into the habits of the Yoruba language to express himself. "In using the habits of a language familiar to him," she wrote, "Tutuola overcomes the problem of linguistic alienation which plagues other Nigerian writers, some of whom have at first to wrestle with the English language, before they can begin to try to say what they mean. . . . Unwittingly (for Tutuola is not like James Joyce, a conscious inventor) he has created a language which enables him to express himself" (Lindfors 1975, 153). Leslie did not, however, acknowledge or address the question her argument immediately raises, perhaps because she was not aware of any possible question. But one has to ask, was Tutuola unable to express himself in Yoruba? If he was, why did he need to "unwittingly" create another language? One might also ask if the effort involved in forcing English into unfamiliar habits did not perhaps equate to other Nigerian writers' wrestling with English. Furthermore, how could one sustain an argument that a writer who abandons the language in which he has native fluency in favor of an alien tongue he must wield with an effort, and imperfectly, has thus avoided linguistic alienation?

Finally, Leslie had an explanation for the stance of Nigerian critics on Tutuola's version of English. "Middle-class Nigerians," she wrote, "are ashamed of his language since oddly enough, among both the British and the Nigerians, inability to use the English language indicates some mental deficiency" (Lindfors 1975, 150). Unfortunately she did not think it necessary to explain why Nigerians, who almost invariably have highly respected elders in their families who do not speak or understand English, would consider the inability to use English or use it properly as indicative of mental deficiency, or, if indeed they so considered it, why Tutuola's affliction should be a matter for shame on the part of other Nigerians, middle-class or not.

Endorsement for Tutuola also came from scholars such as Irele, and the three collaborators on *Toward the Decolonization of African Literature*,

Chinweizu, Onwuchekwa Jemie, and Ihechukwu Madubuike. In a study of the works of three Yoruba writers (Fagunwa, Soyinka, and Tutuola), Irele first detailed the great accomplishments of Fagunwa, who is universally accepted as the father of Yoruba fiction and as a consummate artist. When Irele came to the subject of Tutuola, he acknowledged his indebtedness to Fagunwa but, as I have already mentioned, went on to commend him for "the extension he has given to the traditional fantasy in Yoruba folk tale, and to the mythical novel in Yoruba created by Fagunwa" (Irele 1971, 17).

Chinweizu and his coauthors of *Toward the Decolonization of African Literature* devoted considerable space to virtually unreserved praise for Tutuola and dismissal of criticisms of him by other critics, even others such as Larson who are themselves diehard fans of the writer. Their major point was that the world of Tutuola's works, its "cosmography," is authentically Yoruba, and the works should therefore not be excluded from established categories of literature. Because these works embrace the worlds of the living, the dead, and the unborn, and admit of traffic among them, they are not therefore to be "downgraded and dismissed as ghost novels, quest romances, fantasies and the like, but must be accepted as legitimate African novels—as extended written fictional prose narratives whose subject is African man in African society, rendered in accordance with the social realities and cosmography of the African bourgeoisie" (Chinweizu and Madubuike, 22). They cite Tutuola's first two books as "examples in which aspects of our modern literature have been successfully grafted onto traditional trunks" (258).

With regard to Tutuola's English, they first applaud its simplicity in comparison to the sometimes impenetrable style of Soyinka's poetry. Soyinka, they contend, is in this matter "dancing after the march of British opinion." Anyone who is able to "read . . . the works of Amos Tutuola . . . should be able to read whatever our other poets write in English." Any writer who adopts simple English will be appreciated by "most literate Africans," who will give him all the audience he needs. "In addition, foreigners will also appreciate him (as they appreciate Tutuola and Okot p'Bitek), and rather than have less of each audience he will have more" (Chinweizu and Madubuike, 246).

What is significant in those passages is not the preference for Tutuola's style over Soyinka's but the insistence on coupling Tutuola with, and comparing him to, artists such as p'Bitek, who deliberately experimented with English by forcing it into the syntax of African languages, in his case Acholi. One is not surprised that the trio chose to construe Tutuola's idiosyncratic English as a regional variant of the language, thus enabling themselves, as in the following passage, to argue for its right to exist alongside other Englishes:

> We would like to point out that the King's English, or the English of schoolmen, is not the only kind of English. Writing in an English different from standard English should not be construed as "letting Africa down." Africans have no business speaking the King's English indistinguishably from an English don; and they have no business trying to prove to Europeans that Africans can speak or write European languages indistinguishably from Europeans. (Chinweizu and Madubuike, 264)

Much like their European precursors, the African scholars who have in a sense discovered Tutuola have sought to explain disagreements with their own assessment of the writer's excellence as resulting from some handicap on the part of the holdouts, usually attributed to inattentive or faulty reading habits or, indeed, sheer negligence. Achebe's conclusion that those who disagree with him on the moral purpose in *Drinkard* must not have read it, or must have read it inattentively, is a case in point. When they do concede that the dissenting critics perhaps read Tutuola after all, they explain their failure to see the light by postulating the theory that one requires special powers, special training, and special facilities to "properly" understand, enjoy, and appreciate him; the equipage that would suffice for the understanding, enjoyment, and appreciation of any other writer would simply not do. Moreover, although they maintain that Tutuola is preeminently Yoruba, living right at the heart of the Yoruba experience that he documents, they contend further that even Yoruba readers cannot apprehend him; only Europeans such as the Moores, the Roscoes, and the Collinses—and among Nigerians, the Achebes, and such specially equipped Yoruba readers such as Omolara Leslie and Abiola Irele—can.

In *The African Experience,* Irele wrote, "If we are to ask an African audience, for instance, to recognize the work of Tutuola, we must then be armed with an insight into his works which enables us to relate it to its African context and therefore to an African audience" (Irele 1981, 39). He continued:

> Because our writers are using mainly foreign languages, our own people do not catch their African accent which is unmistakably there. This problem is well dramatized by the curious position of Fagunwa and Tutuola: the one recognized by his own people as a great writer but unknown

abroad; the other praised abroad—largely for the wrong reasons. The
lesson here, of course, is that Tutuola will in the long run be the loser in
this situation and I would consider this to be a tragedy. (Irele 1981, 40)

He further stressed that "Tutuola possesses a power of the imagination
which breaks through the limitations of his language and which, *properly
considered,* compels our adhesion to his vision and our recognition of him
as an original artist" (Irele 1981, 184; italics mine).

On the issue of language, however, Irele distanced himself from
Tutuola's other African admirers. Although conceding that the violence
Tutuola does to English "gives to his novels the appeal of novelty of language in addition to that of theme," he concluded that it remains "an
exceptional phenomenon" (Irele 1981, 163). He took issue with Europeans who compared Tutuola favorably to his more educated compatriots who use "pretentious" English, "as if there was necessarily merit in
doing violence to English, and a corresponding demerit in using that
language with an acceptable measure of competence!" (182). He further
wrote:

> On the specific point of language, the limitations of Tutuola are limita-
> tions and constitute a real barrier, sometimes even a formidable one, both
> for him as an artist, and for his readers. Tutuola obviously does not dom-
> inate his linguistic medium and there is no pretending that this is an
> advantage. The truth is that we arrive at an appreciation of Tutuola's
> genuine merit, *in spite of* his imperfect handling of English, not because of
> it. (Irele 1981, 183; italics in original)

Because Yoruba lay "nearer the heart of his inspiration and of his sensibility than English," Irele thought that Tutuola would perhaps have
been better off writing in "the language that came most easily to him
and most naturally, as it were, to his material" (Irele 1981, 183).
Whereas foreign readers might be fascinated by "the very pressure of
the Yoruba language upon the *peculiar* idiom Tutuola wrung out of the
English language" (italics mine), it does not produce a sufficiently creative tension, only imbalance. The explanation for the circuitousness of
the foregoing observation soon becomes evident: it is that Irele for some
reason felt a necessity to hedge somewhat. It came in tandem with a
reassertion of the necessity of special powers to appreciate Tutuola. In
his words, "It needs to be said and recognized that the shift from
Fagunwa in Yoruba to Tutuola in English cannot but represent, *at least
at the first flush,* a disappointing experience for the Yoruba-speaking

reader familiar with the work of Fagunwa, so that it needs closer attention to arrive at a response to the writings of Tutuola adequate to his *peculiar* genius" (183; italics mine).

An Imputation of Jealousy

Another suggestion Tutuola's admirers offer to explain why certain African intellectuals withhold their applause from Tutuola is that they are acting out of jealousy, and a reluctance to share their space as members of the literary elite with someone who had not gone through a university. Taban Lo Liyong is a good example, and his tone in the following passage is eloquent testimony to his regard for such recalcitrant academics:

> To our surprise, one day, into the hall of the fame walks a primary school boy, a naughty boy, a boy who knows no grammar, almost a total villager, and he claims a seat among immortals. What? We shout. Who are you? When were you in Achimota? Perhaps you were at Ibadan with me? Have you been-to? In a land where school knowledge is extremely important, our drop-out is meticulously analyzed, weighed, and found insolvent. Our analysts pull their *agbada* up and set to jollof-rice and gari with chicken legs in their university halls and blame the whole thing on Dylan Thomas, Gerald Moore, and the whole White world.[10]

In Lo Liong's essay, in which he flailed at several Nigerian and African nonadmirers of Tutuola—Lewis Nkosi, Christina (Ama Ata) Aidoo, and the Yoruba Wale Olumide among them—he excused Tutuola's ungrammatical English by asserting that "James Joyce is more ungrammatical" (Lo Liyong 1969, 157). "Today when the machine is taking up more and more of man's former dominion, isn't it refreshing," he asked, "to find a man who is man enough to stand up against the machines? For what is language but a machine, and learning grammar makes us more and more slavish to it?" (161). He went on to declare flatly that Tutuola

> is a genius and the Father of Modern African Literature: West Africans woke up to write nervously because he was already in the field, and he is still ahead, far ahead; . . . One day, and I wish it comes sooner, the Swedish Academy might begin to think seriously about awarding the Nobel Prize for literature to first-rate writers, and not to second-rate Peace fighters as they have done frequently. When that day comes, they should seriously consider Tutuola for the Nobel Prize for Literature. He

merits it more than half-a-dozen winners I know. Why should we continue to honour Homer dead and deny the laurel to a Homer alive? (Lo
Liyong 1969, 168)

As did Taban Lo Liyong, Sunday Anozie saw jealousy as the motivation for African critics who declared themselves unimpressed by
Tutuola. They did not hesitate to underestimate Tutuola and were not
anxious to admit him into their circle, Anozie charged, because of their
"literary and intellectual snobbishness." He also found fault with
Tutuola's European admirers, though. "In Europe especially," Anozie
wrote, "one ascertains in the enthusiasm of English-speaking readers a
certain current of paternalistic conservatism which seeks to magnify
everything bizarre and exotic, whether in African art or African literature" (Lindfors 1975, 238). And in a passage that betrays a certain
degree of insensitivity to terminological nuances, Anozie first compared
Tutuola to Proust and Kafka and then concluded:

> Belonging to the Yoruba tribe of Western Nigeria, a tribe renowned for
> the richness of its folklore, Tutuola naturally finds in folklore a fertile
> source for his creative demands. However, the imagination which gets
> hold of this traditional world is not an inventive or an original imagina-
> tion but one which seeks to give the illusion of coherence to disconnected
> facts. This is all the more true because the world of folklore and—
> Tutuola's world also—is a disturbed world, *prelogical* and sometimes cre-
> puscular, in which, moreover, events take place by themselves without
> any logical, intellectual connection. Nevertheless, in traditional African
> society, these are events which, in the *primitive* context of the collective
> consciousness, provide an ethical perspective and constitute an efficacious
> means of education. (Lindfors 1975, 239–40; italics mine)

Readers of the foregoing opinions on Tutuola expressed by African
scholars will not be mistaken if they recognize in them echoes of views
earlier expressed by European critics.

Lacuna about Fagunwa

Every knowledgeable reader of Tutuola's work has remarked that D. O.
Fagunwa is an inescapable presence in it; he is also a permanent fixture
in its criticism. Although Fagunwa's *Ogboju Ode* came out in 1950, Wole
Soyinka's translation *(Daemons)* was not published until 1968; and for
another 20 years, there would be no other work by that renowned

Yoruba author available to non-Yoruba readers. Consequently Tutuola's early champions adopted their positions without the ability to assess one of the major criticisms of his works: that they were poor and garbled reproductions of concepts and episodes with which Fagunwa had testified to Yoruba inventiveness and dramatized Yoruba values. Having committed themselves in print, sometimes incautiously and sometimes cavalierly, before gaining access to the materials on which their challengers based many of their objections, Tutuola's apologists have subsequently found retreat awkward or impossible, even in the face of new and better information. Nigerians who were familiar with Fagunwa, or at least knew about him, did not always take advantage of their knowledge. Some insisted on Tutuola's debts to Fagunwa but in a manner that sanitized what others saw as plagiarism, a practice consistent with that of Tutuola's European backers. Others, while acknowledging the debt, nevertheless contrived to downplay Fagunwa's stature in favor of Tutuola, even while faulting Europeans for doing the same thing.

Beier's early writing on Fagunwa and Tutuola noted the connection between the two. For example, writing on Fagunwa, Beier quoted the following description of death: "His eyes are as big as a food bowl, round like moons and red like fire; and they are rolling about like ripe fruit dangling in the wind. The teeth in his mouth look like lion's fangs, and they are bright red, for it is not yam he likes, nor bananas nor *okra,* nor bitter leaf; he likes nothing but human flesh" (Beier 1979, 201). He then followed with the observation, "It is in passages like these that Fagunwa is closest to Tutuola. *Drinkard* and *My Life* abound with descriptions like this and they may well have been directly influenced by Fagunwa" (201). Again, after an extended quotation describing Olowo-Aiye's fight with Eshu Kekere Ode (in Soyinka's translation), Beier wrote, "Here again Fagunwa is not unlike Tutuola" (201). Because Fagunwa preceded Tutuola, and it was he who influenced Tutuola and not vice versa, Beier should normally have said Tutuola was like Fagunwa.

Irele has pointedly disapproved of the tendency in critical circles to play Tutuola up at Fagunwa's expense. He objected, for example, to Beier's curious phraseology, which, Irele said, gave one the impression that Beier wished to acknowledge Fagunwa's achievement, but in such a manner as would protect Tutuola's foreign reputation. Worse than Beier's ploy, Irele thought, was the behavior of Fagunwa's own publishers, "who seem to have appreciated his value as a source of profitable business rather than as a writer in his own right." The blurb on Soyinka's translation of *Ogboju Ode,* Irele noted, was designed to place the translator in the limelight and relegate the author to the background. He was convinced that Nelson, the publishers, were more interested in the revenue they could generate from having Soyinka on their list than in exposing Fagunwa to a wider world of readers, a cynical preference that led them to suppress Fagunwa's name in advertisements of Soyinka's translation (Irele 1981, 176). Irele acknowledged Fagunwa's place at the head of creative writing in Yoruba language and his pervasive influence on all Yoruba writing, declaring that much of the praise and acclaim critics had lavished on Tutuola more properly belonged to Fagunwa, "who provided not only the original inspiration but indeed a good measure of the material for Tutuola's novels" (184).

In a statement that testified to the determining role European authorities played (and still play) in the formation of African opinions even on African matters, Irele observed that if Ulli Beier (one of Tutuola's original promoters) and other European critics had acknowledged Tutuola's dependence on Fagunwa earlier, much would have been gained. "The echoes of Fagunwa in Tutuola's works are numerous enough to indicate that the latter was consciously creating from a model provided by the former," Irele wrote, adding that in "some cases, these echoes have the sound of straightforward transcriptions, not to say plagiarisms" (Irele 1981, 184). But he went on to argue:

> There is no disparagement of Tutuola's achievement in pointing out the immediate derivation of his work from that of Fagunwa. It would indeed have been to Tutuola's advantage if this connection had been disclosed earlier, and when subsequently noticed, more overtly acknowledged. This omission in Beier's consideration of the two writers appears to me particularly regrettable. (Irele 1981, 184)

It is not correct, however, to say that Beier did not mention the connection between the two writers, as Irele's own citation from Beier's essay demonstrates. What one can say is that he minimized it. Unfortunately Nigerians, especially Yoruba, who had all the facts to make a more forceful case, failed to do so, and their later capitulation to European critics' views compounded the problem. If Beier was at fault, then these Nigerians should also share the blame, perhaps even be assigned the major part of it.

Ayo Bamgbose's *The Novels of D. O. Fagunwa,* published in 1974, did mention Tutuola's dependence on Fagunwa, but without making too much of it. Bamgbose identified Tutuola as the most successful of the

Yoruba writers "in the Fagunwa tradition." Although Tutuola wrote in English, Bamgbose said, the English was essentially a literal translation of Yoruba to English, for which reason Tutuola could still be regarded as a direct descendant of Fagunwa. Bamgbose added, "Tutuola's debt to Fagunwa is considerable. Like the other writers in the tradition, he has borrowed the framework of Fagunwa's novels, particularly in *The Brave African Huntress* and *Feather Woman of the Jungle.*"[11]

After all his corrective observations, Irele himself went on to praise the "special vigor of Tutuola's imagination, its considerable sharpness, as it is inscribed within the framework in which, after Fagunwa, he too operates," and to contend that although the "echoes" of Fagunwa have the sound of straightforward transcriptions, not to say plagiarisms, Tutuola's work achieved "an independent status that it owes essentially to the force of his individual genius" (Irele 1981, 184). Irele also cited "the development that he has given to the form he took over from the earlier writer [which] has the character of a brilliant confirmation" (184). Discounting the echoes that he said approximated plagiarism, Irele argued that imitation was normal in creative writing, and that the only problem was that the critics he faulted for not revealing Tutuola's use of Fagunwa had not acknowledged the "echoes," for it would in fact have been to Tutuola's advantage if critics had openly conceded them. One is left to wonder why they felt it necessary to hide them.

In a discussion in the early 1980s, the Brazilian dancer and student of dance Inaysira dos Santos expressed to me her anger at European scholars who insisted on referring to (and implicitly disparaging) art forms, including the dance, from non-European (and especially African) cultures as "primitive." By the term, she asserted, they implied that a form was naive, wild, undisciplined, and requiring little study or deliberate artistry. She insisted that these so-called "primitive" forms are often every bit as deliberate, disciplined, and artistic as the best-regarded European examples. But although the European critics distinguished between European "art" and spontaneous, undisciplined expressions that coexist alongside "art," they lumped corresponding undisciplined expressions in non-European cultures together with what those in the cultures would regard as art, sometimes even substituting the former for the latter. European undisciplined forms coexisted free, without being confused with bona fide art (allowing for the problems of terminological indeterminacy and varying conceptions about the relationship between the beautiful and the utilitarian, of course). The appeal of Tutuola's wildness, his primitivism, for Europeans who regard those qualities as the essence of African art is precisely the sort of thing that so angered dos Santos.

Am I in the foregoing suggesting that there is absolutely no merit in Tutuola's work? Absolutely not. No matter how much of his material he takes from Fagunwa, Tutuola still works it all into an extended narrative. In addition, he has done a considerable amount of invention himself, like the Supreme Second and the Minds in *Herbalist*. There also was some reason for the School of Drama at the University (College) of Ibadan to select his *Drinkard* for translation and dramatization. It was certainly not because the idea of a person journeying to heaven to satisfy a need that had to do with living, or that originated with living, was innovative, for it was already familiar in the well-known story of Àwòdórun. What was appealing was the audaciousness of the reason, of the idea of risking all the peril involved in going to heaven simply to satisfy a habit that most people regard as unworthy of a responsible man.

The Nigerian sculptor Bruce Onobrakpeya, when charged by the coordinating body of Africa 95, the 1995 London Festival of African Arts, to arrange a Nigerian drama entry, selected Bode Sowande's Odu Themes Meridian to perform an adaptation of Tutuola's *My Life*. Onobrakpeya's regard for the book was such that he had contemplated making carvings based on Tutuola's images in the book. Although the choice was challenged by the National Association of Nigerian Theatre Arts Practitioners (NANTAP), who did not think the work represented Nigeria's image well enough, and the minister of information and culture, who thought a work that accounted for the country's experience with colonialism and imperialism (such as Ola Rotimi's *Ovoramwen Nogbaisi*) would have been more appropriate, Onobrakpeya and others championed *My Life,* and Sowande's adaptation won the right to represent Nigeria at the festival.[12] Odu Themes has retained the work in its repertory and has performed it on other occasions.

Nor do I see (as some others apparently do) the use of materials from Yoruba folktales or European folktales as necessarily bad. I might, of course, object that Tutuola's versions sometimes fail to do justice to the Yoruba imagination. On the other hand, I do not believe that closeness to Yoruba culture is in itself necessarily any reason to applaud a fictional work as great or excellent.

Chapter Six

Aspects of Tutuola's Art

Unarticulated Episodes and Internal Inconsistencies

Chinweizu and his fellow *bólèkájà* critics chose Tutuola as their cause célèbre in their challenge to Western critics for insisting on the conventions of the Western novel as the models that would apply universally. To the *bólèkájà* critics, the issue was one of autonomy, "the autonomy of African literature" (Chinweizu and Madubuike, 17). It is a complicated issue, though, whose full examination is beyond the scope of this study. My interest in the challenge is limited to their contesting the refusal of the Western critics in question to accept Tutuola's books as "novels pure and simple," preferring to regard them instead as "ghost novels, romances, quest romances, fantasies, allegories, etc." (17–18). Donatus Nwoga did not think it was inappropriate to apply those conventions to Tutuola, especially if what he writes are labeled as novels. It was for that reason, among others, that Nwoga criticized Harold Collins for his lack of rigor in his apologetics for Tutuola. Collins, Nwoga observed, correctly identified the critical issues that must be settled if discussion of Tutuola's art was to be meaningful and productive. These include "those of language, the relation of oral traditions to modern African literature, the appropriate mode of fiction, the desirable forms of literary acculturation, how modern African writing should come to terms with the African past, and the question of the audience of African writing." Nwoga also mentioned the critical adjustments necessary in moving from conventional writers to Tutuola. Unfortunately, Nwoga continued, Collins failed to follow through on his own prescription as a result of critical inconsistency on his part: he excused the episodic nature of the romances because it was consistent with the structure of the "naive romance," then justified it on the grounds of "creditability" consistent with the standards for "the romantic mode of fiction." Implicitly rejecting suggestions that Tutuola was operating in any genre other than the novel, Nwoga stressed the a priori necessity of establishing whether one can transfer the "syncretic techniques" of the oral performance before a live audience to "the medium of the long novel with all the expectations which centuries of the form have given rise to" (Nwoga, 96).

Collins was handicapped by a zealot's admiration for Tutuola that disposed him to find rationalizations for everything Tutuola did. To his credit, though, Collins was able to concede that no matter what standard one applied to the "romances," some of the episodes were superfluous and irrelevant (Collins 1969, 39). Lindfors's analogy of the episodes to railroad boxcars comes to mind once again; none of the cars that make up the train is indispensable to the others; apart from the fact that they can be arranged in any order without any adverse effect on the train or the others, cars can also be added or detached without any ill effect.

As good an illustration as any of the autonomy of the episodes in Tutuola's novels is his practice of sometimes excerpting a part of a longer work for publication as a self-standing short story. The best example is the concluding episode of *Ajaiyi,* which later becomes a short story, "The Village Witch Doctor," in the collection *The Village Witch Doctor and Other Stories.*[1] More interesting than the reuse of the material, though, are the modifications Tutuola made to the original for its later publication. In the earlier version, the reader is told simply that Ajaiyi's (and Aina's) parents are desperately poor, and that the children inherited poverty from them. In the short story, the poverty originated with Ajaiyi's grandfather Aro, whose inherited fortune was stolen by Osanyin, the witch doctor. Aro passed the poverty on to his son Jaye, who passed it in turn to Ajaiyi. Thereafter the stories follow essentially the same lines, except that there is no sister in the latter one. Incidentally, it is evident that Ajaiyi is another incarnation of Pauper, or vice versa.

Tutuola handled the exposure of the fraudulent witch doctor with far greater imagination the second time around, achieving a far more humorous spectacle. In the earlier version, when Ajaiyi surprises the rogue, who has come to the grave with his servants in hopes of collecting three more rams, Ajaiyi says to the surprised culprit, "Hun-un! So you have taken my rams for yourself and not my dead father!" Later on, Ajaiyi threatens to kill the rogue, proclaiming (despite the frightened man's declaration of his true identity), "But I believe, you are my dead father who had taken my rams on top of the grave! Therefore, you are to set me free from my chronic poverty this midnight" (*Ajaiyi,* 231). But the reader knows, as does the witch doctor, that Ajaiyi does not really believe that he is confronting his father's ghost, because his first words distinguish between the man before him and his dead father. The witch doctor has no real reason to believe that Ajaiyi truly mistakes him for the dead man, and there is no reason for the reader to think that the unfortunate man is really in a panic that misidentification of himself might bring disaster on his head.

In the later version, Ajaiyi's first words to the surprised witch doctor are "Hun-un! My rams, because of which I have pawned myself to the third pawnbroker, and you—my dead father." He ignores the witch doctor's protestations that he is not the dead father and continues, "But I believe you are my dead father. . . . Therefore you are to set me free of my poverty this midnight" (*Witch Doctor,* 10). The panic of the witch doctor can be imagined when he thinks that Ajaiyi really believes him to be his father's ghost with powers to relieve abject poverty. The scene is also much funnier.

We can also find in the same work representative examples of digressive irrelevance, of episodes that fail to meet even the standard of connection to the lifeline of a common hero. One is the episode that constitutes the chapter "Don't Pay Bad for Bad," and the other is the sequence in "The Witch Mother Turned into the Pupil of the Eyes," in which the witch mother engages in a battle of witchery with some spirits (*Ajaiyi,* 137–66). The first is a retelling of the folktale in which a jealous woman, by forcing her friend to destroy a valuable property, puts the life of her own precious child at risk. The other episode begins with the witch mother's son Ishola's marketplace encounter with three spirits, Ajala, Bola, and Fola. In their anger at the boy's impudence toward them, they revive the dead rat he is selling and cause it to scramble off into the bush. After some irrelevant passages (in which Ishola finds out that his mother is a witch, and the coven of witches insist that Ajaiyi and his companions must be fattened and then killed for them), the witch mother impresses the spirits with her own magical powers. They thereafter invite her to their home, intending to kill her, but she manages to get them to kill their mother instead. She subsequently escapes, with the spirits in hot pursuit, and when she is about to be caught, she jumps into a blacksmith's eyes, becoming the pupil of the eye. There ends the career of the witch mother. The episode has nothing to do with Ajaiyi and his friends, except that they are the witch mother's captives at that point. What we have is a mini-adventure with the witch mother as the heroine while Ajaiyi and his story are held in abeyance.

This episode also highlights one of the peculiarities of Tutuola's plots—their tendency to be internally inconsistent. The witch mother demonstrates her superior powers, and the spirits are so impressed that they shake hands with her and invite her to their home. There they attempt to murder her, but after she tricks them into killing their mother, she seems powerless before them, and she can find safety only in losing herself permanently in the eye.

The red bird, red fish, red people episode in *Drinkard* is equally intriguing in its dispensing with the logic of common experience. It refuses to acknowledge death as a means of finally escaping from the prospect of dying. The red fish and red bird that the young man (who narrates the experience to the Drinkard) killed before he and his people turned red materialize in the red people's after-death abode to demand annual human sacrifice, until the Drinkard kills them, again (*Drinkard*, 80). The red people themselves, who had died before settling in the new place, also meet their death, again, at the hands of Give and Take and his cohorts (91).

In chapter 5, I have alluded to the Drinkard's account of his and his wife's final arrival and entry into Deads' Town as another example of Tutuolan (il)logic, because having said that the town would not permit their entry in daylight, because they were not yet dead, he also said that they had to await daylight to enter the town, because it was a strange town to them.

Here again I will not list all instances of bungled details but will cite only one more. The reader knows that the Drinkard lost his father (by death) some six months before he set out on his adventure. He reports, nevertheless, that on his return home with his magic egg, he "met" his *parents* (plural) in his town (*Drinkard*, 117). And he is able to procure 200 kegs of palm wine to drink with his friends. Why the trip to the Deads' Town? (117–18). Apart from the reincarnation of his father, the availability of palm wine in abundance recalls the Yoruba saying *"Ohun tó wá lo sí Sókótó wà lápòo sòkòtò"* [What he sought all the way to the city of Sokoto was all the while in the pocket of his trousers *(sòkòtò)*].

Tutuola's Women

As I conceded earlier, Tutuola deserves commendation for certain accomplishments, important among them being his service to the women's cause. Simbi can hold her own against any adversary, male or female, human or nonhuman; her beheading the king who was about to behead her and her fellow captives, her defeating the phoenix and the satyr and forcing Dogo to give up his life of crime all certify her as a genuine heroine. But Adebisi, the heroine of *Huntress*, is even more fearsome and more formidable. She breaks the male monopoly of the hunting profession by succeeding her father after his retirement as the head of his town's hunting fraternity and inheriting his hunting paraphernalia. She also reverses the traditional gender roles by venturing into the Jungle of the Pigmies to rescue her four older brothers, who had disappeared during a hunting trip, whereas the normal expectation would be for male stalwarts to embrace terrifying ordeals to rescue women in distress. (Incidentally, the same idea is played out in brief in *Feather Woman,* where the hero's sister goes after him after his long absence resulting from his detention by the Feather Woman.)

With regard to both of these heroines, but especially to Adebisi, the reader must constantly remind himself or herself that he or she is reading about the exploits of a woman, that is, must consciously vacate the habit of thought that reserves warrior roles and capabilities to men. In rescuing not only her brothers but also the thousands of people the pigmies have imprisoned, Adebisi kills all the pigmies and dispatches a strange wild animal with "about sixteen horns on forehead . . . a kind of two fearful eyes which had a kind of powerful light, as well as a kind of boa constrictor" (*Huntress,* 16), not to mention all the other dangerous animals and formidable adversaries. She returns home with precious metals, and after selling them, she "became a rich lady at once" (150). In accomplishing these feats, Adebisi is spectacularly violent and bloody, a hallmark she shares with Tutuola's other leading characters. Whether she represents a victory for feminism or an erasure of a desirable feminine difference is a judgment the reader must make according to his or her predilections.

The foregoing caveat notwithstanding, Tutuola deservedly scores some points as an empowerer of women. He scores even more with the Witch-Herbalist, whom he invests with godlike qualities and functions, this at a time when better-regarded and better-educated African writers were justifiably being criticized for their chauvinistic portrayal of women, or for their exclusion of women from their works, and long before Achebe would embrace the feminist agenda with the (not entirely successful) Beatrice gambit in *Anthills of the Savannah* (1987), and before non-Nigerian male writers such as the Kenyan Ngũgĩ wa Thiong'o would do the same with characters such as Jacinta Warĩĩnga in *Devil on the Cross* (1982).

Unfortunately, however, Tutuola does not permit statements, on any topic, that would be generally applicable to all his work. His characteristic inconsistency, his slapdash habit of thought, is evident in this regard also. His nonsexist, female-empowering portrayal of the aforementioned female characters is counterbalanced by his depiction of figures such as the Drinkard's wife, the youngest wife of the Devil Doctor of *Ajaiyi,* and Brawler and Popondoro in *Pauper.* The Drinkard's wife is in fact not much more than a trophy, and she plays no meaningful role in the adventure, aside from spouting cryptic prescience of little significance on occasion, beginning with "This would be a brief loss of woman, but a shorter separation of a man from lover" when the red king invites one of them to volunteer to be sacrificed to the red bird and the red fish (*Drinkard,* 78). The trophy idea becomes elaborately fleshed out in *Pauper* when the maiden Popondoro constitutes a bridal price for the better of two competitors—Pauper and Slanderer (*Pauper,* 50–72). The Devil Doctor's youngest wife, by accusing Ajaiyi of plotting to rob the Devil Doctor of both his coral treasure and his wife, functions as the nemesis that causes Ajaiyi to be reunited with the burdensome iron lump the Doctor had relieved him of in return for his services (*Ajaiyi,* 216).

These women, then, along with such others as the Faithful-Mother in *Drinkard,* Victoria Juliana in *My Life,* the witch mother in *Ajaiyi,* and even the helpful old woman whose mucus helps Pauper win Popondoro in the contest against Brawler, play more or less traditional roles, mainly as supports for men, or as sources of difficulties. It seems as though Tutuola toyed with the possibility of making Aina a companion for Ajaiyi throughout his adventures, just as the Drinkard's wife accompanies him in his, and as Brawler would dog Pauper (for the most part) in the later work; but after some distance into the story, the author discards Aina, marries her off so that she can be tied down, in favor of male companions such as Ojo and Alabi for the hero.

The portrayal of Popondoro and Brawler deserves some fuller discussion. As I mentioned earlier, Popondoro's role is a later version of that which the nameless wife of the Drinkard plays. Just as she winds up as a trophy the Drinkard wins for rescuing her from the complete gentleman-skull, so Popondoro is a trophy for whoever wins her in a contest of brawn. Her predicament, though, is very unlike that of the Drinkard's future wife. Popondoro's misfortune is her extreme beauty, the "beauty of magnet," beauty that "needs to be glorified and honoured greatly" and that "attract[s] people with full force like the magnet which attracts another iron forcibly" (*Pauper,* 50). It is a beauty that has become a threat to public peace in the town of Abalabi. On account of her, men leave their farmwork to engage in bloody fights for the right to have her. The contest is organized to marry her off to someone that the entire community sanctions and thus end the bloodshed (55). But although she is depicted as a person of celestial beauty, and although on the day of the contest, "the golden rays of the sun formed a strange beautiful crown on Popondoro's head" (60), Tutuola endows her with little in the way of agency in the story. She has no part in the decisions and arrangements for securing a husband for her, a proceeding that is not unusual in the traditional contest; but in addition, Tutuola—by not recording her songs of flattery, encouragement, and revival—minimizes even the little she does. Tutuola says that the songs caused the men who heard them to become "so dejected that many of them fainted and fell down" (61), but one assumes that their dejection is due to jealousy of Pauper, to whom the songs are directed.

As for Brawler, that she shares equal billing in the title with her two male coprincipals leads the reader to expect her agency to compare to that of the other two. In fact, for all her reputed peacocklike beauty (*Pauper,* 9), she is to Pauper very much like the "active lump of iron" Ajaiyi is constrained to carry involuntarily with him everywhere he goes. Brawler's character is in fact an unfortunate stereotyping of womanhood. To be sure, Slanderer is also a bane for Pauper, causing problems and engineering reversals of Pauper's fortune whenever he seems on his way to prosperity. But whatever Slanderer does is articulated and reasoned, even if both his articulation and his reasoning are contrary. Brawler is quite another matter. She has no other purpose in life or in the novel than to engage in "hot brawls," "hotful brawls," and "hurtful brawls," all for absolutely no reason at all. Her affliction apparently developed from her youth, when her brawls "were much more harmful in climax so that her parents and their neighbors were unable to hear any other words with their ears both day and night except for the brawls of this lady" (10). Having failed to stop her brawling, her father expels her from his home, and she eventually marries Pauper. Needless to say, she does not even fulfill the traditional or stereotypical role of wives, that of being helpful to their husbands. She is in every way a deadweight around Pauper's neck. For example, Pauper sends her to the market to sell his wood carvings, but her incessant brawling so aggravates prospective buyers that they go away from her in disgust (144). Moreover, when Creator's *ikò* (messenger) tells Brawler that Creator wishes to help her any way she wants, she responds, "Haaa! This is the happiest day for me since I came to earth! The kind of help that I wish Creator to do for my husband is to slay him for me! That is the only help I want from Him" (31). After Pauper puts Death (whom Creator sent to carry out her wish) to flight, she turns next to Peace and

Joy, who refuse her request because they perform only peaceful and joyful tasks (39).

Brawler and Popondoro are certainly not designed to please feminists. Even in the town of women, where all authority including the choice of who rules and under what conditions is in the hands of women, its own herald announces, "all of you know well that a town without men is an insignificant town and by that it is useless!" (*Pauper*, 124). So much, one might say, for the feminist quip that a woman without a man is like a fish without a bicycle.

A major instance of Tutuola's favoritism toward men is his different treatments of the deaths of Ajaiyi's mother and father. Of his mother's death, Tutuola writes:

> Immediately she was dead Aina and I started to weep loudly and we were staggering about in the house as our neighbours and my father took our dead mother to the backyard and they buried her there. After she was buried, my father staggered back to the sitting room as our four neighbours went back to their houses. (*Ajaiyi*, 16)

That is the sum of the account of the obsequies accorded the dead woman. The impression the reader gets is that the burial came immediately, and unceremoniously, after the death. The treatment of the father's death is much different: Tutuola devotes a whole chapter to it, and it spills into the next. He shows the dying father calling his son and daughter to him, blessing them, and advising them:

> You will not die in poverty as I am going to die in poverty soon. But furthermore, I shall not forget to advise you again that you must not forget "Remember The Day After Tomorrow." But you must put in your mind always that "Remember The Day After Tomorrow" shall come back to you soon after death. . . . After my death and when I reach heaven, your mother and I shall be looking after you from heaven. Goodbye, my dear son and daughter. Goodbye, goodbye, goodbye to y-o-u. (*Ajaiyi*, 20)

There follow episodes in which the survivors make arrangements for the funeral. First, Ajaiyi searches for and succeeds in finding a wood-carver to make a coffin for the dead man. Because he has no money to pay the man, Ajaiyi offers to work off the cost after the funeral. But the wood-carver agrees to make the coffin for free because the dead man, though poor, had been kind to him (*Ajaiyi*, 23). Similarly, Aina finds a cloth seller who gives her some white cloth for her father's shroud for free, refusing her promise to work off the cost later because, as the cloth seller tells Aina, "Your father was well known to me and I was well known to him as well as the money is well known to every person. Although he was in great poverty throughout his life time, but he was very kind to every person throughout his life time. Now, for your father's kindness when he was alive, take this piece of cloth for free of charge. But do not come back to me with the hope to do work for the cost of the cloth!" (26). Finally, Ajaiyi approaches a tailor to sew the shroud, and he too agrees to do the work for free, also refusing the offer of later work because "Your father was kind to me and to other people when he was alive. Therefore, I am not going to take anything from you as my workmanship, but I shall sew the cloth for free of charge. Although your father was in poverty throughout his life time but he was kind!" (27).

The obsequies for the father include his lying in state and being visited by mourning neighbors, and a procession to the burial ground a mile outside the town, complete with dirge singing and dancing. Later on, the neighbors advise Ajaiyi to pawn himself for some money to finance the funeral ceremony for their *father*, not their father and mother, which is to take place a few days later (*Ajaiyi*, 28).

Tutuola's Construction of Heroism

Heroism, either in fiction or in real life, customarily connotes exceptional bravery and resourcefulness in accomplishing all but impossible tasks. Tutuola's heroes and heroines undoubtedly qualify on the grounds of what they accomplish, and even arguably on that of bravery. But for the most part, he substitutes good luck and good chance for resourcefulness. He succeeds marvelously in getting his leading characters into difficult and dangerous situations, into confrontations with seemingly deadly adversaries, but he never abandons them to their own resources, contriving instead to extricate them almost magically, and no thanks to their own endowments. He thus, in a significant way, redefines the concept of heroism. Any one of his novels will do for a case study, and *Ajaiyi* offers several good examples.

The first instance of modified heroics in that work comes when the slaver who had bought Ajaiyi and Aina from their kidnapper has them placed before his idol before sacrificing them. Their hands are tied behind them as they lie prone before the shrine, but from where Ajaiyi lies, he can see many long swords hung around the idol. When before dawn "the slave-buyer or the chief idol worshipper, his family, servants

and his followers" approach the shrine to carry out the sacrifice, Aina
cries, "Hah, they are coming to kill us now for this idol." As matters
turn out, she need not have feared. When the worshipers all "began to
dance round the shrine like a mad person," the hero springs to action:

> Then this time, I did my best to loose the rope away from my hands and
> God was so good the rope cut unexpectedly. Then without hesitation, I
> took one of the swords which were hung round the idol. I hastily cut off
> the rope which was on Aina's arms. . . . I rushed against the Chief Idol
> Worshipper (slave-buyer) but as I was about to behead him with the
> sword. All of them were so feared that they run away from the shrine.
> (*Ajaiyi*, 39)

He asks Aina to follow, and he chases the whole congregation around
town, intending to kill them, but they fortunately escape into the bush
"without their wish."

The unlikely turn of events recalls Simbi's equally unlikely derail-
ment of the attempt by the king of the Sinners' Town to sacrifice her
and other female slaves to his head. Here Simbi, herself next in line to be
beheaded by the king, is

> laid down before them (gods) . . . and immediately he (king) raised up
> the sword just to behead her as he had beheaded many others, she
> jumped up and grasped the sword from him. Without hesitation she
> beheaded him with that sword and some of the chiefs, etc. as well who
> attempted to hold her for killing. And the rest chiefs, the prominent peo-
> ple and the common people who were dancing at the outside of the
> shrine, having seen this, they were disordered. (*Simbi*, 39)

On another occasion, Ajaiyi and his sister escape from a tight spot
through what the hero construes to be intervention by God. He is held,
again with Aina, in a room under guard and without food for three days
on orders of the Spirit of Fire, king of the town of fire. "But in the midnight of the fourth day that we were in this room. The Almighty Creator was so good, this guard fell asleep. Then without hesitation, as I
held my sword, I whispered to Aina to follow me and she did so. So in
darkness, we escaped from the palace to another part of the town"
(*Ajaiyi*, 51). They hide in ashes for many days, and finally an obliging
torrential rain falls and sweeps them with the ashes into the safety of an
underwater city.

Luck again comes to aid Ajaiyi, along with his companions Ojo and
Alabi, after they have been captured by two one-legged ghosts who

intend to roast them for food. When the captives discover the ghosts' intentions, a fight ensues. "After a while," says Ajaiyi, "we were so lucky, they became tired. They were so tired that they fell down and began to struggle to die but of course they were immortal creatures. As soon as both of them fell down helplessly, we took all their fighting weapons." The heroes eat the ghosts' food after some rest. "Then we came out from their hole and we continued our journey at the same time in the same jungle. It was like that we were safe from these one legged ghosts" (*Ajaiyi*, 92). These, by the way, are the same ghosts who earlier captured the three, the same ghosts who were so strong that when they were boxing the ears of these same victims, the victims "were falling down ten times in a second because they were as strong as a giant" (91).

I will cite just one instance of heroic deeds by one of Tutuola's female leads, the brave huntress Adebisi. When the pigmies capture her, they take away her gun, her hunting bag, her poisonous cudgel, and the head of the lamp-eyed animal she had been wearing as a hunting lamp to light her way. She escapes from the pigmies' custody by pretending to be a corpse and getting them to throw her away. Because she needs food, she sneaks back into the town every midnight to steal food from the kitchens. The most heroic part of the story, à la Tutuola, comes when she wants to recover the articles taken from her. Afterward Adebisi tells her own story:

> I had noticed the part of the ceiling of the palace in which all were kept the very day that I was brought from the jungle. So after I hesitated for a while and I saw that all the people in this palace had slept deeply. Then I hastily climbed this ceiling. Luckily I met all there and I took them at once. But when I came down and as I was leaving the palace I smashed a part of the king's arms and he woke at the same moment. He looked right round but he did not see me, for his eyes had already dimmed and he could not see well of course. . . . And I was very lucky as he was in this condition or if he had the clear eyes and if he caught me there was no doubt I would be killed at once. (*Huntress*, 96)

With regard to this characteristic of Tutuola's art, as with others, his admirers have not been remiss in proclaiming it as a mark of genius. In a highly creative and inventive interpretation of *Drinkard,* John Coates— referring to the escape by the Drinkard and his wife from the Spirit of Prey (which was facilitated by the providence that "God [was] so good" that the spirit did not close his eyes, an eventuality that would have proved fatal for the couple) and similar lucky escapes—conceded, "Ingenuity has little part to play in the Drinkard's eventual escape from 'Unreturnable Heaven's Town.' Tutuola is careful to connect the continuous specifically detailed physical cruelties practised here with the complete irrationality of the town's inhabitants. . . . The tortures must be borne, escape being mainly an affair of luck."[2] Tutuola's narrative, Coates said, "accepts with an easy grace the existence of events absolutely beyond human control."

Humor

Tutuola's sense of humor has not failed to impress his readers, although it is fair to say that humor presents itself in different guises to different readers. For example, when the Drinkard reports that when he first saw the complete gentleman he ran to a corner of the market and cried for a few minutes "because I thought within myself why was I not created with beauty as this gentleman" (*Drinkard*, 25), some readers might see humor whereas others see pathos. But Simbi's self-transformation into an *iromi* (a water insect) and lodging in the satyr's nostril does result in the spectacle of the satyr "running about, . . . crying loudly, . . . jump[ing] up and down, . . . and dash[ing] to the trees and rocks" (*Simbi*, 124). It is certainly slapstick material. Without doubt, also, a scene from *My Life* that seems somewhat incomprehensible is intended to be humorous. The hero is fleeing ghosts intent on killing him when he comes on an ugly ghostess. She is so ugly that the hero forgets why he is running and begins to chase her, the better to see her ugliness:

As I was chasing her to and fro to look at the ugliness it was so this bush was blowing various fearful alarms and this was pointing out how I was running and how far reaching in the bush to the ghosts who were chasing me at the back to kill me. (*My Life*, 86)

Apart from those instances that derive from the situations (and those in descriptions), a good deal of Tutuola's humor comes in his dialogue. One humorous formulation that he is rather fond of is the humorous Yoruba expression of incredulity in the form of the question "Àbí bóo?" or "Àbí báwo?" (literally, something like "How was that again?"). Idiomatically, it means something like "What did I hear you say?" or "You must be kidding!" For example, when Brawler introduces herself as "Brawler" to Pauper, the following dialogue ensues:

"Brawler or what?" Pauper wondered and was startled in fear.

"Surely, Brawler is my name!" Brawler shrugged and replied fast and then she continued her brawls. (*Pauper,* 13)

And when Creator's *ikò* tells Pauper and his wife Brawler, "Creator sends a message of happiness to you, Pauper and your wife, Brawler," Pauper's response is, "Creator sends a message of happiness to me and my wife or what?" The reader is told that "Pauper was greatly startled and then he moved back a bit from the Iko before he asked" (*Pauper,* 29). Finally, in *Ajaiyi,* when the two orphaned children tell the kidnapper they mistake for a relative that their father has died, he responds, "Died or what?" (*Ajaiyi,* 32).

Sometimes the humor results from the sheer dissonance between expression, situation, and expectation, as when Brawler tells the messenger from Creator that the boon she seeks is the slaying of her husband (*Pauper,* 31). When after Pauper has got the better of Death (with some help from Creator, who sent Death to kill Pauper in the first place) and has put him to flight, Brawler turns to Peace and Joy to do the dastardly deed, the dialogue has a humorous quality:

"Please, Joy, help me bite my husband! Please, I beg you!"

"Haa! Never shall I bite a person. I am Joy and I do only things which are joyful!" thus Joy declined to help Brawler bite her husband.

"Well, it is not bad yet! But Peace, please help me bite my husband, he is running away!" Brawler waved her hands and shouted to Peace hurriedly.

"No! I shall not bite a person! But I do only peaceful things!" Thus Peace and Joy refused to help Brawler. But instead they hastily entered their house in which they lived in peace and joy which had no end. (*Pauper,* 39)

Also humorous is the demeanor with which the carcass-eating creature in *Ajaiyi* asks the hero to give up his vigil by the corpse of his friend Ade: "Will you please leave this place now! I want to eat this deadbody; it is my food!" (*Ajaiyi,* 66). And, finally, also in *Ajaiyi,* Ishola, the witch mother's son, is somewhat discomfited when he is confronted by the prospect of being killed as a meal for the witches. But the Vice-President of the Witches thus commiserates with him: "Ishola, look at my eyes well. I have killed the whole of my own sons and daughters only on whom I relied and your mother, who is the chairwoman for us, ate from their flesh! So, you should not be afraid if your mother is preparing to kill you soon for us!" (151).

On occasion, though, Tutuola's humor slips into grossness. Consider the following passage from *Pauper* on the type of food that desperate hunger reduces Pauper and his wife to eating:

> And Pauper was carrying one dead she-goat along to his house, from which he and his wife, Brawler, were going to eat as their dinner. The dead she-goat had been thrown in the incinerator and it had already swelled out to the state of bursting just in a few hours' time. (*Pauper*, 22)

One is reminded of the treatment the feeble old woman gives Pauper's hoe to keep it from breaking in his contest with Slanderer—anointing it with mucus she blows on it from her nose. One surmises that little puts Tutuola off, for his imagination accommodates such things as impaling the heads of Laketu's executed thieves on a tree on the way to the market as a warning to other would-be thieves (*Pauper*, 17), and the brandishing of the severed heads of the two-headed monster as a trophy and indispensable prop in *Herbalist*.

Language and Editors

I referred earlier to Mark Axelrod's comparison of Tutuola's and Daniel Kunene's use of English, in which Axelrod praised Tutuola for doing what Kunene fails to do in his collection of short stories *From the Pit of Hell to the Spring of Life*. Kunene, Axelrod observed, did not "alter the prose, as Amos Tutuola does, to make it sound less Anglicized and more African" (Axelrod, 18). That late in the day, the information had not become generally known that Tutuola was never deliberately manipulating language for effect. The best analysis of his usage to date has remained Afolayan's, published in 1971. He pointed out that the "vigor and freshness" Moore saw in Tutuola's language derived from the fact that he first organized his materials in his mind in Yoruba and then expressed them, as already organized, in English—not, as Moore posited, from Tutuola's "refusal to be merely correct." Afolayan added, "One may even suggest that Tutuola thinks that he is correct when he writes" (Afolayan, 206).

Afolayan's instructive and most helpful discussion of the subject applies, necessarily, to the author's works published before 1971, that is, from *Drinkard* to *Ajaiyi*. Tutuola's language in these novels, he suggested, was "a temporary intermediate point in the bilingual evolution of a dialect—the dialect being the rather undefined abstraction 'Nigerian English' or at least 'Yoruba English' " (Afolayan, 200–201). Its idiosyncrasies resulted from the expression of "either Yoruba deep grammar with English surface grammar, or Yoruba systems and/or structures in English words" (194–95). He offered the following examples from *Drinkard* for the first type: "But when I entered the room, *I met a bed*" (*Drinkard*, 13); and "I wanted him to *lead* me a short distance" (*Drinkard*, 15), examples that have "lexical and syntactic features different from similar items in standard English, though the structures in which they occur are normal English ones." The other examples Afolayan cited, with regard to tense, aspect, transitivity, and modality, all demonstrate the influence of Tutuola's Yoruba on his tenuously apprehended English.

This is no place to question Tutuola's choice of English, a subject I have already addressed in an earlier chapter. At this point, I am interested in his editors' apparent preference, at least in the early going, for preserving Tutuola's ungrammatical usage over correcting it, once it was clear that he was not engaged in linguistic experimentation. Geoffrey Parrinder, in the foreword to *My Life*, considered Tutuola's limited education an asset because better education would have forced him into "a foreign style" (as though English was not foreign), similar to "the correct but rather stiff essays that some more highly educated Africans produce" (*My Life*, 10). Parrinder also noted that Tutuola's publishers edited his manuscript "to remove the grosser mistakes, clear up some ambiguities, and curtail some repetition" (15). The original flavor of the style, Parrinder said, had been left "to produce its own effect."

There are reasons, however, to wonder what effect the publishers were after. Formulations such as "Unreturnable-Heaven's Town," "dead-babies on the road-march to the Deads' Town," and "before we rose up our heads, we were in the centre of a market" (*Drinkard*, 44) might strike some readers as fresh and forceful, but what effect is expected from "but I lied down there awoke" (14), "my wife and myself betraited ourselves" (66), and "a piece of land did not be near there" (75)? After reading *Huntress*, the reviewer Akanji (Beier) was perplexed enough by the editors' choices to question them. He could appreciate their not wanting to tamper with Tutuola's style, he wrote, for translating *Drinkard* into correct English would destroy its rhythm. But he thought their leaving even spelling mistakes uncorrected was unfair. Tutuola's language and poetry would suffer no adverse effect if he was told that "gourd" was not spelled "guord," and "it is mere sensationalism on the part of the publishers not to correct a mistake like the following: 'I thank you all for the worm affection you have on me.' " In such cases, Akanji continued, the publishers were "no longer interested to preserve Tutuola's originality [but] are inviting the readers to have a good laugh at his expense" (Lindfors 1975, 84).

The editors certainly leave enough room for readers to suspect their motives. How would one otherwise explain the fact that Tutuola goes from words such as "belong" (as in "he reached a village which also *belonged* to the smelling-town") in *My Life* (38); to "were blonged," "blong," and "blongings" in *Huntress* (15, 17, 116, 125); to "belong" in *Feather Woman* (89); back to "blong" in *Ajaiyi* (46) and then, in the same work, to "belongings" (92)? Similar movement from "save" to "safe" as a verb occurs from work to work in the Tutuola opus. In *My Life,* the hero says he told his older brother, who was trying to carry the younger to safety, "to leave me on the road and run away for his life perhaps he might be *safe* so that he would be taking care of our mother as she had no other sons more than both of us and I told him that if God *saves* my life too then we would meet again, but if God does not *save* my life we should meet in heaven" (20; italics mine). But in *Simbi* we have passages such as "Because this hunter is a person like yourself, therefore, you are trying now to *safe* him alone among us. . . . So the more you *safe* him out, the more you will *safe* us out as well, though we are bush animals . . . and she was thinking what to do next to *safe* the hunter alone" (55; italics mine).

At times one cannot be sure if the editors' interest in the outlandish might not have prevented them from recognizing typographical errors. Such is the case in the passage in *Simbi:* "Immediately they entered this town without their wish, they entered a big house and met an old womans at with sorrow in one of the rooms that were in that house" (51). Tutuola most probably intended "met an old woman sat with sorrow," a construction that recalls "I was seriously sat down" in *Drinkard* (8). The same goes for "beyond the knowledge of human begins" in *Pauper* (126). The errors in "quicker than to swallow my spat," "dumps who could not speak," "the thick forg covered the whole village" (*Feather Woman,* 63, 99, 100), and "as I was mistakingly dashing to both trees and rocks and all these things were distopping me to go out of this fearful smoke in time" (*Huntress,* 61) could also easily be attributed to bad spelling and could have been corrected at no other cost to the reader than a giggle.

Perhaps one can argue serendipitous artistry in certain passage that would justify the preservation of Tutuola's usage. For example,

> A few months later from when the properties of the king had brought to her room by the hole dwelling animal, rat, as called, one day, when the king wanted to go somewhere, he opened the door of his property room just to take some of the gold, etc., that which he wanted to wear to the place that he wanted to go. (*Simbi*, 57)

Moreover, one could perhaps credit Tutuola with logical interrogations of the inconsistencies in the English language, for if one can say, "to my astonishment," "to my sorrow," "to my shame," and the like, why not "to my fear"?

Tutuola's Self-Improvement Efforts

Because Tutuola chose to write in English, he cannot very well complain if even his editors and publishers hold his gaffes up to ridicule. Perhaps one should not argue in his defense, either. But to his credit, he readily acknowledged his shortcomings in that regard and actively embarked on self-improvement, which is evident in the marked improvement in his style beginning with *Herbalist* (despite its twinklings). If, as Afolayan testified, Tutuola's English in the earliest novels approximated that of contemporary secondary class two students, and in the later ones (from *Huntress* to *Ajaiyi*) that of secondary class four users (Afolayan, 198–99), certainly by *Witch Doctor* he was writing at a level that compares easily with that of high school certificate holders.

Tutuola's self-conscious efforts at self-improvement, which included his eclectic reading and enrollment in evening classes, resulted in such innovations as a marked increase in dialogue use (beginning with *Simbi*); the use of the third-person voice (in *Simbi*, *Pauper*, and the short story collections);[3] a broadening of scope (in the quest for materials) beyond Fagunwa and Yoruba tales; the deliberate effort to infuse a Yoruba flavor into his novels, for example, by the increasing use of proverbs (in *Pauper* and *Herbalist* especially); and the particularization (proper names for his characters and towns, especially in *Pauper*).

Throughout his career, Tutuola attempted to increase and improve his vocabulary by consulting the dictionary for new words, just as he borrowed characters from Greek mythology. Already in *My Life* he was using terms such as "reverberating" (18), "portico" (19, 23), "risible" (48), "incognito" (63), and "sceptical" (73), sometimes malapropos, to be sure. In *Simbi,* to take later examples, he contrived to include expressions such as "the necroses of the boa bites" (93), and, in *Ajaiyi,* words, phrases, and sentences such as "wheezing" (45), "squabbled" (45, 56), "an odium" (46), "recluses" (88), "dexterous" (94), "people who are misanthrope, misadvisers, misadventurers, deceivers, debasers, etc, etc. etc.!" (100), "the three of us were complainants who had come to the Creator for complacency" (106), "he was just decoying us to kill us" (116), "cantankerous" deputy of the devil (119), "we hastily engrafted her with fear" (130), "This disciple was his Augur" (185), "it was a great petulance to Devil" (197), and "she came to my room with the altercation" (213).

Concluding Comments

Regardless of the naïveté or sophistication one accords Tutuola's novels, critics have recognized their potential as reflectors of the human psyche. The reviewer of *Simbi* for the *Times Literary Supplement* of October 21, 1955, wrote that the novel would be interesting to psychoanalysts, "in, for instance, the tale of Bako, a girl who steals goats, rams and cocks, and when questioned says they have been stolen by her Siamese twin sister at home" (Lindfors 1975, 77). John Updike saw "a certain psychological realism" in the "subdivision" of the hero of *Herbalist* (the hero, his two minds, and his Supreme Second), illustrating that humans "are all more persons than the unitary conventions of social proceedings acknowledge."[4]

Available evidence points to the fact that Tutuola has been attentive to the controversy his work has occasioned. For example, his concern about the debate surrounding his language prompted him to write *Pauper, Brawler, and Slanderer* in Yoruba, with the title *Ìsé, Òsì àti Asò,* before translating it into English for publication. He wrote it in Yoruba to prove a point, he said:

> The reason is that many people thought I could not write stories in my own language. To write in one's own language is a little better than to write in English though we will translate it into English later. If we keep on writing in English it won't take so long before we forget our tradition and customs. (Ilesanmi, 2041)

He used expressions such as "crab's winks,"[5] he further explained, because he wanted his international audience to know that the Yoruba have their own manner of speaking.

Anthony West wrote of Tutuola's "good luck in being a castaway on a little island in time where he can be archaic without being anachronistic." He occupied a unique situation, though, according to West, "and it would be as fatal for a writer with a richer literary inheritance to imitate him as it would be for a sculptor to adopt the idioms of Benin or Mycenae."[6] West was certainly premature and obviously mistaken in his judgment, as readers of Ben Okri's highly acclaimed novels and short stories will testify. There can be no doubt that Okri is a consummate stylist blessed with a fecund imagination, nor that his application of these to materials similar to Tutuola's in works such as *The Famished Road* (1991), but more especially in "Worlds that Flourish"(1988) and "What the Tapster Saw" (1988), has been far from fatal. That fact leaves one wondering if Collins did not have a point after all when he suggested that Tutuola might be something of a trailblazer "leading the West African novel" (Collins 1969, 64).

Chapter Seven

Epilogue

Amos Tutuola died on Saturday, June 7, 1997, at his home at Odo-Ona, a village near Ibadan. He died as he had lived, amid uncertainties, contradictions, and controversy. The causes and circumstances of his death reflect a major contradiction in his life and career. Diabetes and hypertension, the conditions to which he succumbed, need not prove fatal to a patient able to afford proper medical care; unfortunately Tutuola was not, for despite his literary successes and international fame, at the time of his death, he was destitute. In the view of many who mourned him, a view with which he concurred (according to his last interviews), he got far less from life and much less from his society than he deserved.

His virtual local anonymity in his last days, despite his international fame, is also something of a contradiction. Although until days before his death, visitors from Nigeria and abroad periodically sought him out at his home for interviews, he was not by any means a locally famous personality. Five years before Tutuola's death, Dapo Adeniyi observed that

> in the noisy suburb of Ibadan, Odo-Ona, in which the famous novelist lives, few of the residents—made up of mostly peasants and petty-traders—knew of the presence of such a personality in their neighbourhood. This writer once entered in error into a house some two electric poles from the house of the author and enquired after him mentioning his name but no one present [had] heard of that name before.[1]

Even when he died, it took some time for the country to acknowledge his passing. As a commentator wrote, "Like a pin-drop in a deep ocean, the news of Amos Tutuola's death came quite unceremoniously to Nigerians early this week. His passage became almost unnoticed following little celebration of his existence by the mass media."[2] Another remarked on the country's indifference to Tutuola's death, accusing the media of ignoring the event, turning their faces the other way and sleeping off. It mattered nothing, this commentator added, that Tutuola's oldest daughter was employed in the media:

Nigeria's qualification [in soccer] for France '98 at the expense of Kenya's Harambee Stars, politics and . . . suchlike engaged their attention. And even when the media woke up to the shocking news of the renowned and world acclaimed folklore writer, they didn't give it the deserved prominence—a piece tucked in one of the inside pages here, a short, almost unnoticeable promo on the front page there.[3]

Nor were the media alone in ignoring his demise. The Association of Nigerian Authors (ANA), which one would have expected to lead the mourning for the pioneering English-language author, was as remiss as the rest of the public. A fortnight after the event, Tony Biakolo reported that the organization was at last in the process of making "almost belated efforts to organize something memorable to mark the exit of this literary icon" and called on the government and other bodies to at least confer posthumous honors on him. A day earlier, Femi Osofisan, a prominent dramatist and onetime president of the ANA, had proposed that the country redeem itself for its neglect of Tutuola and "give this man a proper farewell." The veteran author Cyprian Ekwensi also called on Sani Abacha, Nigeria's military ruler, to honor Tutuola.[4]

The Osun/Oyo chapter of the association did assemble at the Arts Faculty of the University of Ibadan on Saturday, July 26, to commemorate Tutuola's passing, and as one would expect, the mood was not celebratory. An observer reported on the evident pain the participants felt, because Tutuola's achievements notwithstanding, his society did not recognize him: "He was derided at home while abroad he received nearly unparalleled encomiums, at least, for daring."[5] That was precisely the point that the scholar and poet Niyi Osundare made at the gathering. Quoting Tutuola as once saying, "First I was rejected at home but when white people accepted me, the people at home started accepting me," Osundare described the late author's experience as representative of that of other Nigerian writers; for like him, he said, they received no recognition from their compatriots, except in response to adulation of them abroad. "The fate of Nigerian writers is a very pathetic one," Osundare said. "We suffer a terrible complex in this country. Tutuola said it and he is so eternally right. We do not value what is ours. Who is Osofisan, Ola Rotimi, Sowande, Iyayi, Osundare and others? They are nobody until they have been published in *Times Literary Review* before we begin to talk about them" ("Homage," 37).

Another member of the organization, most likely without intending to, offered a comment that went a long way toward explaining the phenomenon Osundare cited. The initial reception of Tutuola at home should not have surprised anyone, Pius Omole said, "because the critics at that time were products of colonialism and the dominant culture was that of the coloniser. So if Tutuola didn't write within that culture, there was no way they could have appreciated what he was doing." The implication that Tutuola responded to colonialist tastes and interest in the exotic is reinforced by Tutuola himself, who told an interviewer,

> Probably if I had more education, that might change my writing or improve it or change it to another thing people would not admire. Well, I cannot say. Perhaps with higher education, I might not be popular as a writer. I might not write folktales. I might not take it as anything important. I would take it as superstition and not write in that line.[6]

Leaving the general public's lack of excitement at Tutuola's death aside, perhaps the ANA's slowness to react was not so inexplicable or extraordinary after all. In spite of the recent embrace of Tutuola by Nigerian literati and critics (Achebe, for example), relations between the man and the association had apparently not been the most cordial or supportive. It should be recalled that the selection of Tutuola's *My Life* for adaptation as Nigeria's drama entry at Africa 95 in London had provoked vocal opposition from the National Association of Nigerian Theatre Practitioners (NANTAP), and also from the minister of information and culture. One cannot assume, of course, that the ANA shared NANTAP's or the minister's reservations about the book—and, by extension, Tutuola's art—but, asked in a 1996 interview why he did not travel to London to attend the festival, Tutuola placed the blame (at least partly) on an ANA official. "I did not go," Tutuola told his interviewer; "my publishers had already prepared a place for me but (an official of the Association of Nigerian Authors [ANA], name withheld) did not help much. The British High Commission did not give money for ticket."[7] Tutuola would not spell out how the ANA official had failed to help him, but the message that the withheld help was instrumental in keeping the author away from the festival is clear.

In calling on the country to honor Tutuola, Osofisan elaborated that he "did not mean just a burial ceremony, but I am also talking of the even more important rites of remembrance by giving his works a greater prominence in our curriculum, enshrining his memory in some permanent symbol and so on" (Balogun, June 13, 1997, 2). Others were somewhat more realistic, for few among Tutuola's champions would go so far as to claim that his writing was a good model for students of literature.

At the Oyo/Oshun ANA gathering to honor his memory, Tutuola received sympathy for the neglect he had suffered, for his dying, as the playwright Chief Wale Ogunyemi put it, "unsung and in abject poverty," and especially for his daring (Adeniji, "Homage," 37). Osundare added that Tutuola's achievement was that he had demonstrated that "it is actually possible to make something out of nothing" (37). Daring and audacious defiance of limits are the qualities another admirer commended in him. Koye Fadayiro wrote in a tribute:

> The role of Tutuola in the genre of emergent African literature in English is that of a cultural catalyst; his legacy is the defiant courage to believe in oneself as a writer and to believe in one's culture and its universal potentiality. Tutuola's essence was . . . entertaining the world from a solid undoubtable home base. Our own roots are the only sources we can lay claim to.[8]

True to the public perception of him as shy, diffident, and intensely private, Tutuola kept the public off balance until the end by teasing them with revisions of supposedly settled facts, or by withholding significant information. For example, whereas his 1947 marriage to Victoria Alake was public knowledge, the fact that he in fact had four wives, who bore him 11 surviving children, was not generally known.[9] The most significant new knowledge about him to come to light, however, is that his real family name is not Tutuola but Odegbami. The truth was revealed by one Mr. Jacob Oluwole Odegbami, an elderly family member among the relatives gathered at Tutuola's home at the news of his death. Odegbami was the family name, he said, but Tutuola was the first name of Amos's father, which Amos adopted "for some reasons in his writing career" (Ukanah, 21). The reason is really not difficult to divine. I recall a sermon a Methodist minister delivered at a Sunday service in Osogbo some time in the early 1950s. Some church members, he said, had presented their children for baptism and, on being asked the names by which the children were to be baptized, had proposed the likes of Sàngóbùnmi, Ifágbàmí, and Ògúnjìnmí (names meaning, respectively, Sàngó gave me this child; Ifá redeemed me; and either Ògún overlooked my failings or Ògún blessed me [with this child]). Such names were an outrage, the minister said, an affront to the Christian God to whom the parents were presenting the children. Candidates for baptism must have names that acknowledged the Christian God as the only giver and protector, preferably names from the Bible. The central role of a Christian organization in the inception of Tutuola's writing career would explain his wish not to be saddled with a name such as Odégbàmí (literally "The hunting profession saved me," but really "Ògún saved me" or "Erinlè saved me," because names beginning with "Ode" signal that the bearers worship one or the other of the two gods). Significantly, descriptions of Tutuola's last days picture a man who "spends the cool of the evening attending prayer meetings at his home church, a branch of the Christ Apostolic Church (CAC) nearby."[10]

Tutuola also kept his interviewers guessing with regard to his sources and inspiration. In my discussion of the subject, I cited inconsistencies in his accounts of how he came by his stories, especially those he worked into his earliest novels. At the end of his life, he gave new accounts that deepen the mystery around the subject. In what was billed as his "last formal interview with any Nigerian newspaper," he reportedly had the following to say:

> We used to tell folktales to our school mates and teachers. Each time we got our holidays, I used to go to my people in the village. There was no radio or television but our source of amusement was to tell folktales after dinner. I used to listen to old people and the folktales they told. Each time I returned to the school, I told the story [sic] to the other school mates and I became a very good story teller. They used to give me presents for telling incredible folktales.[11]

Tutuola also told another interviewer an incredible story regarding his use of D. O. Fagunwa. Tutuola credited the earlier author as influencing him, saying that *My Life in the Bush of Ghosts* was Tutuola's rendering of Fagunwa's *Ogboju Ode Ninu Igbo Irunmale*. Then, according to the interviewer, "he recalled that as a pupil at Salvation Army Infant School, he was fascinated with the book by Fagunwa but, having no money to buy it at the cost of 1s 3d (13 kobo), he borrowed it from a classmate and read it within an hour" (Awoyinfa, 6). Fagunwa's book runs 102 pages of not-easy-to-read Yoruba, and it would be quite a feat for even the most accomplished reader of Yoruba to read it in an hour.

Tutuola's Legacy

Harold Collins's monograph on Tutuola drew criticism for its highly partisan defense of Tutuola, and for its tendency to dismiss or rationalize even legitimate objections to aspects of the author's art. Yet one can fairly say that at the time of its writing, Tutuola still generated enough enthusiasm among readers to afford Collins the comfortable feeling that he wrote and spoke for a sizable community of "Tutuola freaks." Collins was not alone among critics who, while dismissing criticisms of Tutuola by his compatriots and other West Africans as paranoid and wrongheaded, predicted with some confidence that Tutuola would have the last laugh, after his delayed but certain universal recognition and acclaim as a literary genius destined to lead West African fiction into parity with the best in the world. Others such as Gerald Moore, and after him Abiola Irele, Omolara Leslie, Taban Lo Liyong, and even more recently Chinua Achebe, discovered and proclaimed Tutuola's genius, which they said was hidden from only those handicapped by poor training or inadequacies as readers. Within the space of a few years, however, some of his early admirers were reversing themselves, proclaiming his diminishing literary powers or expressing irritation with the very qualities and affectations they had earlier applauded. As Ebele Eko observed in 1971, the general trend in Tutuola's reputation was downward from a peak after the publication of *Drinkard*,[12] the exceptions I have noted notwithstanding. She offered some sound explanations for the phenomenon:

> An important factor in the trend of Tutuola's reception was time. From 1952 until 1958 when Achebe's *Things Fall Apart* was published, Tutuola had virtually the English West African literary scene all to himself. By 1958, he ceased to be a literary novelty, Cyprian Ekwensi had published two novels, although not as internationally well known, but Achebe's first book was of such import that much critical attention was diverted from Tutuola to him. Other writers joined the arena in quick succession, and Tutuola was never again to enjoy the very favorable reception he got for his first two works. (Eko, 41)

But the emergence of new writers would not ordinarily preclude the continued enjoyment of acclaim by an established writer: Soyinka's emergence has not relegated Achebe to oblivion, nor has Ben Okri's tarnished Soyinka's glory.

The rationalizations that Tutuola's old admirers have offered simply do not seem convincing enough. Moore was representative in seeing Tutuola's drive to improve his English and his self-education as a letdown, a betrayal of those "Tutuola freaks" for whom the magic was in his "furiously non-standard" English (Collins 1969, 97) and his nightmarish African world. One cannot help but wonder if such proffered reasons were not simply a convenient way to vacate an embarrassing position. Especially in the face of Tutuola's tendency to tell and retell the same story again and again with slight variations over a span of 40 years, critics would have a difficult task maintaining claims like Lo Liyong's that Tutuola was a "Homer alive" who deserved the Nobel Prize for literature. Besides, his happy embrace of colonial fashioning, his utter obliviousness to the pressing social issues around him, and his childlike and playful fascination with escapism were bound to relegate him in time to irrelevance: employing folkloric and mythical materials for significant commentary on life and the human condition is one thing; using them to pander to the European taste for exotic African light entertainment is quite another.

In a perceptive 1971 article, Paul Neumarkt, referring to Harry Slochower's *Mythopoesis,* judged Tutuola's work "a psychological antithesis." Myth, Neumarkt said, addressed the question of identity, which was the great preoccupation of contemporary African writers. Tutuola was an exception; he did not "go beyond the question 'where do I come from?' In other words: Tutuola shares the commitment to the past, but does not ask the questions of 'where am I bound' and 'what must I do to get there?' "[13] Neumarkt continued:

> A study of Tutuola's work reveals that he is an antithetical voice in the African chorus, and it is for this reason that one should look at his predicament as one of personal psychological dimensions. His work does not depict a social struggle or an involvement with the white man's culture *per se.* Even the Reverend Devil in his book *My Life in the Bush of Ghosts* with its Methodist Church and Sunday School instruction are marginal reflections which have no vital bearing on the development of the theme. (Neumarkt, 185)

That it is the world outside Africa that has sustained Tutuola and his reputation attests to the suggestion that he symbolizes the African condition during the twentieth century, which has been characterized by the phenomena of extraversion, and the determination (and manipulation) of African tastes, desires, and developments by European interests. On a human level, one might feel Tutuola's pain for the neglect about which he complained to an admiring Yoruba interviewer:

> Abroad people told me I am more known in other countries than in my own country. I know that I deserve honours for the past 10 years. Because I don't boast. Even if you go through many magazines that reviewed my books they would say Amos Tutuola is the first African author to get international fame. Because of this, I deserve honour. Perhaps the reason the Nigerian government does not give me any honour is

because of my education. Because those who followed me have been given honours. I think it is because of my education. If the government thinks of that and they don't recognise me as an author or a good author, well, they are wrong. (Ilesanmi, 2043)

On the same personal grounds, though, as well as on cultural ones, one is tempted to dismiss his pathos with a shrug. One can hardly fault those who decide on worthy recipients of the Order of Merit for passing over a writer who, by his own admission (before he was apparently instructed to say something more fashionable) was motivated by boredom and playfulness, who really had no intention of publishing his stories, let alone of using them to instruct or edify anyone, and who, at least in some views, was exposing himself to ridicule, whether deliberately or out of innocence.

Tutuola told the same interviewer that he wrote *Pauper* in Yoruba before he translated it into English for publication. Significantly, though, the work has not been published in Yoruba, a move that would have put claims that he is attuned to the Yoruba imagination, or that Yoruba readers are clamoring for his writing, to the test. Furthermore, unlike works by Achebe and Soyinka, Tutuola's would not be adopted for use in Nigerian classrooms, and it is quite unlikely that he would be so adopted anywhere else in Africa. Although Tutuola has proved more durable than students of African literature could have imagined in the 1960s, Martin Tucker, for example, was already saying in 1967 that Tutuola was passé (Tucker, 67). And although scholars and writers such as Robert Plant Armstrong, Sunday Anozie, Chinua Achebe, and Taban Lo Liyong have conferred some significance on Tutuola's work by subjecting it to brilliant, often creative analyses, one might make bold to suggest that he is likely to remain a testimony to the anomalous African condition in the twentieth century, a testimony to what Tucker described as the African defeat "by the self-Europeanization of Africans themselves" (Tucker, 67), and Jean-Paul Sartre as a "nervous condition" willingly acquiesced to.[14] The survival of Tutuola's reputation (already much tarnished) into the twenty-first century is as unlikely as the persistence of the African condition into it would be lamentable.

Notes and References

Chronology

  1. Ebele Ofoma Eko, "The Critical Reception of Amos Tutuola, Chinua Achebe, and Wole Soyinka, in England and America, 1952–1974" (Ph.D. diss., University of North Carolina at Greensboro), 1974.

  2. This is a detail that needs resolution. It would have been highly unusual for someone who has completed only two years of primary school (grade school) to have been admitted to a high school, whatever his age. The fact that on his return to Abeokuta in 1936 he enrolled again in his old grade school makes his account all the more problematic.

Chapter One

  1. Harold R. Collins, *Amos Tutuola* (New York: Twayne Publishers, 1969); hereafter cited in the text as Collins 1969.

  2. Amos Tutuola, *My Life in the Bush of Ghosts* (New York: Grove, 1954), 152; hereafter cited in the text as *My Life*.

  3. Amos Tutuola, *The Palm-Wine Drinkard and His Dead Palm-Wine Tapster in the Deads' Town* (New York: Grove, 1953), 68; hereafter cited in the text as *Drinkard*.

  4. Eric Robinson, letter to *West Africa,* in *Critical Perspectives on Amos Tutuola,* ed. Bernth Lindfors (Washington, D.C.: Three Continents Press, 1975), 29.

  5. Simon Gikandi, introduction to *Things Fall Apart,* by Chinua Achebe, expanded edition (Oxford: Heinemann, 1996), ix.

  6. V. Y. Mudimbe, *The Idea of Africa* (Bloomington and Indianapolis: Indiana University Press, 1994), 132; hereafter cited in text as Mudimbe 1994.

  7. Agboola Ologunde, "The Yoruba Language in Education," in *Yoruba Language and Literature* (Ibadan: University Press and University of Ife Press, 1982), 289.

  8. Wole Soyinka, *Aké: The Years of Childhood* (London: Rex Collins, 1981), 33.

  9. "M.A., he got it; Ll.D, he ate it; Ph.D., he knocked it down, the degrees he did not work for, they gave him!"

  10. I have not been able to find the meaning or derivation of this word. I do know of the Yoruba insulting ditty that goes:

Yò bíládè fuùlù
konkobílitì
Bó bá di kôòtù
Ma gbéya e tà
[You bloody fool
concobility
If it comes to a court case
I'll sell your mother.]

11.   Wole Soyinka, *Ibadan: The Penkelemes Years. A Memoir: 1946–1965* (London: Methuen, 1994), 99.

12.   Onwuchekwa Jemie Chinweizu and Ihechukwu Madubuike, *Toward the Decolonization of African Literature,* vol. 1 (Washington, D.C.: Howard University Press, 1983), 182; hereafter cited in the text.

13.   Chinua Achebe, "Africa and Her Writers," in *Morning Yet on Creation Day* (Garden City, N.Y.: Anchor, 1976), 35; hereafter cited in the text as Achebe 1976.

14.   Eric Larrabee, "Palm-Wine Drinkard Searches for a Tapster," in Lindfors, *Critical Perspectives on Amos Tutuola,* 14; hereafter cited in the text.

15.   V. S. Pritchett, review of *The Palm-Wine Drinkard and His Dead Palm-Wine Tapster in the Deads' Town,* in Lindfors, *Critical Perspectives on Amos Tutuola,* 23.

16.   Adeagbo Akinjogbin, letter to *West Africa,* in Lindfors, *Critical Perspectives on Amos Tutuola,* 41.

17.   Charles Larson, *The Emergence of African Fiction* (Bloomington and London: Indiana University Press, 1972), 11; hereafter cited in the text as Larson 1972.

18.   Abiola Irele, "The Criticism of Modern African Literature," in *Perspectives on African Literature,* ed. Christopher Heywood (New York: Africana, 1971), 10; hereafter cited in the text as Irele 1971.

19.   Paul Gilroy, *The Black Atlantic: Modernity and Double Consciousness* (Cambridge, Mass.: Harvard University Press, 1993).

20.   Dylan Thomas, "Blythe Spirits," in Lindfors, *Critical Perspectives on Amos Tutuola,* 8; hereafter cited in the text.

21.   Kingsley Amis, review of *My Life in the Bush of Ghosts,* in Lindfors, *Critical Perspectives on Amos Tutuola,* 26.

22.   Robert Plant Armstrong, *The Affecting Presence: An Essay in Humanistic Anthropology* (Urbana: University of Illinois Press, 1971), 151; hereafter cited in the text.

23.   O. R. Dathorne, "Amos Tutuola: The Nightmare of the Tribe," in *Introduction to Nigerian Literature,* ed. Bruce King (New York: Africana, University of Lagos, 1972), 72; hereafter cited in the text.

Chapter Two

1.   Amos Tutuola, *The Witch-Herbalist of the Remote Town* (London: Faber and Faber, 1981), 93; hereafter cited in the text as *Herbalist.*

2.   Amos Tutuola, *The Wild Hunter in the Bush of Ghosts* (Washington, D.C.: Three Continents Press, 1989), 147; hereafter cited in the text as *Wild Hunter.*

3.   Amos Tutuola, *Feather Woman of the Jungle* (San Francisco: City Lights, 1988), 62; hereafter cited in the text as *Feather Woman.*

4.   *Pauper, Brawler, and Slanderer* (London: Faber and Faber, 1987); hereafter cited in the text as *Pauper.*

5.   Amos Tutuola, *Ajaiyi and His Inherited Poverty* (London: Faber and Faber, 1967); hereafter cited in the text as *Ajaiyi.*

6.   James S. Coleman, *Nigeria: Background to Nationalism* (Berkeley and Los Angeles: University of California Press, 1958), 97.

7.   Amos Tutuola, *Simbi and the Satyr of the Dark Jungle* (San Francisco: City Lights, 1983), 15; hereafter cited in the text as *Simbi.*

8.   Amos Tutuola, *The Brave African Huntress* (New York: Grove, 1958); hereafter cited in the text as *Huntress.*

Chapter Three

1.   Arthur Calder-Marshall, review of *The Palm-Wine Drinkard and His Dead Palm-Wine Tapster in the Deads' Town,* in Lindfors, *Critical Perspectives on Amos Tutuola,* 9.

2.   References in the text are to Wole Soyinka's translation, *The Forest of a Thousand Daemons: A Hunter's Saga* (London: Nelson, 1968); hereafter cited in the text as *Daemons.*

3.   Ayo Bamgbose, *The Novels of D. O. Fagunwa* (Benin City: Ethiope Publishing, 1974), 6.

4.   A. Afolayan, "Language and Sources of Amos Tutuola," in Lindfors, *Critical Perspectives on Amos Tutuola,* 204–5; hereafter cited in the text.

5.   Bernth Lindfors, "Amos Tutuola: Literary Syncretism and the Yoruba Folk Tradition," in *European Language Writing in Sub-Saharan Africa,* vol. 2, ed. Albert S. Gérard (Budapest: Akadémiai Kiadó, 1986), 635.

6.   Chinua Achebe, "Work and Play in Tutuola's *The Palm-Wine Drinkard,*" in *Hopes and Impediments: Selected Essays, 1965–1987* (New York: Doubleday, 1989), 109; hereafter cited in the text as Achebe 1989.

7.   D. O. Fagunwa, *Igbo Olodumare: Apa Keji Ogboju Ode Ninu Igbo Irunmale* (The forest of the almighty: part two of the forest of a thousand daemons) (Lagos: Nelson, 1949), 55; hereafter cited in the text as *Igbo.* The translations are mine.

8.   See Oyekan Owomoyela, "Àjàpá, Ajá the Dog, and the Princess," in *Yoruba Trickster Tales* (Lincoln and London: University of Nebraska Press, 1998).

9. Donatus Nwoga, review of Harold Collins's *Amos Tutuola, Research in African Literatures* 2, no. 1 (Spring 1971): 94–98; hereafter cited in the text.

10. See "Àjàpá's Instant Pregnancy," in Owomoyela, *Yoruba Trickster Tales*.

Chapter Four

1. John Parrinder, foreword to *My Life in the Bush of Ghosts* (London: Faber and Faber, 1954), 11.

2. Chinua Achebe, "The African Writer and the English Language," in *Morning Yet on Creation Day*, 82.

3. *Hopes and Impediments* (the collection of essays in which Achebe includes the lecture) is dedicated to Chinweizu, a vocal Marxist literary critic, and Mike Thelwell.

4. The sort of storytelling that Donald Cosentino describes among the Mende (1982), in which the main (sometimes sole) purpose is to concoct a plot different from the one an earlier teller has formulated, and where any other significance is absent, is an exception.

5. Daniel Biebuyck and Kahombo C. Mateene, *The Mwindo Epic* (Berkeley and Los Angeles: University of California Press, 1969), 144.

6. Amos Tutuola, "Ajantala, the Noxious Guest Is Born," in *Yoruba Folktales* (Ibadan: Ibadan University Press, 1986), 1–6; hereafter cited in the text as *Folktales*.

7. Amos Tutuola, "Ajantala and the Three Brothers," in *Yoruba Folktales*, 7–14.

8. The reading of the he-goat's fate—to live among humans—must accord with Yoruba values, in which it is (even for an animal) preferable to live in the forest. Consider in this regard the proverb "Agbéòdè bí òfé, amoaraáré bí oóde; a débo fún òfé, òfé ò rú; agánrán gbébo, ó rúbo; àsèhìnwá àsèhìnbò òfé di ará Òyó, agánrán di ará oko; wón rò pé òfé ò gbón" [*Òfé* , dweller-in-the-corridor, forward as *oóde;* a sacrifice was prescribed for *òfé* but he ignored it; agánrán offered the sacrifice; in the end *òfé* became a native of Oyo while *agánrán* wound up in the bush. And yet they had thought *òfé* was a fool].

9. Amos Tutuola, "Antere, the Child of the Goddess of the River," in *Yoruba Folktales*, 15–20.

10. The error is conceivable, but barely, for *Ojó òla* (the Yoruba formulation for the day after tomorrow or the future) could be a person's name.

11. Ulli Beier, ed., *Introduction to African Literature*, new edition (London: Longman, 1979), 201–2; hereafter cited in the text as Beier 1979.

12. Omolara (Ogundipe) Leslie, "*The Palm-Wine Drinkard:* A Reassessment of Amos Tutuola," in Lindfors, *Critical Perspectives on Amos Tutuola*, 149.

13. Abiola Irele, *The African Experience in Literature and Ideology* (London: Heinemann, 1981), 35; hereafter cited in the text as Irele 1981.

14. Gerald Moore, *Seven African Writers* (London: Oxford University Press, 1962), 43; hereafter cited in the text as Moore 1962.

15. Mike Awoyinfa, who interviewed Tutuola in 1983, reported that the author had translated *The Palm-Wine Drinkard* into Yoruba and had sent it to Fagbamigbe Publishing Company for publication ("Amos Tutuola: Nigeria's Nobel Literature Laureate Who Never Won," *Weekend Concord,* 14 June 1997, 7). In a later interview with Tajudeen Yussuf in December 1986, Tutuola, complaining that publishers had lately shown no interest in his work, cited Olaiya Fagbamigbe as an exception: "He was in the process of interpreting most of my scripts into Yoruba language," Tutuola said, "but no sooner he asked me to obtain my copy rights than he died as result of the riots which greeted the results of the last general elections in Ondo State" ("Encounter with Amos Tutuola," *SNN,* 25 January 1987, 14).

16. William Bascom, *The Yoruba of Southwestern Nigeria* (New York: Holt Rinehart and Winston, 1969), 101.

17. V. Y. Mudimbe, *Parables and Fables: Exegesis, Textuality, and Politics in Central Africa* (Madison: University of Wisconsin Press, 1991), 63; italics mine; hereafter cited in the text as Mudimbe 1991.

18. Fagunwa describes him thus: "This man had four heads: one was human enough and faced the East; the second was like the head of a lion and was turned to the West; the third was a serpent's, its tongue darted incessantly and spouted venom—this was to the North, and the fourth was the head of a poisonous fish from whose mouth flared huge flames—and this was turned southwards. Myriad snakes were coiled around his neck and innumerable scorpions had made his shoulders their home: he was excessively hairy. Wasps and stinging bees flew round him in thousands and he caressed them as he walked" (*Daemons,* 84).

19. Michael Thelwell, introduction to *The Palm-Wine Drinkard and His Dead Palm-Wine Tapster in the Deads' Town* (New York: Grove Press, 1994), 188–89; hereafter cited in the text.

20. The following is Beier's translation of Olowo-Aiye's paean to his father, which includes examples of personification:

> And the epileptics were cured by my father, and those who suffered from guinea worm were cured likewise, and thousands of lepers became healthy people in our house. And my father punished small pox, and attacked malnutrition; he spoiled the reputation of rheumatism, and turned stomach ache into a pauper; and headache became a helpless child, and backache was speechless; cough went into hiding and pneumonia fled; the tiny itching worms kept dead silent and fever was lost in thought; dysentery bent its head, the sore wept and the stomach ulcer was disgusted; the rash wrinkled

its brow and the cold cried for help. (Beier, *Introduction to African Literature,* 200)

Chapter Five

1.   Camara Laye, *The Radiance of the King* (New York: Collier, 1971), 24; hereafter cited in the text.

2.   Gerald Moore, "Amos Tutuola: A Nigerian Visionary," in Lindfors, *Critical Perspectives on Amos Tutuola,* 49.

3.   Adrian A. Roscoe, *Mother Is Gold: A Study in West African Literature* (London: Cambridge University Press, 1971), 112.

4.   Chinua Achebe, "The Role of the Writer in a New Nation," *Nigeria Magazine* 81 (1964): 160; hereafter cited in the text as Achebe 1964.

5.   Harold R. Collins, "A Theory of Creative Mistakes and the Mistaking Style of Amos Tutuola," *World Literature Written in English* 13 (1974): 155–56; hereafter cited in the text as Collins 1974.

6.   Raoul Granqvist, "Orality in Nigerian Literature," *Moderna Språk* 77, no. 4 (1983): 335.

7.   Martin Tucker, *Africa in Modern Literature: A Survey of Contemporary Writing in English* (New York: Frederick Ungar, 1967), 72; hereafter cited in the text.

8.   Simon Raven, review of *Feather Woman of the Jungle, Spectator,* 4 May 1962, 597.

9.   Mark Axelrod, "The Will to Freedom," review of *From the Pit of Hell to the Spring of Life,* by Daniel Kunene, and *End Papers: Essays, Letters, Articles of Faith, Workbook Notes,* by Breyten Breytenbach, *Bloomsbury Review,* March–April 1987, 18; hereafter cited in the text.

10.   Taban Lo Liyong, "Tutuola, Son of Zinjanthropus," in *The Last Word: Cultural Synthesism* (Nairobi: East African Publishing House, 1969), 159–60; hereafter cited in the text as Lo Liyong 1969.

11.   Ayo Bamgbose, *The Novels of D. O. Fagunwa* (Benin City: Ethiope Publishing, 1974), 6.

12.   "Tutuola's Last Battle: Why Nigerian Govt. Rejected His Story," *Daily Times,* 14 June 1997.

Chapter Six

1.   Amos Tutuola, *The Village Witch Doctor and Other Stories* (London: Faber and Faber, 1990); hereafter cited in the text as *Witch Doctor.*

2.   John Coates, "The Inward Journey of the Palm-Wine Drinkard," *African Literature Today* 11 (1980): 127.

3.   Tutuola told an interviewer that he preferred to write in the first person because he took himself as the hero of his stories; that way, he could explain things better. He wrote *Pauper, Brawler, and Slanderer* in the third person because he wished to prove that he could write in that voice. See Obafemi Ile-

sanmi, "The Folklore Fantasist," *West Africa* 3716 (31 October 1988): 2043; hereafter cited in the text.

4. John Updike, "Three Tales from Nigeria," *The New Yorker*, 23 April 1984, 123.

5. The Yoruba expression *ìséjú àkàn* (a crab's wink) is a play on *ìséjú kan* (literally, one blink), meaning one minute.

6. Anthony West, "From the *New Yorker*, Dec. 5, 1953," in Lindfors, *Critical Perspectives on Amos Tutuola*, 17–18.

Chapter Seven

1. Dapo Adeniyi, "A Day with Amos Tutuola," *Daily Times*, 11 July 1992, 11.

2. Sola Balogun, "Time Out for the Fabulist," *The Guardian on Saturday*, 14 June 1997, 25.

3. Phillip Oluwole Ukanah, *Sunday Tribune*, 15 June 1997, 4; hereafter cited in the text.

4. Tony Biakolo, "Pioneer Tutuola's Exit," *Sunday Sketch*, 22 June 1997, 20; Balogun, "Tutuola, Novelist, Dies at 77," *Guardian*, 13 June 1997, 1–2; Wale Sokunbi, "Abacha Must Honour Tutuola—Ekwensi," *Weekend Concord*, 21 June 1997, 32.

5. Olayiwola Adeniji, "Homage to an Ancestral Literary Figure," *The Guardian*, 4 August 1997, 37; hereafter cited in the text as Adeniji, "Homage."

6. In Mike Awoyinfa, "Nigerian Nobel Literature Laureate Who Never Won," *Weekend Concord*, 14 June 1997, 7.

7. In Festus Adedayo, "Amos Tutuola: Neglected Palmwine Drinkard," *Sunday Tribune*, 11 February 1996, 11.

8. Koye Fadayiro, "Tutuola and His Palm-Wine," *The Guardian*, 8 July 1997, 33.

9. Kolawole Olabisi, "Amos Tutuola's Unfulfilled Dreams," *Punch*, 18 June 1997, 16.

10. Sunny Oribioye, "Tutuola's Last Battle: Why Nigerian Govt. Rejected His Story," *Daily Times*, 14 June 1997, 15.

11. Olayiwola Adeniji, "The Man and His Art," *The Guardian on Saturday*, 14 June 1997, 25.

12. Ebele Ofoma Eko, "The Critical Reception of Amos Tutuola, Chinua Achebe, and Wole Soyinka, in England and America, 1952–1974" (Ph.D. diss., University of North Carolina at Greensboro, 1974), 40; hereafter cited in the text.

13. Paul Neumarkt, "Amos Tutuola: Emerging African Literature," *American Imago* 28 (1971): 129–45; reprinted in Lindfors, *Critical Perspectives on Amos Tutuola*, 184; hereafter cited in the text.

14. Jean-Paul Sartre, preface to *The Wretched of the Earth*, by Frantz Fanon (New York: Grove Press, 1968), 20.

Selected Bibliography

PRIMARY SOURCES

Novels

Ajaiyi and His Inherited Poverty. London: Faber and Faber, 1967.

The Brave African Huntress. London: Faber and Faber, 1958; New York: Grove, 1958.

Feather Woman of the Jungle. London: Faber and Faber, 1962; San Francisco: City Lights, 1988.

My Life in the Bush of Ghosts. London: Faber and Faber, 1954; New York: Grove, 1954.

The Palm-Wine Drinkard and His Dead Palm-Wine Tapster in the Deads' Town. London: Faber and Faber, 1952; New York: Grove, 1953.

Pauper, Brawler, and Slanderer. London: Faber and Faber, 1987.

Simbi and the Satyr of the Dark Jungle. London: Faber and Faber, 1955; San Francisco: City Lights, 1983.

The Wild Hunter in the Bush of Ghosts. Washington, D.C.: Three Continents Press, 1982; rev. ed., 1989.

The Witch-Herbalist of the Remote Town. London: Faber and Faber, 1981.

Short Stories

"Ajantala, the Noxious Guest." In *An African Treasury,* ed. Langston Hughes. New York: Pyramid, 1961.

The Village Witch Doctor and Other Stories. London: Faber and Faber, 1990.

Yoruba Folktales. Ibadan: Ibadan University Press, 1986.

SECONDARY SOURCES

Books and Parts of Books

Achebe, Chinua. *Morning Yet on Creation Day.* Garden City, N.Y.: Anchor, 1976.

———. *Anthills of the Savannah.* London: Heinemann, 1987.

———. *Hopes and Impediments: Selected Essays, 1965–1987.* Oxford: Heinemann International, 1989.

Adas, Michael. *Machines as the Measure of Men: Science, Technology, and Ideologies of Western Dominance.* Ithaca and London: Cornell University Press, 1989.

Afolayan, A. "Language and Sources of Amos Tutuola." In *Perspectives on African Literature,* ed. Christopher Heywood, 49–63. London: Heinemann, 1971; New York: Africana, 1971; reprinted in Lindfors 1975, 193–208.

Ajisafe, A. K. *Aiyé Àkámarà* (A world of illusions). 2d ed. Lagos: C.M.S. Bookshop, 1929.

Akanji (Ulli Beier). Review of *The Brave African Huntress. Black Orpheus* 4 (October 1958); reprinted in Lindfors 1975, 83–85.

Akinjogbin, Adeagbo. Letter to *West Africa,* 5 June 1954; reprinted in Lindfors 1975, 41.

Amis, Kingsley. Review of *My Life in the Bush of Ghosts. The Spectator,* 26 February 1954; reprinted in Lindfors 1975, 25–26.

Anozie, Sunday O. "Amos Tutuola: Literature and Folklore, or The Problem of Synthesis." *Cahiers d'études africaines* 10 (1970): 335–51; reprinted in Lindfors 1975, 237–53.

Armstrong, Robert Plant. *The Affecting Presence: An Essay in Humanistic Anthropology.* Urbana: University of Illinois Press, 1971.

Awoonor, Kofi. "Amos Tutuola and Yoruba Folklore." In *The Breast of the Earth,* 226–50. Garden City, N.Y.: Anchor, 1975.

Bamgbose, Ayo. *The Novels of D. O. Fagunwa.* Benin City: Ethiope Publishing, 1974.

Banjo, Ayo. "Aspects of Tutuola's Use of English." In *Essays on African Literature,* ed. W. L. Ballard, 155–73. Spectrum Monograph Series in the Arts and Sciences 3. Atlanta: School of Arts and Sciences, Georgia State University, 1973.

Bascom, William. *The Yoruba of Southwestern Nigeria.* New York: Holt Rinehart and Winston, 1969.

Beier, Ulli, ed. *Introduction to African Literature.* New edition. London: Longman, 1979.

Biebuyck, Daniel, and Kahombo C. Mateene. *The Mwindo Epic.* Berkeley and Los Angeles: University of California Press, 1969.

Calder-Marshall, Arthur. Review of *The Palm-Wine Drinkard and His Dead Palm-Wine Tapster in the Deads' Town. The Listener,* 13 November 1952; reprinted in Lindfors 1975, 9–10.

Chinweizu, Onwuchekwa Jemie, and Ihechukwu Madubuike. *Toward the Decolonization of African Literature.* Vol. 1. Washington, D.C.: Howard University Press, 1983.

Collins, Harold R. "Founding a New National Literature: The Ghost Novels of Amos Tutuola." *Critique* 4, no. 1 (1961): 17–28; reprinted in Lindfors 1975, 59–70.

———. *Amos Tutuola.* New York: Twayne Publishers, 1969.

Cosentino, Donald. *Defiant Maids and Stubborn Farmers: Tradition and Invention in Mende Story Performance.* Cambridge: Cambridge University Press, 1982.

Dangarembga, Tsitsi. *Nervous Conditions.* London: The Women's Press, 1988.

Dathorne, O. R. "Amos Tutuola: The Nightmare of the Tribe." In *Introduction to Nigerian Literature,* ed. Bruce King. New York: Africana, University of Lagos, 1972.

Ekwensi, C. O. D. Review of *Simbi and the Satyr of the Dark Jungle. West African Review,* January 1956; reprinted in Lindfors 1975, 79.

Fagunwa, D. O. *Ògbójú Ode Nínú Igbó Irúnmalè.* London: C.M.S., 1938; Edinburgh: Nelson, 1950. Translated by Wole Soyinka as *The Forest of a Thousand Daemons: A Hunter's Saga.*

———. *Igbo Olodumare: Apa Keji Ògbójú Ode Nínú Igbó Irúnmalè* (The forest of the almighty: part two of the forest of a thousand daemons). Lagos: Nelson, 1949.

Gikandi, Simon. Introduction to *Things Fall Apart,* by Chinua Achebe, ix–xvii. Expanded edition. Oxford: Heinemann, 1996.

Irele, Abiola. "The Criticism of Modern African Literature." In *Perspectives on African Literature,* ed. Christopher Heywood, 9–24. New York: Africana, 1971.

———. *The African Experience in Literature and Ideology.* London: Heinemann, 1981.

Johnson, Babasola. Letter to *West Africa,* 10 April 1954; reprinted in Lindfors 1975, 31–32.

Klima, Vladimir. *Modern Nigerian Novels.* Prague: Academia, 1969.

Larrabee, Eric. "Palm-Wine Drinkard Searches for a Tapster." *The Reporter,* 12 May 1953; reprinted in Lindfors 1975, 11–14.

Larson, Charles. *The Emergence of African Fiction.* Bloomington and London: Indiana University Press, 1972.

Laurence, Margaret. "A Twofold Forest." In *Long Drums and Cannons: Nigerian Dramatists and Novelists,* 126–47. New York: Praeger, 1969.

Laye, Camara. *The Radiance of the King.* New York: Collier, 1971.

Leslie, Omolara (Ogundipe). "*The Palm-Wine Drinkard:* A Reassessment of Amos Tutuola." *Journal of Commonwealth Literature* 9 (July 1970): 48–56; reprinted in Lindfors 1975, 145–53.

Lindfors, Bernth. "Oral Tradition and the Individual Literary Talent." In *Folklore in Nigerian Literature,* 23–50. New York: Africana, 1973.

———. "Amos Tutuola: Literary Syncretism and the Yoruba Folk Tradition." In *European Language Writing in Sub-Saharan Africa,* vol. 2, ed. Albert S. Gérard, 632–49. Budapest: Akadémiai Kiadó, 1986.

———. "Tutuola's Latest Stories." In *Short Fiction in the New Literatures in English,* ed. Jacqueline Bardolph, 271–76. Nice: Faculté des Lettres et Sciences Humaines de Nice, 1989.

————, ed. *Critical Perspectives on Amos Tutuola.* Washington, D.C.: Three Continents Press, 1975.

Lo Liyong, Taban. "Tutuola, Son of Zinjanthropus." In *The Last Word: Cultural Synthesism,* 157–70. Nairobi: East African Publishing House, 1969; reprinted in Lindfors 1975, 115–22.

Mackay, Mercedes. "The Books of Amos Tutuola." *West Africa,* 8 May 1954; reprinted in Lindfors 1975, 43–44.

Moore, Gerald. "Amos Tutuola: A Nigerian Visionary." *Black Orpheus* 1 (September 1957): 27–35; reprinted in Lindfors 1975, 49–57.

————. *Seven African Writers.* London: Oxford University Press, 1962.

Mudimbe, V. Y. *Parables and Fables: Exegesis, Textuality, and Politics in Central Africa.* Madison: University of Wisconsin Press, 1991.

————. *The Idea of Africa.* Bloomington and Indianapolis: Indiana University Press, 1994.

Naipaul V. S. From *New Statesman,* April 1958; reprinted in Lindfors 1975, 87

Neumarkt, Paul. "Amos Tutuola: Emerging African Literature." *American Imago* 28 (1971): 129–45, reprinted in Lindfors 1975, 183–92.

Ngũĩ wa Thiong'o. *Devil on the Cross.* London: Heinemann, 1982.

A Nigerian Correspondent. "Portrait: A Life in the Bush of Ghosts." *West Africa,* 1 May 1954; reprinted in Lindfors 1975, 35–38.

Obiechina, Emmanuel N. "Amos Tutuola and the Oral Tradition." In *Language and Theme: Essays on African Literature,* 21–52. Washington, D.C.: Howard University Press, 1990.

Ogunmola, Kola. *The Palmwine Drinkard.* Adaptation of Amos Tutuola's *The Palm-Wine Drinkard and His Dead Palm-Wine Tapster in the Deads' Town.* Transcribed and translated by R. G. Armstrong, Robert L. Awujoola, and Val Olayemi. Occasional Publication no. 12. Ibadan: Institute of African Studies, University of Ibadan, 1968.

Okri, Ben. *Stars of the New Curfew.* New York: Penguin, 1988.

————. *The Famished Road.* New York: Nan A. Talese/Doubleday, 1991.

Ologunde, Agboola. "The Yoruba Language in Education." In *Yoruba Language and Literature,* ed. Adebisi Afolayan, 277–90. Ibadan: University Press and University of Ife Press, 1982.

Owomoyela, Oyekan. *Yoruba Trickster Tales.* Lincoln and London: University of Nebraska Press, 1998.

Oyedele, Adekanmbi. *Aiyé rèé* (What a world!). Ibadan: Western Nigerian Literature Committee, 1947.

Oyono, Ferdinand. *Houseboy.* London: Heinemann, 1966.

Palmer, Eustace. *The Growth of the African Novel.* London: Heinemann, 1979.

Parrinder, John. Foreword to *My Life in the Bush of Ghosts,* by Amos Tutuola, 9–15. London: Faber and Faber, 1954.

Priebe, Richard K. "Tutuola the Riddler." In Lindfors 1975, 265–73.

————. *Myth, Realism, and the West African Writer.* Trenton: African World Press, 1988.

Pritchett, V. S. Review of *The Palm-Wine Drinkard and His Dead Palm-Wine Tap-ster in the Deads' Town. New Statesman and Nation,* 6 March 1954; reprinted in Lindfors 1975, 21–23.

Raven, Simon. Review of *Feather Woman of the Jungle. Spectator,* 4 May 1962, 597.

Review of *Simbi and the Satyr of the Dark Jungle. Times Literary Supplement,* 25 May 1962; reprinted in Lindfors 1975, 77.

Robinson, Eric. Letter to *West Africa,* 17 April 1954; reprinted in Lindfors 1975, 33–34.

Rodman, Selden. Review of *The Palm-Wine Drinkard and His Dead Palm-Wine Tapster in the Deads' Town. New Yorker,* 5 December 1953; reprinted in Lindfors 1975, 15–16.

Roscoe, Adrian A. *Mother Is Gold: A Study in West African Literature.* London: Cambridge University Press, 1971.

S. D. D. Review of *Feather Woman of the Jungle. West African Review,* August 1962; reprinted in Lindfors 1975, 93.

Sartre, Jean-Paul. Preface to *The Wretched of the Earth,* by Frantz Fanon, 7–31. New York: Grove Press, 1968.

Soyinka, Wole. *The Forest of a Thousand Daemons: A Hunter's Saga* (transla-tion of Fagunwa's *Ògbójú ode nínú igbó irúnmalè*). London: Nelson, 1968.

———. *Aké: The Years of Childhood.* London: Rex Collins, 1981.

———. *Ibadan: The Penkelemes Years. A Memoir: 1946–1965.* London: Methuen, 1994.

Thelwell, Michael. Introduction to *The Palm-Wine Drinkard and His Dead Palm-Wine Tapster in the Deads' Town,* 177–90. New York: Grove Press, 1994.

Thomas, Dylan. "Blythe Spirits." *The Observer,* 6 July 1952; reprinted in Lind-fors 1975, 7–8.

Tucker, Martin. *Africa in Modern Literature: A Survey of Contemporary Writing in English.* New York: Frederick Ungar, 1967.

Dissertation

Eko, Ebele Ofoma. "The Critical Reception of Amos Tutuola, Chinua Achebe, and Wole Soyinka, in England and America, 1952–1974." Ph.D. diss., University of North Carolina at Greensboro, 1974.

Articles and Reviews

Achebe, Chinua. "The Role of the Writer in a New Nation." *Nigeria Magazine* 81 (1964): 157–60.

Adedayo, Festus. "Amos Tutuola: Neglected Palmwine Drinkard." *Sunday Tri-bune,* 11 February 1996, 9–11.

Adeniji, Olayiwola. "The Man and His Art." *The Guardian on Saturday,* 14 June 1997, 25.

————. "Homage to an Ancestral Literary Figure." *The Guardian,* 4 August 1997, 37.

Adeniyi, Dapo. "A Day with Amos Tutuola." *Daily Times,* 11 July 1992, 11.

Awoyinfa, Mike. "Amos Tutuola: Nigeria's Nobel Literature Laureate Who Never Won." *Weekend Concord,* 14 June 1997, 6–7; first published in *Sunday Concord,* 29 May 1983.

Axelrod, Mark. "The Will to Freedom." Review of *From the Pit of Hell to the Spring of Life,* by Daniel Kunene, and *End Papers: Essays, Letters, Articles of Faith, Workbook Notes,* by Breyten Breytenbach. *Bloomsbury Review,* March–April 1987, 18.

Balogun, Sola. "Tutuola, Novelist, Dies at 77." *The Guardian,* 13 June 1997, 1–2.

————. "Time Out for the Fabulist." *The Guardian on Saturday,* 14 June 1997, 25.

Biakolo, Tony. "Pioneer Tutuola's Exit." *Sunday Sketch,* 22 June 1997, 21.

Beilis, Viktor. "Ghosts, People, and Books of Yorubaland." *Research in African Literatures* 18, no. 4 (Winter 1987): 447–57.

Coates, John. "The Inward Journey of the Palm-Wine Drinkard." *African Literature Today* 11 (1980): 122–29.

Collins, Harold R. "A Theory of Creative Mistakes and the Mistaking Style of Amos Tutuola." *World Literature Written in English* 13 (1974): 155–71.

Edwards, Paul. "The Farm and the Wilderness in Tutuola's *The Palm-Wine Drinkard.*" *Journal of Commonwealth Literature* 9, no. 1 (1974): 57–65.

Elder, Arlene A. "Paul Carter Harrison and Amos Tutuola: The Vitality of the African Continuum." *World Literature Written in English* 28 (Autumn 1988): 171–78.

Fadayiro, Koye. "Tutuola and His Palm-Wine." *The Guardian,* 8 July 1997, 33.

Ferris, William R. "Folklore and the African Novelist: Achebe and Tutuola." *Journal of American Folklore* 86, no. 339 (January–March 1973): 25–36.

Granqvist, Raoul. "Orality in Nigerian Literature." *Moderna Språk* 77, no. 4 (1983): 329–43.

Ilesanmi, Obafemi. "The Folklore Fantasist." *West Africa* 3716 (31 October 1988): 2041, 2043.

Jones, Eldred. "*The Palm-Wine Drinkard*—Fourteen Years On." *Bulletin of the Association for African Literature in English* 4 (1966): 25–27.

King, Bruce. "Two Nigerian Writers: Tutuola and Soyinka." *Southern Review* 6, no. 3 (July 1970): 843–48.

Larson, Charles. "Ten Years of Tutuola Studies, 1966–1976." *African Perspectives* 1 (1977): 67–76.

————. "Third World Writing in English." *World Literature Today* 57, no. 3 (Summer 1983): 418–19.

Lindfors, Bernth. "Amos Tutuola and His Critics." *Abbia* 22 (May–August 1969): 109–18.

————. "Amos Tutuola and D. O. Fagunwa." *Journal of Commonwealth Literature* 9 (July 1970): 57–65.

————. "Amos Tutuola's Earliest Long Narrative." *Journal of Commonwealth Literature* 16, no. 1 (1981): 45–55.

————. "Amos Tutuola's Search for a Publisher." *Journal of Commonwealth Literature* 17, no. 1 (1982): 90–106.

Nkosi, Lewis. "Conversation with Amos Tutuola." *The Classic* 1, no. 4 (1965): 57–60.

Nwoga Donatus. Review of Harold Collins's *Amos Tutuola: Research.* In *Research in African Literatures* 2, no. 1 (Spring 1971): 94–98.

Obe, Ad'Obe. "An Encounter with Amos Tutuola." *West Africa,* 14 May 1984, 1022–23.

Ogunyemi, Chikwenye Okonjo. "The Africanness of *The Conjure Woman* and *Feather Woman of the Jungle.*" *Ariel* 8, no. 2 (1977): 17–30.

Olabisi, Kolawole. "Amos Tutuola's Unfulfilled Dreams." *Punch,* 18 June 1997, 16.

Omotoso, Kole. "Interview with Amos Tutuola." *Afriscope* 4, no. 1 (1974): 62, 64.

Oribioye, Sunny. "Tutuola's Last Battle: Why Nigerian Govt. Rejected His Story." *Daily Times,* 14 June 1997, 15; first published in *Glendora Review* 1, no. 2 (n.d.).

Palmer, Eustace. "Twenty-Five Years of Amos Tutuola." *International Fiction Review* 5, no. 1 (1978): 15–24.

Sokunbi, Wale. "Abacha Must Honour Tutuola—Ekwensi." *Weekend Concord,* 21 June 1997, 27, 32.

Tucker, Martin. "Three West African Novelists." *Africa Today* 12, no. 9 (November 1965): 10–14.

Ukanah, Phillip Oluwole. "The Last Wishes of Amos Tutuola—Son." *Sunday Tribune,* 15 June 1997, 4, 21.

Updike, John. "Three Tales from Nigeria." Review of *The Forest of a Thousand Daemons* (Wole Soyinka's translation of Fagunwa's *Ògbójú ode nínú igbó irúnmalè*), *The Witch-Herbalist of the Remote Town,* by Amos Tutuola, and *Double Yoke,* by Buchi Emecheta. *The New Yorker,* 23 April 1984, 119–29.

Yussuff, Tajudeen. "Encounter with Amos Tutuola." *SNN,* 25 January 1987, 8, 14.

Index

Page numbers followed by n refer to the note number on that page. Page numbers in parentheses refer to the page on which the discussion is located.

169

The Author

Oyekan Owomoyela, a Nigerian by birth, is a professor of English at the University of Nebraska. His publications include *African Literatures: An Introduction* and the edited volume *A History of Twentieth-century African Literatures*.

The Editor

Bernth Lindfors is a professor of English and African literatures at the University of Texas at Austin. He has written and edited more than 30 books, including *Black African Literature in English* (1979, 1986, 1989, 1995), *Popular Literatures in Africa* (1991), *Comparative Approaches to African Literatures* (1994), *Long Drums and Canons: Teaching and Researching African Literatures* (1995), *Loaded Vehicles: Studies in African Literary Media* (1996), and (with Reinhard Sander) *Twentieth-century Caribbean and Black African Writers* (1992, 1993, 1996). From 1970 to 1989, he was editor of *Research in African Literatures*.

BAKER & TAYLOR